Minors : The Law and Practice
The Juvenile Courts — The Offences —
The Role of the Local Authorities

by Kenneth W. Pain, Barrister
Justices' Clerk for Mid Hants

London
Fourmat Publishing
1987

ISBN 1 85190 030 6

First published 1982 under the title *Practice and Procedure in Juvenile Courts*
This edition 1987

© Fourmat Publishing
27 & 28 St Albans Place Islington Green London N1 0NX
Printed in Great Britain by
Billing & Sons Ltd, Worcester

Foreword

The law relating to minors is complex and wide ranging and busy lawyers, police officers and social workers can find that they are spending much valuable time on research when called upon to deal with a problem involving a minor. My purpose in writing this book has been to bring together the more important aspects of the law in relation to minors in a comparatively short, clear guide to the subject. The work does not contain all of the law relevant to those under 18 and from time to time the reader may have to refer to other reference books for greater detail. In particular, it does not deal with adoption, wardship and custodianship — all covered in companion volumes. I believe, however, that this book contains a basic explanation of the most important aspects of the relevant law and that readers ought to be able to deal with most problems without further extensive research.

Part I contains a concise but comprehensive account of the practice and procedure in juvenile courts. Emphasis has been given to the special considerations which apply in the juvenile court whenever a child or young person is brought before it in criminal proceedings or in relation to care proceedings.

Part II is focused upon specific offences that can be committed by minors or by others in relation to minors. Each offence is examined and relevant case law is quoted together with the penalties that may be imposed in respect of each offence discussed.

Part III is devoted to aspects of the law that relate particularly to the welfare of minors. The role of the local authorities is examined in detail, not only in relation to children in their care but also in relation to such establishments as homes provided by voluntary organisation, registered children's homes, foster homes and nurseries.

I hope that all who are involved from time to time with the law relating to minors — solicitors and barristers, local authority staff, social workers, police, prosecutors and court administrators — and others who are concerned with the welfare of young people will find the book useful.

My aim has been to produce a work that will be both a concise introduction to the subject for those who are coming to it for the first time and a useful remembrancer for those who are already familiar with it.

KWP
April 1987

Contents

Table of cases

List of abbreviations

AA 1958	Adoption Act 1958
AA 1976	Adoption Act 1976
AEA 1971	Attachment of Earnings Act 1971
AMA 1929	Age of Marriage Act 1929
BG&LA 1963	Betting, Gaming and Lotteries Act 1963
CA 1975	Children Act 1975
CAA 1984	Child Abduction Act 1984
CCA 1980	Child Care Act 1980
CCR 1982	Crown Court Rules 1982
CHA 1982	Children's Homes Act 1982
CJA 1961	Criminal Justice Act 1961
CJA 1982	Criminal Justice Act 1982
CLA 1977	Criminal Law Act 1977
CPPA 1875	Conspiracy and Protection of Property Act 1875
C(P)R 1968	Children (Performances) Regulations 1968
CUC(C)O 1977	Certificates of Unruly Character (Conditions) Order 1977
C&YPA 1933	Children and Young Persons Act 1933
C&YPA 1963	Children and Young Persons Act 1963
C&YPA 1969	Children and Young Persons Act 1969
C&YP(HP)A 1955	Children and Young Persons (Harmful Publications) Act 1955
EA 1875	Explosives Act 1875
EA 1944	Education Act 1944
EA 1971	Education Act 1971
EA 1980	Education Act 1980
EA 1981	Education Act 1981
ECA 1973	Employment of Children Act 1973
EWYP&CA 1920	Employment of Women, Young Persons and Children Act 1920
FA 1961	Factories Act 1961
FA 1968	Firearms Act 1968
FCA 1980	Foster Children Act 1980

FLRA 1969	Family Law Reform Act 1969
GA 1968	Gaming Act 1968
GA 1973	Guardianship Act 1973
GAL&RO(P)R 1983	Guardian Ad Litem and Reporting Officers (Panels) Regulations 1983
GMA 1971	Guardianship of Minors Act 1971
HASSASSA 1983	Health and Social Services and Social Security Adjudications Act 1983
H&SWA 1974	Health and Safety at Work Act 1974
HS&PHA 1968	Health Services and Public Health Act 1968
JCCR 1954	Juvenile Courts (Constitution) Rules 1954
JCR 1970	Justices' Clerks' Rules 1970
JPA 1949	Justices of the Peace Act 1949
LA 1902	Licensing Act 1902
LA 1964	Licensing Act 1964
LAA 1974	Legal Aid Act 1974
LAA 1982	Legal Aid Act 1982
LACPR 1968	Legal Aid in Criminal Proceedings (General) Regulations 1968
LGA 1958	Local Government Act 1958
LGA 1972	Local Government Act 1972
LG(MP)A 1982	Local Government (Miscellaneous Provisions) Act 1982
MA 1949	Marriage Act 1949
MCA 1980	Magistrates' Courts Act 1980
MCCR 1970	Magistrates' Courts (Children etc) Rules 1970
MCR 1981	Magistrates' Courts Rules 1981
MHA 1983	Mental Health Act 1983
MSA 1970	Merchant Shipping Act 1970
M&QA 1954	Mines and Quarries Act 1954
N&CMRA 1948	Nurseries and Child-Minders Regulation Act 1948
NHA 1975	Nursing Homes Act 1975
NHSA 1977	National Health Service Act 1977
OA 1978	Oaths Act 1978
PACEA 1984	Police and Criminal Evidence Act 1984
PCA 1978	Protection of Children Act 1978
PCCA 1973	Powers of the Criminal Courts Act 1973
PC(T)A 1986	Protection of Children (Tobacco) Act 1986
SA 1950	Shops Act 1950
SAR 1983	Secure Accommodation (No 2) Regulations 1983

SOA 1956	Sexual Offences Act 1956
SSA 1975	Social Security Act 1975
TA 1968	Theft Act 1968
TMA 1969	Tattooing of Minors Act 1969

Part I

THE JUVENILE COURTS

Chapter 1

Introduction

1. Constitution of Juvenile Court

Only members of the juvenile court panel for a petty sessions area may sit in the juvenile court. As a general rule three members of the panel will sit. The court is properly constituted if two members of the panel are in attendance, but only if one is a man and the other a woman. The court may not be constituted of more than three members of the panel (JCCR 1954 r.12(1)).

A stipendiary magistrate who is a member of the panel may sit alone if he thinks it inexpedient in the interests of justice for there to be an adjournment (JCCR 1954 r.12(2)).

The court may be constituted without a man, or as the case may be, without a woman if no man or no woman is available owing to circumstances that were not foreseen when the bench was arranged. Similarly, the court may continue to sit if the only man or the only woman present cannot properly sit as a member of the court. In each case it is in order for the remaining members of the panel to adjudicate only if they think that it is inexpedient in the interests of justice for there to be an adjournment (JCCR 1954 r.12(3)).

Notwithstanding the restrictions referred to above, a member of the panel may act alone in any case in which a single justice has by law jurisdiction to act (JCCR 1954 r.12(4)).

Generally, each juvenile court must sit under the chairmanship of the chairman or deputy chairman of the panel. If, however, neither chairman nor deputy chairman is available owing to circumstances that were not foreseen when the justices to sit were chosen, the members of that court must choose one of their number to preside (JCCR 1954 r.13).

Although generally a juvenile court panel will serve a single petty sessions area, two or more petty sessional benches may agree (subject to the consent of the Secretary of State signified by the making of a Statutory Instrument) to the forming of a combined panel to deal with the juvenile court work in both their areas. An application will be directed to the Secretary of State via the county's Magistrates' Courts Committee.

The Lord Chancellor is concerned that all members of juvenile court panels should sit sufficiently frequently to ensure that they have enough experience to deal properly with the business of the juvenile court. In a letter to courts dated 18 April 1986 the Lord Chancellor, having accepted recommendations made by the Judicial Studies Board, required a minimum of 12 sittings per annum for each panel member, with a suggested target of 15 sittings per annum.

In smaller, rural divisions, sittings of the order required by the Lord Chancellor can rarely be achieved if there is a panel sufficiently large to ensure that a properly constituted court is always available. The answer will often be the formation of a combined panel for two or more petty sessional divisions.

Justices are appointed to juvenile court panels every third year, beginning with the Bench annual general meeting in October 1955. Any proposal to establish a combined panel can be more conveniently dealt with when a new panel falls to be appointed, since this allows sufficient time for inter-bench consultations, and for magistrates' courts committee agreement and the approval of the Secretary of State to be obtained.

2. Juvenile etc. defined

(a) Juvenile

A person who has not yet attained his seventeenth birthday is a juvenile. Exceptionally, a person who is seventeen but who has still to attain his eighteenth birthday may be regarded as a juvenile. Children and young persons together make up the wider group of persons known as juveniles.

(b) Child

Generally a person under the age of 14 is to be regarded as a child for the purposes of the Children and Young Persons Acts 1933 to 1969. One must always have regard to certain important exceptions to the general rule. They are as follows:

(i) for the purposes of the Education Act 1944, 'child' means a person who is not over compulsory school age;

(ii) for the purposes of the Child Care Act 1980, 'child' means a person under the age of eighteen years and any person who has attained that age and is the subject of a care order.

(c) Infant

In the C&YP Acts the term 'infant' is sometimes used to describe persons who have not attained the age of eighteen years.

(d) Relevant infant

Throughout Part I of the C&YPA 1969 and the rules made thereunder 'relevant infant' is used to describe the child or young person who is the subject of the proceedings.

(e) Young person

A person who has attained the age of fourteen years but has still to attain the age of seventeen years is a 'young person'. A person attains a particular age at the start of the relevant anniversary of his birth (FLRA 1969, s.9).

3. Venue

Juvenile courts are petty sessional courts sitting for the purpose of hearing any charge against a child or young person (C&YPA 1933 s.45). Sometimes juvenile courts are held in juvenile court buildings set apart for the purpose, but are more usually held in petty sessional court houses. In either case, a juvenile court may not sit in a room in which sittings of a court other than a juvenile court have been or will be held within one hour before or after the sitting of the juvenile court (C&YPA 1933 s.47).

4. Who may be present in court?

Juvenile courts are not public courts in the same way that adult courts are. The proceedings are not secret; indeed *bona fide* representatives of newspapers and news agencies are entitled to be present. However, the general public is not allowed to be in a court that is sitting as a juvenile court. In addition to press and other news agency representatives, only the following categories of people are allowed to be present in court:

(a) members and officers of the court. This group includes justices, the justices' clerk and his staff, probation officers and social services officers;

(b) parties to the case, their solicitors and counsel, witnesses and other persons directly concerned in the case;

(c) such other persons as may be specially authorised by the court to be present. Under this category consent is frequently given for students with an interest in the work of the court and of the various agencies connected with the court to be present.

(C&YPA 1933 s.47 as amended by C&YPA 1963 s.17(2)).

5. Restrictions on reports of proceedings

The information that can be contained in a newspaper or news agency report of proceedings in a juvenile court is very tightly controlled. The restrictions are applied in the interest of the young persons who are involved in the proceedings, and relate to sound and television broadcasts as well as to newspaper reports.

The court and the Secretary of State may in any particular case make an order dispensing with the restrictions or with such part of them as may be specified in the order, if satisfied that it is appropriate to do so for the purpose of preventing an injustice to a child or young person. In the absence of such an order, the media are prohibited from revealing the name, address, school or any particulars calculated to lead to the identification of any child or young person concerned in proceedings before a juvenile court.

The prohibition applies to children and young persons who are witnesses as well as to those who are before the court as defendants.

The restriction is not limited to the written or spoken word and any picture which is of or includes a picture of a juvenile concerned in any proceedings is also covered (C&YPA 1933 s.49(1)).

Any person who publishes the matter in contravention of the controls is liable on summary conviction to a fine not exceeding Level 5 for each offence (C&YPA 1933 s.49(2)).

In addition to the general restriction placed upon the media by virtue of this section of the Act, the court may specifically prohibit the publication of any matter that could lead to the identification of a child or young person who has been before the court, whether as defendant or witness (C&YPA 1933 s.39).

T' ess Council is able to deal with complaints about improper
ℨ of information relating to juveniles as well as with other
eral complaints. It is important to remember that the
ıy only hear a complaint if it is made within one month of
ion that is the source of the complaint.

6. Methods of address, court layout etc.

The layout of juvenile courts varies a great deal from court to court and from area to area. This is in part due to the great variety of court buildings used as juvenile courts; some are purpose built, but most were built for other uses and serve as juvenile courts when the need arises. There is, therefore, nothing about the layout of the court that is a clear indication that it is in use as a juvenile court, although in some of the purpose built juvenile courts, the layout has been designed with a view to softening, to a certain extent, the impact that an appearance before the court might otherwise have upon children and young persons. In some courts, for example, there is no 'dock'. In others the bench has been brought down to a lower level so that the justices do not appear to be as remote from the parties as might otherwise be the case.

It is the differences in procedure, language and methods of address that really serve to distinguish juvenile courts from other types of court. Procedures that are special to juvenile courts will be dealt with in later chapters. At this point it is enough to draw attention to the language used in juvenile courts and to methods of address.

The first principle in juvenile courts should be to ensure that those who appear before the court understand what is going on and what is expected of them. This is a principle that should be high in the order of priorities in any court but it is of paramount importance in juvenile courts.

When the court is addressing a juvenile it must bear in mind his age and level of understanding. Great care must be taken to ensure that complicated expressions and legal jargon are avoided as much as possible. Solicitors appearing before the court should, of course, also modify their approach in this way.

It may be necessary for the court to explain the nature of the charge to the defendant in very simple terms indeed. The court has a special duty when dealing with juveniles to ensure that they fully understand what is happening at every stage of the proceedings.

Specific statutory provision has been made to stop the use of the words 'conviction' and 'sentence' in juvenile courts. In the case of children and young persons dealt with summarily, the expression 'finding of guilt' is used instead of 'conviction' and the expression 'order made upon a finding of guilt' is used instead of 'sentence' (C&YPA 1933 s.59).

The forms of address used in juvenile courts have been designed to make any juvenile appearing in court, perhaps for the first time, feel more relaxed in an environment that is, in all probability, totally foreign to him.

It is quite usual in juvenile courts for the justices, the justices' clerk, solicitors and counsel, probation officers and social services officers to refer to the defendant and to juvenile witnesses by their first name rather than by title and surname.

7. Jurisdiction

(a) The general rule

Save in certain exceptional circumstances all charges against a child or young person must be heard in a juvenile court (C&YPA 1933 s.46). In addition, any application assigned to the juvenile court under rules made under s.46, C&YPA 1933 may only be dealt with by that court.

(b) Juveniles charged with adults

A charge preferred against a child or young person *must* be heard by a magistrates' court if that child or young person is charged jointly with an adult; or if, although the adult and the child or young person are charged with different offences, both offences arise out of the same incident or set of circumstances. Additionally, a magistrates' court *may* hear a charge preferred against a child or young person, if an adult is charged at the same time with aiding, abetting, causing, procuring, allowing or permitting that offence (C&YPA 1933 s.46(1)).

(c) Defendants found to be or believed to be juveniles

If, during the course of any proceedings in a magistrates' court, it appears that the person to whom those proceedings relate is a child or young person, that court may, if it thinks fit, continue with the proceedings and determine them (C&YPA 1933 s.46(1)).

A juvenile court sitting for the purpose of hearing a charge against a person who is believed to be a child or young person may, if it thinks fit, continue to hear and determine the charge even though it becomes clear during the proceedings that the person in question is an adult (C&YPA 1933 s.48(1)).

(d) Juveniles attaining age of seventeen during proceedings

If proceedings in respect of a young person are begun under s.1 of the Children & Young Persons Act 1969 or for an offence, and he attains the age of seventeen before those proceedings have been concluded, the juvenile court can deal with the case and make any order which it could have made had he not attained that age (C&YPA 1963 s.29 as amended by Schedules 5 and 6 C&YPA 1969). If the defendant becomes seventeen before an either way offence (see page 15) has been put to him, he must be given the right to choose trial by jury.

(e) Written pleas from children and young persons

As a general rule pleas of guilty are not accepted from juveniles. If a notification has been received from an accused person that he wishes to plead guilty to the offence without appearing in court in pursuance of MCA 1980 s.12, and the court has no reason to believe that he is a child or young person, then, if he is a child or young person, he shall be deemed to have attained the age of seventeen (C&YPA 1933 s.46 (1A)). It is, however, unlikely that s.12 procedures will be accepted in a juvenile court since in such courts there is always reason to believe that the accused is a child or young person. In practice, the provision referred to above is only relevant where a juvenile is concerned in a case with an adult, and both have taken advantage of s.12 procedures.

(f) Bail and remand applications

The various provisions that restrict the right of justices sitting in a magistrates' court other than a juvenile court to hear or determine matters relating to children and young persons do not prevent any justice or justices entertaining remand applications and requests for the grant of bail. A justice or justices may hear such applications and receive such evidence as may be necessary even though they are not sitting as a juvenile court. Indeed, in these circumstances the justices adjudicating need not be members of the juvenile court panel (C&YPA 1933 s.46(2)).

8. Criminal cases and care proceedings distinguished

The jurisdiction of juvenile courts is not limited to dealing with crimes alleged to have been committed by juveniles. A large part of the court's time is devoted to dealing with the many applications that must be made in the interests of ensuring that juveniles in need of care, guidance or control get the sort of help they need.

Throughout the chapters of this book comparisons are made between criminal cases and the civil proceedings that, for ease of reference, are called care proceedings. In the book the expression 'care proceedings' includes applications for care orders, for supervision orders and for the discharge or variation of these types of order.

When dealing with a juvenile, the court is required to have regard to his welfare. In a proper case, the justices must take steps to see that he is removed from undesirable surroundings and that he gets the benefit of proper education and training (C&YPA 1933 s.44 as amended by C&YPA 1969 Sched. 6).

When they are adjudicating in a criminal case, justices must have due regard to this general consideration but must also keep in mind many other principles of sentencing. It is necessary, therefore, for the court to have regard to the nature of the offence. It must consider the seriousness of the offence and any matters that aggravate it on the one hand or mitigate it on the other, eg provocation. The circumstances of the juvenile before the court must also be taken into account.

In addition, the justices must weigh in the balance such other matters as the character and history of the offender, his family and his work, the matters put forward in mitigation and the likely effect of any sentence that they might consider imposing.

The court must also consider whether it is possible or desirable to apply any of the principles of sentencing laid down in *R* v *Sargeant* (1974); namely, retribution, deterrence, prevention and rehabilitation. It is because of the numerous, and often diametrically opposed, principles of sentencing that there will inevitably be cases in which courts will deal with young offenders in ways that cannot easily be recognised as welfare promoting.

In contrast, whenever the court is dealing with a care proceedings application it is under a duty to deal with the case in the manner that it judges to be in the best interests of the relevant infant. In such cases, the court is not concerned with deterrent measures or with courses of action designed to demonstrate a determination to uphold the rule of law. The court's attention can be focused upon the needs of the relevant infant and upon the best method of ensuring that those needs are met.

Chapter 2

Starting proceedings

1. Who may institute proceedings?

The answer to this question will depend upon whether the proceedings under consideration are criminal proceedings or care proceedings. It is necessary to consider each type of case separately.

(a) Criminal case

At the present time there is no restriction of law that limits the persons who may lay an information with a view to commencing criminal proceedings against a juvenile.

Criminal proceedings may not be instituted against children who have not attained the age of ten years (C&YPA 1933 s.50 as amended by C&YPA 1963 s.16(1)).

A person who decides to lay an information in a case in which he has reason to believe that the alleged offender is a young person, is under a duty to give notice of his decision to the local authority (C&YPA 1969 s.5(8)). For these purposes the appropriate local authority is the local authority for the area in which the young person resides or, if the young person does not appear to reside in the area of a local authority, the local authority in whose area the offence was allegedly committed (C&YPA 1969 s.5(9)). Subsections 8 and 9 of s.5 are the only subsections in force at the time of going to press. For the time being, informations can be laid by private citizens (this is most likely in cases of assault or similar conduct) although generally they are laid by the police.

If the other parts of s.5 are brought into force at some future date it will then only be possible for qualified informants to lay informations against young persons.

Section 5(9), C&YPA 1969 defines a 'qualified informant' as a 'servant of the Crown, a police officer and a member of a designated police force acting in his capacity as such a servant, officer or member; a local authority; the Council of a county district and any body designated as a public body for the purposes of the section'. 'Designated' means designated by an order made by the Secretary of State. The section also makes it clear that a qualified informant may act by an agent.

If the remaining parts of C&YPA 1969 s.5 are brought into force, qualified informants will not be able to lay an information alleging an offence if the suspected offender is a young person, unless the informant is of the opinion that the offence is of a description prescribed by the Secretary of State in accordance with the powers vested in him by virtue of C&YPA 1969 s.5(4); and that it would not be adequate for the case to be dealt with by a parent, teacher or other person, or by means of a caution from a constable or through the exercise of the powers of a local authority or other body not involving court proceedings; or by means of care proceedings taken in accordance with the provisions of C&YPA 1969 s.1 (C&YPA 1969 s.5(2)).

A qualified informant will not be able to come to a decision to lay an information unless:

(i) he has told the appropriate local authority that the laying of an information is being considered and has invited observations from the authority; and

(ii) the local authority have indicated that they do not wish to make any observations or have not made any during the period or extended period allowed by the qualified informant for the receipt of observations, or he has considered the observations made by the authority during that period.

A qualified informant will be entitled to disregard these provisions in any case in which it appears to him that the requirements of C&YPA 1969 s.5(2) (above) are satisfied and will continue to be satisfied notwithstanding any observations that might be made by the local authority (C&YPA 1969 s.5(3)).

Any information that is laid by a qualified informant will have to be in writing and shall:

(i) state the alleged offender's age to the best of the informant's knowledge; and

(ii) contain a certificate signed by the informant stating that the requirements of C&YPA 1969 s.5(2) and (3) are satisfied, or that the case is one in which the requirements of C&YPA 1969 s.5(2) are satisfied and he is entitled to disregard the requirements of C&YPA 1969 s.5(3) (C&YPA 1969 s.5(5)).

If, when the justices begin to inquire into a case, either as examining justices or on the trial of an information, they have reason to believe that the alleged offender is a young person and either:

(i) it appears that the person who laid the information was not a qualified informant at the time the information was laid; or

(ii) the information is not in writing and does not contain the certificate required by virtue of the provisions of C&YPA 1969 s.5(5)(b),

they will be under a duty to quash the information. The order made by the justices will be without prejudice to the laying of a further information in respect of the matter in question.

However, no proceedings shall subsequently be invalidated because a contravention of any requirement of C&YPA 1969 s.5 has been discovered; and no action may be taken in respect of any such proceedings on the ground that a contravention has been discovered (C&YPA 1969 s.5(6)).

None of the provisions of C&YPA 1969 s.5(1) to (6) will apply to an information laid with the consent of the Attorney General or laid by or on behalf of or with the consent of the Director of Public Prosecutions (C&YPA 1969 s.5(7)).

(b) Care proceedings

At the present time care proceedings applications may only be brought by the local authority, a constable, or officers of the NSPCC. The Secretary of State does have the power to authorise other persons to make these applications, but to date he has not done so. The authority for officers of the NSPCC to make applications is contained in SI 1970 No 1500.

Care proceedings may not be begun by any person other than a local authority, unless that person has given notice of the proceedings to the appropriate local authority, ie the local authority for the area in which the relevant infant resides. If it appears that the infant does not reside in the area of a local authority, the notice must be given to the local authority for the area in which it appears the circumstances giving rise to the proceedings arose (C&YPA 1969 s.2(3)).

Care proceedings brought as a result of a failure to attend school regularly may only be brought by a local education authority (C&YPA 1969 s.2(8)).

It is not possible for the parent or guardian of a child or young person to bring him before a juvenile court on the ground that he is unable to control him. Any parent or guardian who believes that for this reason the child or young person in question ought to be brought before a juvenile court may give notice in writing asking the local authority in whose area that child or young person lives to bring him before a juvenile court under C&YPA 1969 s.1.

The local authority is under no *obligation* to bring the child or young person before the court following the service of such notice, but should the local authority refuse to do so within twenty-eight days from the date on which the notice is given, the parent or guardian may apply to a juvenile court, by way of complaint, for an order directing them to do so (C&YPA 1963 s.3(1)).

Where a complaint has been made for an order directing a local authority to bring a child or young person before the juvenile court under C&YPA 1969 s.1, the local authority must make available to the court such information as to home surroundings, school record, health and character of the child or young person as appears to them to be likely to assist the court. In order to be able to do so the local authority must make such investigations as may be necessary (C&YPA 1963 s.3(2)).

The child or young person who is the subject of the complaint shall not be present in court when the application for an order requiring the local authority to bring proceedings is heard (C&YPA 1963 s.3(3)).

Care proceedings are commenced by the local authority (or other officer) serving upon the clerk to the juvenile court, the relevant infant, and his parent or guardian, a notice of care proceedings, in the form set out at page 230. On receipt of the notice, if a date was not arranged in advance, the clerk of the juvenile court will arrange a date for the hearing of the application before the court.

2. Time limits

(a) Criminal case

There are no special time limits placed upon the commencement of criminal proceedings when juveniles are involved. Proceedings for summary offences must, therefore, be commenced within a period of six months starting with the date upon which the offence was committed, unless the particular statute by which the offence was created provides otherwise (MCA 1980 s.127). The time limit does not apply to either way offences.

An either way offence is an offence which, in the case of an adult, can be tried in the magistrates' court or in the Crown Court.

The circumstances in which it is possible to commit a juvenile to the Crown Court for trial are very strictly limited. A person who is under the age of 17 must be tried in the juvenile court or in the magistrates' court (if concerned with an adult), unless:

(i) he has attained the age of 14 and the offence is such as is mentioned in C&YPA 1933 s.53(2) (see below) and the court considers that if he is found guilty of the offence it ought to be possible to sentence him in pursuance of that subsection; or

(ii) he is charged jointly with a person who has attained the age of 17 and the court considers it necessary in the interests of justice to commit them both for trial. (MCA s.24)

Section 53(2), C&YPA 1933 provides that 'where a child or young person is convicted on indictment of any offence punishable in the case of an adult with imprisonment for fourteen years or more, not being an offence the sentence for which is fixed by law, and the court is of the opinion that none of the other methods in which the case may be legally dealt with is suitable, the court may sentence the offender to be detained for such period, not exceeding the maximum term of imprisonment with which the offence is punishable in the case of an adult, as may be specified in the sentence; and where such a sentence has been passed the child or young person shall, during that period, be liable to be detained in such place and on such conditions as the Secretary of State may direct'.

(b) Care proceedings

There is no time limit applied by statute to the commencement of care proceedings. Before the proceedings can be brought the applicant must reasonably believe that one of the conditions set out in C&YPA 1969 s.1(2) is satisfied and that the juvenile is in need of care or control which he is unlikely to receive unless an order under the section is made. The proceedings are, by their very nature, designed to deal with situations that exist at the time the application is made. This being so, time limits do not arise.

3. Securing attendance in a criminal case

(a) Defendant

The attendance of a juvenile defendant at court can be secured either by the issue of a summons (see page 245) requiring him to attend

15

court on a given date and at a given time, or by the issue of a warrant for the arrest of the defendant. In either case, the process issued will be based upon an information laid within the appropriate time limits. (MCA 1980 s.1).

If a warrant is issued for the arrest of the defendant it may direct that the defendant be brought before the court immediately or it may direct that upon arrest the defendant shall be released on bail (MCA 1980 s.117). A defendant released on bail is under a duty to surrender to custody on the date and at the time specified in the warrant. Additional conditions, both pre-release and post-release, may be imposed in appropriate cases (Bail Act 1976 s.3).

(b) Parent or guardian

Where a child or young person is charged with an offence, any parent or guardian of his may be required to attend court during all the stages of the proceedings where the court thinks it desirable, unless the court is satisfied that it would be unreasonable to require his attendance (C&YPA 1933 s.34).

A summons (see page 246) or a warrant may be issued to secure the attendance of any parent or guardian at court and a summons to the child or young person may include a summons to his parent or guardian (MCCR 1970 r.26).

4. Securing attendance in care proceedings

(a) Relevant infant

A justice may issue a summons or a warrant for the purpose of securing the attendance of the relevant infant before the court in which care proceedings are brought or to be brought in respect of him (C&YPA 1969 s.2(4)). Section 55(3) and (4) MCA 1980 apply to warrants issued for the purpose of securing the attendance at court of a relevant infant. The effect is that no warrant may be issued unless the court is satisfied that a summons cannot be served on the relevant infant, or that a summons was served on him within a reasonable time before the hearing and he has not appeared in answer to it. If he has appeared on a previous occasion, a warrant may only be issued at an adjourned hearing if the court is satisfied that he has had adequate notice of the time and place of the adjourned hearing. These subsections are applied by s.2(4) C&YPA 1969 as amended.

Where the relevant infant is arrested by virtue of a warrant issued under the provisions of the above section and cannot be brought before the court immediately, he may be detained in a place of safety for a period of not more than seventy-two hours from the time of the arrest. Unless the infant is brought before the court he shall be brought before a justice within that time. The justice shall either make an interim order in respect of him (see page 105) or direct that he be released forthwith (C&YPA 1969 s.2(5)).

(b) Parent or guardian

Any parent or guardian of an infant brought before the court in connection with care proceedings may be required to attend court during all stages of the proceedings, unless the court is satisfied that it would be unreasonable to require his attendance (C&YPA 1933 s.34).

A summons or a warrant may be issued to secure the attendance of any parent or guardian of an infant before the court in connection with care proceedings (MCCR 1970 r.26).

Chapter 3

Legal aid

1. Availability

In most respects the law relating to legal aid is the same whether the person who is to appear in court is an adult or a juvenile. There are certain procedural differences if the application is made in respect of a person who has not attained the age of *sixteen*, and these are detailed below. The availability of legal aid to a juvenile varies a little depending upon whether his impending court appearance is in connection with a criminal matter or with care proceedings.

(a) Criminal case

Legal aid is available to any juvenile who is to appear before a court in respect of a criminal offence. A legal aid order may be made in respect of a person who has been charged with an offence before the court; a person who is brought before the court to be dealt with; or in respect of a person who has been charged before a magistrates' court and remitted to the juvenile court to be sentenced in accordance with the provisions of s.56(1) C&YPA 1933 (LAA 1974 s.28(1) and (2)). In criminal proceedings there is no provision for legal aid to be granted to the parents of the juvenile before the court.

(b) Care proceedings

A legal aid order may be granted to a juvenile who is or is to be brought before a juvenile court in connection with a care proceedings application (LAA 1974 s.28(3)(a)). Similarly, legal aid is available to juveniles who are to appear before the juvenile court in connection with an application for the variation or discharge of a supervision order under the provisions of C&YPA 1969 s.15 or on an application for an order authorising detention in accommodation provided for the purpose of restricting liberty under CCA 1980 s.21A (LAA 1974 s.28(3)(b)). Legal aid is also available in the case of a juvenile who is or is to be brought before the juvenile court in connection with an application to remove him from care and place him in a Borstal institution pursuant to C&YPA 1969 s.31 (LAA 1974 s.28(3)(c)).

(c) Appeals

Legal aid is available to a juvenile who wishes to appeal to the Crown Court from a decision of the juvenile court, whether that decision was made in the course of a criminal trial or during the course of care proceedings.

In the case of an appeal by a juvenile who has been found guilty of and sentenced for a criminal offence, legal aid may be granted by the juvenile court or by the Crown Court (LAA 1974 s.28(5)).

Legal aid may also be granted to a juvenile who wishes to appeal from the juvenile court in respect of any of the following matters:

(i) any finding or order made under the provisions of C&YPA 1969 s.1, except an order requiring his parent or guardian to enter into a recognizance to take proper care of him and to exercise proper control over him (C&YPA 1969 s.2(12)) (see page 89);

(ii) a finding that an offence condition alleged in care proceedings is satisfied with respect to him in consequence of an offence which was not admitted by him before the court (C&YPA 1969 s.3(8)) (see page 90);

(iii) an order made following an application to vary or discharge a supervision order (C&YPA 1969 s.16(8)) (see page 79);

(iv) an order made following an application to vary or discharge a care order (C&YPA 1969 s.21(4)) (see page 90);

(v) an order under CCA 1980 s.21A authorising detention in accommodation provided for the purpose of restricting liberty (see page 178).

Once again, the power to grant legal aid for the appeal is vested in both the juvenile court and the Crown Court (LAA 1974 s.28(6)).

(d) Parents and guardians

It is not possible for the parent or guardian of a child or young person brought before the juvenile court in connection with care proceedings to be granted legal aid. It is the child or young person who is the 'person brought before a juvenile court'.

Legal aid may be granted to a parent or guardian when an order has been made under the provisions of C&YPA 1969 s.32A (LAA 1974 s.28(6A)) (see page 43). Such an order prevents the parent or guardian representing the child or young person in the course of proceedings:

(i) under s.1 C&YPA 1969 (care proceedings);

(ii) on an application under s.15(1) C&YPA 1969 for the discharge of a supervision order;

(iii) on an application for the discharge of a care order under s.21(2) C&YPA 1969;

(iv) on appeal to the Crown Court under s.2(12) C&YPA 1969;

(v) on appeal to the Crown Court under s.16(8) C&YPA 1969; or

(vi) on appeal to the Crown Court under s.21(4) C&YPA 1969

if it appears to the court that there is or may be a conflict, on any matter relevant to the proceedings, between the interests of the child or young person and those of his parent or guardian.

If an application under (i) or (ii) above is unopposed the court must make an order in respect of the parent or guardian, unless it is satisfied that it is not necessary to do so to safeguard the interests of the child or young person (s.32A(2) C&YPA 1969).

Any order that is made under this section on an application within (i), (ii) or (iii) above shall continue to have effect for the purposes of any appeal to the Crown Court arising from those proceedings (s.32A(3) C&YPA 1969).

The power to make an order under this section in relation to applications within (i), (ii) or (iii) above may be exercised by a single justice, before the hearing of the application (s.32A(4) C&YPA 1969).

The power to grant legal aid to a parent or guardian in such a case is in addition to the power to grant legal aid to the child or young person. Where legal aid has been granted to the parent or guardian it is good practice to grant it to the child or young person as well.

2. Eligibility

A legal aid order may be granted in respect of an applicant if it appears desirable to grant the order in the interests of justice (LAA 1974 s.29(1)).

When determining whether it is desirable to grant the order in the interests of justice, courts find the guidelines laid down by the former Lord Chief Justice Widgery — the 'Widgery Criteria' — most helpful. The 'Widgery Criteria' suggest that, unless the defendant has adequate means to provide representation at his own expense, legal aid should be granted if:

(a) the charge is a grave one in the sense that the accused is in real jeopardy of losing his liberty or livelihood or suffering serious damage to his reputation; or

(b) the charge raises a substantial question of law; or

(c) the accused is unable to follow the proceedings and state his own case because of his inadequate knowledge of English, mental illness or other mental or physical disability; or

(d) the nature of the defence involves the tracing and interviewing of witnesses or expert cross-examination of a witness for the prosecution; or

(e) legal representation is desirable in the interest of someone other than the accused as, for example, in the case of sexual offences against young children when it is undesirable that the accused should cross-examine the witness in person.

The court is obliged to grant legal aid in certain circumstances. In the case of juveniles these may be summarised as follows:

(a) where the defendant is committed for trial on a charge of murder;

(b) where the defendant is brought before the court after a period of remand in custody and may again be remanded in custody, if he is not represented and wants to be and was not represented before the court when he was first remanded;

(c) where a defendant who is to be sentenced for an offence is to be kept in custody to enable inquiries or a report to be made to assist the court in dealing with him; and

(d) where a child is brought before a juvenile court under CCA 1980 s.21A (application for an order authorising the keeping of a child in accommodation provided for the purpose of restricting liberty) and is not but wishes to be legally represented.

(LAA 1974 s.29(1)).

Legal aid does not have to be granted in the circumstances at (b) above if the defendant has been found guilty of the offence charged; here there is no obligation placed upon the court to grant legal aid for the purposes of the proceedings before the court. The court is *obliged* to grant legal aid only for the purposes of so much of the proceedings as relate to the grant of bail (LAA 1974 s.29(1A)).

The court may not grant legal aid to any person unless it appears that his means are such that he requires assistance in meeting the costs he may incur (LAA 1974 s.29(2)).

Legal aid may not be granted to an applicant who has not furnished a written statement of his means in the prescribed form (see page 254) with his application, unless it appears that he is incapable of doing so by reason of his physical or mental condition (LAA 1974 s.29(4) and LACPR 1968 r.1(3)).

When the application for legal aid is made by or on behalf of a person who has not attained the age of sixteen, the court is not *obliged* to obtain a statement of means, but may require a statement of means (see page 254) from the applicant and from a person who is an appropriate contributor in relation to him, eg a parent or guardian, or from such of them as the court selects (LAA 1974 s.29(5)).

2. Who may consider applications?

Legal aid applications may be considered by the court or a justice of the peace (LAA 1974 s.28), or by a justices' clerk (LACPR 1968 r.1(1)).

An application may be made orally to the court but no order shall be made until a statement of means has been considered, unless the applicant is not required under LAA 1974 s.29(4) or (5) to furnish a statement of means (LACPR 1968 r.1(3)).

The powers of the court to determine an application may be exercised by the justices' clerk or by a justice of the peace to whom he has referred it (LACPR 1968 r.1(4)).

Where an application is made orally to the court, the court may refer it to the justices' clerk for determination (LACPR 1968 r.1(5)). When an application is considered by a justices' clerk he may:

(a) make an order; or

(b) refer the application to the court or to a justice of the peace; or

(c) if the review allowed by r.6H would be available to the applicant, refuse the application

(LACPR 1968 r.1(6)).

The review procedure referred to above is available to an applicant where:

(a) the applicant is charged with an indictable offence or an offence triable either way; and

(b) the application has been refused on the ground that it does not appear to the court or the proper officer of the court desirable to make an order in the interests of justice (r.6C(1)(a)); and

(c) the application was made no later than 21 days before the date fixed for the trial of an information or the inquiry into the offence as examining justices, where such a date has been fixed at the time that the application was made

(LACPR 1968 r.6E).

Where a justices clerk refuses to make a legal aid order unless the applicant and/or the appropriate contributor makes a payment or payments on account of any contribution towards costs, the applicant may ask for the application to be determined by a court or a justice of the peace as the clerk thinks fit (LACPR 1968 r.1(7)).

4. Forms of application

Except in the special circumstances referred to above, an applicant for the grant of legal aid must complete and submit an application for legal aid and a statement of means. Juveniles who have not attained the age of sixteen may also be asked to supply a statement of means completed by an appropriate contributor.

Application forms and statement of means forms may vary a little in appearance from court to court but they will follow the prescribed forms in substance. The forms are to be found in LACPR 1968 Sched 1. Specimen forms are also set out in Appendix A, page 252 *et seq*.

Applicants for legal aid and practitioners assisting them to complete the various forms should take care to ensure that all relevant information is given. The statement of means supplied will be used not only to determine whether the applicant's means are such that he requires assistance in meeting the costs he may incur, but also to assess the amount, if any, of the contribution that he may be ordered to pay at the end of the case if the legal aid is granted. The information contained in the application form will be taken into account when the court turns its attention to the question of whether it appears desirable to grant the application in the interests of justice. The application should contain all the information needed to establish whether it falls within the bounds of the 'Widgery Criteria'.

Some practitioners have expressed concern about the existence in application forms of questions designed to establish whether an applicant has previous findings of guilt recorded against him. They argue that if this information is included in an application for legal aid, the applicant may be prejudiced at his trial. In practice there is no such danger. Justices and justices' clerks are only too well aware of the importance of ensuring that a court dealing with a contested case has no knowledge of previous findings of guilt. Great care is taken to ensure that if it has been necessary to refer an application to a justice, that justice does not hear the case. If information about previous court appearances is not given when an application is submitted, legal aid may be refused in a case in which it ought properly to have been granted.

5. Assessment of resources

The court or the proper officer of the court (the justices' clerk) must consider the statement of means of the applicant, legally assisted person or appropriate contributor in accordance with LACPR 1968 r.19, and determine that person's income and disposable capital in accordance with the Second Schedule of those regulations, unless he is in receipt of supplementary benefit. The disposable capital (but not the disposable income) must be determined in a case in which the applicant, legally assisted person or appropriate contributor is in receipt of family income supplement (LACPR 1968 r.19(1) and (2)). No legal aid order shall be made unless it appears that the disposable income and disposable capital of the applicant are such that he requires assistance in meeting the costs which he may incur (LAA 1974 s.29(2)).

6. Legal aid contribution orders

(a) Duty to order

If on assessment it is determined that a person's disposable income or disposable capital exceeds prescribed limits a legal aid contribution order must be made. A contribution order may require payment to be made in one sum or by instalments (LAA 1982 s.7(1) and (2)).

A contribution towards the costs must be made if disposable income exceeds the average of £48 weekly and if disposable capital exceeds £3,000 an order equal to the excess should be made (LACPR 1968 r.19(3)).

The amount of the weekly instalment to be paid out of disposable income is determined in accordance with the Third Schedule of the regulations. At the time of going to press (April 1987) the figures are:

Average weekly disposable income	Weekly contribution
Exceeding £48 but not exceeding £54	£1
" £54 " " " £58	£2
" £58 " " " £62	£3
" £62 " " " £66	£4
" £66 " " " £70	£5
" £70 " " " £74	£6
" £74 " " " £78	£7

The weekly contribution increases for every £4 or part of £4 by £1 for disposable incomes exceeding £78 weekly.

Contributions of sums in excess of £3,000 disposable capital should be paid in one sum.

The resources to be taken into account when legal aid applications are considered are set out in LACPR 1968 Sched. 2 as amended.

(b) Variation and revocation of contribution orders

In any case in which a legal aid contribution order is made it may be varied or revoked if further information is given about the disposable income or capital of those persons whose means were assessed when the order was made. The order may be varied:

(i) in the light of further information as to disposable capital or income; or

(ii) in the light of any change in the disposable capital or income (LAA 1982 s.8(1)).

An order may be made in a case in which no order was originally made if subsequently it appears that the relevant disposable income or capital exceeds or exceeded the prescribed limits (LAA 1982 s.8(2)).

In any case in which a contribution order has been made it may be revoked if it subsequently appears that the relevant disposable income or capital at the time the order was made was such that no order should have been made. Where this happens a new contribution order may be made if changed circumstances make it appear that the specified income and capital limits are then exceeded (LAA 1982 s.8(3)).

At the conclusion of the relevant proceedings the court in which they are concluded may, if it thinks fit:

(i) remit any sum that remains due from the assisted person or, if the assisted person is acquitted, remit or order the repayment of any sum due or paid; or

(ii) remit or order the repayment of any sum due from or paid by an appropriate contributor under the order

(LAA 1982 s.8(5)).

(c) Disclosure of change in resources

The legally assisted person or any appropriate contributor is under a duty to inform the court or the justices' clerk of any change in his financial circumstances which has occurred since his statement of means was submitted which he has reason to believe:

(i) make him liable to pay a contribution when none has been ordered; or

(ii) might affect the terms of any legal aid contribution order that has been made

(LACPR 1968 r.24).

Chapter 4

Court procedure — preliminary matters

1. Failure to appear — criminal case

(a) Prosecutor

If, at the time and place appointed for the trial of a juvenile in connection with a criminal matter, the prosecutor does not appear, the court may dismiss the information or adjourn the hearing until a later date. If evidence has been given on an earlier occasion, the court may proceed with the case notwithstanding the absence of the prosecutor.

In any case in which the court adjourns the trial due to the absence of the prosecutor, the court may not remand the defendant in custody or to the care of the local authority unless he has been brought from custody or cannot be remanded on bail because he is unable to find satisfactory sureties (MCA 1980 s.15).

If the prosecutor is represented by counsel or solicitor, he shall be deemed not to be absent from the proceedings (MCA 1980 s.122).

(b) Defendant

Should the defendant fail to appear at the date and time fixed for the hearing of a criminal case the court may, if the prosecutor is present, proceed in the absence of the defendant. If a summons has been issued the court may not proceed to try an information in the absence of the defendant unless it is proved to the satisfaction of the court that the summons was served on the defendant a reasonable time before the trial, or the defendant has appeared on a previous occasion to answer the information (MCA 1980 s.11).

These provisions apply both in the adult court and in the juvenile court. In the juvenile court, however, it is less likely that the court

27

will be disposed to try the information in the absence of the accused. Many of the options that will be available to the court in the event that the accused is found guilty of the offence charged will give rise to a need for the accused to be present.

More will be said on this subject when the procedure in a criminal trial in the juvenile court is discussed in the next chapter. It is sufficient at this stage to mention, by way of example, that the court may not order that a defendant be detained in a detention centre if he is not present in court (MCA 1980 s.11(3)).

In the adult court there is power to deal with a case in the absence of the accused on the basis of a written plea of guilty entered under the provisions of MCA 1980 s.12 (see also page 9). This section does not apply to informations that are to be tried in the juvenile court (MCA 1980 s.12(1)).

If, instead of proceeding in the absence of the accused, the court (whether it is the adult or the juvenile court) determines to adjourn or further adjourn the trial, it may, if the information has been substantiated on oath, issue a warrant for the arrest of the accused (MCA 1980 s.13(1)).

Where a summons has been issued, the court may not issue a warrant unless it is proved to the satisfaction of the court that the summons was served on the accused within what appears to the court to be a reasonable time before the date for the trial or adjourned trial (MCA 1980 s.13(2)).

In the juvenile court further restrictions are placed upon the court's power to issue a warrant for the arrest of the accused following his failure to appear. No warrant may be issued in respect of a person who has not attained the age of seventeen unless:

(i) the offence to which the warrant relates is punishable (but for the restrictions that are placed upon the imprisonment of young offenders) with imprisonment; or

(ii) the court, having found the accused guilty, proposes to impose a disqualification on him.

(MCA 1980 s.13(3)).

In any case in which the accused fails to appear at the time set down for trial of the information laid against him and the court determines not to proceed in his absence, and it is inappropriate to issue a warrant for his arrest, it must adjourn the trial and serve notice on the accused of the date and time for the hearing of the trial. In these circumstances, the court is usually able to take steps to see that the parents of the accused are present at the next hearing with the accused.

(c) Parent or guardian

The juvenile court has the power to require the attendance of a parent or guardian, and in some circumstances must require it unless it is satisfied that it would be unreasonable to do so.

When a summons is issued against a juvenile it is addressed to a parent or guardian as well as to the accused and a copy of it is served upon both the accused and his parent or guardian. The attendance of the father of the accused may be required as well as that of the mother. See pages 245 and 246 for the forms of summons.

The attendance of a parent or guardian may be secured by the issue of a warrant and in any case in which the parent or guardian fails to appear in response to a summons, it is likely that the court will issue a warrant to secure attendance at the adjourned hearing.

Whenever a child or young person is arrested, such steps must be taken as may be practicable, by the person who arrested him, to inform at least one of the persons whose attendance might be required before the court (C&YPA 1933 s.34 as substituted by C&YPA 1963 s.25 and amended by C&YPA 1969 Scheds. 5 and 6).

2. Failure to appear — care proceedings

(a) Complainant

If the complainant does not appear at the time and place appointed for the hearing of the complaint but the defendant is present, the court may dismiss the complaint.

In any case in which evidence has been received on a previous occasion the court may proceed notwithstanding the absence of the complainant (MCA 1980 s.56).

The court is not bound to dismiss the complaint if the complainant does not appear but may instead adjourn the hearing of the complaint to a later date (MCA 1980 s.54).

(b) Relevant infant

Where at the time and place appointed for the hearing or adjourned hearing of a complaint the defendant is not present the court may use the power granted to it by C&YPA 1969 s.2(4) to issue a warrant for the purpose of securing his attendance.

Although the court has a general power to proceed in the absence of the defendant to a complaint (MCA 1980 s.55), it would not be appropriate to use this power in the case of a complaint made under the provisions of C&YPA 1969 s.1. Many of the orders that might be made by the court should such a complaint be found to be proved are such that the presence of the defendant is essential.

Should the court consider using its powers under C&YPA 1969 s.2(4) (above), it must bear in mind the restrictions placed upon the power to issue warrants for the arrest of a defendant who fails to appear at the time and place appointed for the hearing of a complaint. The court may not issue a warrant unless it is satisfied that a summons cannot be served upon the defendant or the defendant has appeared on a previous occasion to answer the complaint (MCA 1980 s.55(3)).

Where the defendant fails to appear at the adjourned hearing of a complaint, the court may not issue a warrant to secure his attendance unless it is satisfied that he has had adequate notice of the time and place of the adjourned hearing (MCA 1980 s.55(4)).

If a juvenile is arrested by virtue of a warrant issued under C&YPA 1969 s.2(4) and cannot be brought before a court immediately, he may be detained in a place of safety for not more than seventy-two hours. Within that period he must be brought before a justice or before a court.

If the juvenile in question is brought before a justice, the justice shall either make an interim order (see page 105) in respect of him or direct that he be released forthwith (C&YPA 1969 s.2(5)).

It is important to remember that no warrant may be issued for the purpose of securing the attendance of a juvenile at the hearing of a complaint unless that complaint has been substantiated on oath (MCA 1980 s.55(2)).

In certain circumstances it is possible for the court to hear an application for a care order in the absence of the child subject of the application. If the child in question is under the age of five and either:

    (i) it is proved to the satisfaction of the court, on oath or in such manner as may be prescribed by rules under JPA 1949 s.15, that notice of the proposal to bring the proceedings at the time and place at which the application is made was served on the parent or guardian of the relevant infant at what appears to the court to be a reasonable time before the making of the application; or

    (ii) it appears to the court that his parent or guardian is present before the court;

the court may if it thinks fit, after giving the parent or guardian if he is present an opportunity to be heard, give a direction that the relevant infant shall be deemed to have been brought before the court at the time of the direction, and care proceedings in respect of him may be continued accordingly (C&YPA 1969 s.2(9)).

(c) Parent or guardian

The power to issue process to secure the attendance at court of a parent or guardian of a child or young person who is to appear before the court is a general power and applies with equal force whether the proceedings in question are criminal proceedings or care proceedings.

Notice of the application for a care order (see page 230) should be addressed to a parent or guardian as well as to the child or young person in question. The court may require the attendance of both parents and may issue a warrant to secure the attendance of either should they fail to attend in answer to the notice (C&YPA 1933 s.34, as substituted by C&YPA 1963 s.25 and amended by C&YPA 1969 Scheds. 5 and 6).

3. Adjournments

(a) Criminal case

A juvenile court may at any time, whether before beginning to try an information or after it has begun to do so, adjourn the trial. An adjournment may be to a fixed date or to a date to be fixed by the court at a later date. When the time for the adjourned hearing is not fixed the adjournment is said to be an adjournment *'sine die'*. If the defendant is to be remanded the adjournment must be to a fixed date.

The power to adjourn is contained in MCA 1980 s.10. Although the section talks of a magistrates' court, it does apply with equal force whenever justices are sitting as a juvenile court since for the purposes of the statute the expression 'magistrates' court' means 'any justice or justices of the peace acting under any enactment or by virtue of his or their commission or under the common law' (MCA 1980 s.148).

If a trial is adjourned the hearing shall not be resumed unless the court is satisfied that the parties have had adequate notice of the date and time of the adjourned hearing (MCA 1980 s.10(2)).

The court may adjourn a trial after a finding of guilt has been recorded against a defendant whenever it is necessary for the purpose of obtaining reports or otherwise determining the best way of dealing with the case.

(b) Care proceedings

When dealing with a child or young person who is before the court in respect of care proceedings justices may exercise the specific power to adjourn the hearing which is vested in them by virtue of MCCR 1970 r.15. The rule provides that a hearing may be adjourned, whether before or after it has begun. Once again the adjournment may be to a fixed date or to a date to be arranged later. The power to adjourn '*sine die*' does not apply if the justices, on adjourning the hearing, decide to make an interim order (see pages 34 and 105) in respect of the relevant infant.

A hearing that has been adjourned may not be resumed unless the court is satisfied that both the applicant and the respondent (the relevant infant) have had adequate notice of the date and time for the resumed hearing (MCCR 1970 r.15(1)).

4. Remands

(a) Criminal case

Whenever the court adjourns the hearing of the trial of an information it may remand the accused. The remand may be a remand on bail or the accused may be remanded in custody. The provisions of the Bail Act 1976 apply in a juvenile court as they do in an adult court. In any case in which it is decided that the accused should be refused bail the court must, usually, commit him to the care of the local authority in whose area he appears to reside or in whose area the offence or one of the offences appears to have been committed (C&YPA 1969 s.23(1)).

A young person may not be committed to a remand centre or to a prison while on remand unless the court is able to certify that he is of so unruly a character that he cannot safely be committed to the care of the local authority (C&YPA 1969 s.23(2)).

No order may be made under this section in respect of a male under the age of 15 or a female. The Secretary of State has exercised powers granted under s.34(1)(e) of the Act and modified the section so as to include the committal to prison of females under the age of 17 (Children and Young Persons Act 1969 (Transitional Modifications of Part I) Order 1979, SI 1979 No 125).

The court may not certify that a young person is of so unruly a character that he cannot safely be committed to the care of the local authority unless one or more of the following conditions is satisfied in relation to him:

(i) the young person is charged with an offence punishable in the case of an adult with imprisonment for 14 years or more, and:

- the court is remanding him for the first time in the proceedings and is satisfied that there has not been time to obtain a written report from the appropriate local authority on the availability of suitable accommodation for him in a community home, or

- the court is satisfied on the basis of such a report that no suitable accommodation is available for him in a community home where he could be accommodated without substantial risk to himself or others;

(ii) the young person is charged with an offence of violence or has been found guilty on a previous occasion of an offence of violence, and:

- the court is remanding him for the first time in the proceedings and is satisfied that there has not been time to obtain a written report from the appropriate local authority on the availability of suitable accommodation for him in a community home, or

- the court is satisfied on the basis of such a report that no suitable accommodation is available for him in a community home where he could be accommodated without substantial risk to himself or others;

(iii) the young person has persistently absconded from a community home or, while accommodated in a community home, has seriously disrupted the running of the home, and the court is satisfied on the basis of a written report from the appropriate local authority that accommodation cannot be found for him in a suitable community home where he could be accommodated without risk of his absconding or seriously disrupting the running of the home.

(CUC(C)O 1977, SI 1977 No 1037).

Notwithstanding the definition of a young person (see pages 4 and 5), for the purposes of C&YPA 1969 s.23 the Secretary of State has provided by order that the reference to young person shall be construed so as to include a child who has attained the age of 10 years (SI 1970 No 1882).

By virtue of the provisions of MCA 1980 s.128(7) justices may remand to the custody of a constable if the remand is for a period not exceeding three days. This power shall have effect in the case of a child or young person as if the reference to three days were a reference to twenty-four hours (C&YPA 1969 s.23(5) as amended by MCA 1980 Sched. 7).

(b) Care proceedings

Care proceedings are civil proceedings and therefore the court does not have the power to remand a child or young person who is the subject of an application for a care order if it is not in a position to proceed with the application or to make an order. In many cases if it is necessary to adjourn the hearing of the application the relevant infant will simply return home and reside there until the hearing is resumed.

The court may make an interim order if it is not in a position to decide what order, if any, ought to be made in respect of the child or young person in question (C&YPA 1969 s.2(10)). An interim order has the effect of placing the relevant infant in the care of the local authority for the duration of the order.

An interim order may not be made in respect of any person unless either:

(i) that person is present before the court; or

(ii) the court is satisfied that he is under the age of five or cannot be present by reason of illness or accident
(C&YPA 1969 s.22(1)).

Circumstances can arise in which a court that would otherwise have made an interim order placing a relevant infant in the care of the local authority, may direct that the infant in question be committed to a remand centre for a period of not more than twenty-eight days. A relevant infant may only be committed to a remand centre if he has attained the age of fourteen and the court certifies that he is of so unruly a character that he cannot safely be committed to the care of the local authority and the court has been notified by the Secretary of State that a remand centre is available for the reception of persons of his class or description (C&YPA 1969 s.22(5)).

For forms of interim order, see page 203 *et seq.*

Chapter 5

The trial — criminal cases

1. Assistance in conducting the case

In adult courts only solicitors and barristers can, as a general rule, represent a person charged before the court. Justices can allow some other person to sit with a defendant and offer quiet advice as to how he should conduct his case. Any person permitted to give this sort of passive assistance is known as a 'McKenzie friend'.

In the juvenile court it is of the greatest importance that a defendant should have the assistance of a more mature person. A child or young person appearing before the court may, of course, be legally represented, but if he is not, the court must allow his parent or guardian to assist him in conducting his case. The assistance that may be given by a parent or guardian in such a case goes far beyond the quiet suggestions and advice that a 'McKenzie friend' may be permitted to give in the adult court. The parent or guardian concerned may actively assist with such matters as the cross examination of prosecution witnesses (MCCR 1970 r.5(1)).

So great is the importance placed upon the juvenile's receiving adequate assistance that the court may allow a relative of the child or young person before the court or some other responsible person to assist him if his parent or guardian cannot be found or cannot, in the opinion of the court, reasonably be expected to attend (MCCR 1970 r.5(2)).

2. Explaining the charge

In the juvenile court it is a matter of particular importance that the person before the court should, at all stages of the proceedings, fully understand what is happening. It is incumbent upon the court to make sure that the proceedings are explained in language that can be understood by a person of his age and understanding. It is especially important that the child or young person before the court should understand the charge sufficiently; the court must make quite sure that the substance of the charge is explained to him in simple language (MCCR 1970 r.6).

It is not necessary for the court to embark upon a complicated exposition of the constituent parts of the offence. The court should simply satisfy itself that the child or young person fully understands the charge that he is asked to plead to; *R* v *Blandford JJ ex parte G (an infant)* (1966). Clearly, a defending lawyer should adopt the same approach.

3. Taking the plea

In the adult court defendants are invited to plead 'guilty' or 'not guilty' to the charge preferred against them. It is vital that the court, when taking a plea, should be sure that the plea entered is clear and in no way equivocal.

In the juvenile court steps must be taken to ensure that the child or young person before the court fully understands the question he is being asked and is clear in his own mind what his plea should be. A defendant in the juvenile court should not be asked to plead 'guilty' or 'not guilty'; the proper practice is for the defendant to be asked whether he admits the charge that is before the court (MCCR 1970 r.7).

Curiously, despite strict adherence to this rule, the experience of justices' clerks tends to show that most juveniles, when asked whether they admit or deny a charge, reply 'guilty' or 'not guilty' as the case may be. The Magistrates' Association has asked the Secretary of State to revoke the rule in the light of what happens in practice. The Justices' Clerks Society shares the view expressed by the Association, and it is anticipated that it will be revoked in the not too distant future.

4. Procedure when charge is denied

(a) The oath

If the charge is denied by the defendant it will be necessary for witnesses to give evidence under oath or affirmation. Any person giving evidence before a juvenile court under oath must use the following words: 'I promise before Almighty God to tell the truth, the whole truth and nothing but the truth'. The same form of oath must be used by any child or young person called upon to give sworn evidence in any court of law (C&YPA 1963 s.28 as amended by OA 1978 s.2).

Should any person who is to give evidence object to being sworn they must be allowed to give evidence under solemn affirmation instead (OA 1978 s.5(1)). Witnesses who object to being sworn are not now asked to give any explanation of their objection.

(b) Order of speeches

When the charge before the court is not admitted it is the duty of the prosecutor to call the evidence for the prosecution. Before the evidence is called, the prosecutor may address the court.

When the prosecution evidence has been completed, the accused may then address the court, whether or not he afterwards calls evidence or makes an unsworn statement. If the accused does not address the court at this stage, he may address the court at the conclusion of the evidence for the defence.

The court can give leave to either party to address the court a second time, but if leave is given to one party it may not be withheld in the case of the other party. If both parties are allowed to address the court a second time, the second address by the prosecutor must be heard before the second address by the defendant (MCR 1981 r.13).

(c) The prosecution evidence

If the child or young person before the court does not admit the charge, the court must hear the evidence of the witnesses in support of the charge. When each witness has completed his evidence-in-chief, he may be cross-examined by the defendant or by his legal representative or parent, guardian, relative or any responsible person who may have been authorised to assist with the defence (MCCR 1970 r.8(1)).

Circumstances do arise from time to time in which the child or young person is not legally represented or otherwise assisted in conducting his defence. If in this situation the child or young person, instead of asking questions by way of cross-examination, makes assertions, the court is under a duty to ask the witness such questions as it thinks necessary on behalf of the defendant. For this purpose the court may ask the defendant any question that is necessary in order to bring out or clear up any point arising from the assertions (MCCR 1970 r.8(2)).

(d) The defence evidence

If, having heard the evidence for the prosecution, the court is of the opinion that there is a *prima facie* case for the defendant to answer, he must be told that he may give evidence and call any witnesses he may wish to call (MCCR 1970 r.9). The defendant may not make an unsworn statement at this stage (CJA 1982 s.72). Again, in examining any witness who may be called to give evidence for the defence, the defendant may have the assistance of any person who has been authorised to assist by virtue of the defendant's not being legally represented.

5. The finding of the court

Having heard the evidence adduced both by the prosecution and by the defence and listened to the speeches made by or on behalf of both, the court must come to a decision as to guilt or innocence. In the juvenile court, justices are called upon to keep in mind the age of the defendant when arriving at their decision.

Age is of no importance when decisions as to guilt or innocence are being made in an adult court. In the juvenile court the age of the defendant can be of the greatest significance since it can have a bearing on exactly what it is that the prosecution must prove in order to establish the defendant's guilt.

If the defendant before the court is a child, ie he is between the ages of ten and fourteen years, the prosecution must, if there is to be a finding of guilt, prove not only that the crime was committed by him, but also that he knew that what he was doing was wrong; *R* v *Owen* (1830) and *R* v *Kershaw* (1902). The evidence as to the guilty knowledge of the accused must be clear and beyond all possibility of doubt; *R* v *Vamplew* (1862).

If a child commits an act which would amount to an offence in the case of an adult and *animus malus* is an essential ingredient of the offence, it is presumed that he did not have sufficient capacity to know that what he did was wrong. The presumption may be rebutted and it becomes weaker as the defendant gets nearer to his fourteenth birthday.

When the defendant before the juvenile court is a young person, ie he is between the ages of fourteen and seventeen, he is presumed to have sufficient discretion, so as to subject him to criminal prosecution for offences of commission, unless it is clearly shown that he suffers from mental derangement or imbecility.

6. Procedure after finding of guilt or when charge is admitted

The procedure described below is that which should be followed whenever a finding of guilt has been recorded. The procedure should be used whether the finding of guilt has followed an admission of guilt by the child or young person before the court or has been based upon the evidence given in a contested case. A solicitor or barrister representing the juvenile should ensure that this procedure is followed in full.

The procedure is as follows:

> "(*a*) the defendant and his parent or guardian, if present, shall be given the opportunity of making a statement. This statement, made by way of mitigation before sentence is passed, may be made unsworn (CJA 1982 s.72(2));
>
> (*b*) the court shall take into consideration such information as to the general conduct, home surroundings, school record and medical history of the child or young person as may be necessary to enable it to deal with the case in his best interests, and in particular, shall take into account such information which is provided in pursuance of C&YPA 1969 s.9;
>
> (*c*) if such information is not fully available, the court shall consider the desirability of remanding the child or young person for such inquiry as may be necessary;
>
> (*d*) any written report of a probation officer, local authority or registered medical practitioner may be received and considered by the court without being read aloud; and
>
> (*e*) if the court considers it necessary in the interests of the child or young person, it may require him or his parent or guardian, if present, to withdraw from the court."
>
> (MCCR 1970 r.10(1)).

It is necessary to say more about the court's powers to receive and consider reports without their being read aloud, and to require the child or young person before the court or his parent or guardian to withdraw from the court.

Taken as they stand these powers may appear to offend the principles of natural justice since they enable the court to receive information that is not immediately available to the defendant, or to his parent or guardian as the case may be.

In Chapter 7 close attention is paid to the whole question of reports submitted to the court and to the extent to which it is possible for the court to receive information that is withheld from others. At this stage it is sufficient to say that MCCR 1970 r.10 goes on to place significant restrictions upon the court's powers.

MCCR 1970 r.10(2) provides that where a report has been considered without being read aloud or where a child or young person, or his parent or guardian, has been required to withdraw from the court then:

"(a) the child or young person shall be told the substance of any part of the information given to the court bearing on his character or conduct which the court considers to be material to the manner in which the case should be dealt with unless it appears to it impracticable so to do having regard to his age and understanding, and

(b) the parent or guardian of the child or young person, if present, shall be told the substance of any part of such information which the court considers to be material as aforesaid and which has references to the character, conduct, home surroundings or health of the child or young person."

Courts, are, therefore, discouraged from unnecessary use of the power to receive information that is kept from the child or young person or his parent or guardian, by the knowledge that the substance of the information so received must be made known if it is material in the manner in which the case should be dealt with.

In addition, MCCR 1970 r.10(2) further provides that if any person, having been told of the substance of any part of such information, desires to produce further evidence with reference to that information, the court must adjourn the hearing to enable that evidence to be given if it thinks that the further evidence would be material. If the further evidence relates to a report that has been considered by the court it may, if necessary, require the attendance at the adjourned hearing of the person who made the report.

The real value of the power to receive and consider reports without those reports being read aloud lies in the fact that in this way the court may be put in possession of sensitive information that it may not be in the best interests of the child or young person to have broadcast, eg the fact that, unbeknown to the child or young person before the court, his parents are adoptive parents and not natural parents.

When the court exercises its power to ask the defendant, or his parent or guardian, to leave the court while information is received it does frequently happen that the justices are put into possession of material facts that would not otherwise have become known. Sometimes the information gleaned in this way proves to be extremely important when the time comes for the justices to decide upon the sentence or order. The defendant might, for example, make the court aware that he has been habitually ill-treated by one of his parents.

In a case where the defendant is represented, and is asked to leave the court, there is an added safeguard in that his legal representative will be present throughout the proceedings.

7. Explanation of proposed manner of dealing with case

After the justices have heard all the evidence and the speeches, and all the available reports have been considered, they must decide upon the manner in which they are going to deal with the case. Before finally disposing of the case the court is obliged to inform the child or young person before the court, and his parent or guardian if present, of the manner in which it proposes to deal with the case, unless the justices decide that it is undesirable to so inform the child or young person.

After the explanation has been given the court must allow all the persons who have been informed of the proposed manner of dealing with the case to make representations to it (MCCR 1970 r.11). Any such representations may then be made orally.

8. The sentence or order of the court

The emphasis upon ensuring that the child or young person before the court and his parent or guardian understand fully what is happening continues after the court has decided upon its sentence or order.

When the justices have announced their decision the court is under a duty to explain to the defendant the general nature and effect of the sentence passed or order made. The explanation must be given in language that is suitable having regard to the age and understanding of the defendant.

The exception to this general rule is that, should the court have decided to require the parent or guardian of the defendant to enter into a recognizance, it need not explain the general nature and effect of the order to the defendant if it appears to be undesirable to do so (MCCR 1970 r.11(2)).

Footnote: Throughout this chapter much emphasis has been laid upon the court's duty to ensure that the defendant understands what is happening at every stage. It goes without saying that where the defendant is represented, the court will expect the solicitor or barrister concerned to exercise a similar standard of care.

Chapter 6

The hearing — care proceedings

1. Grounds for order

Before a court can make any order in respect of a child or young person brought before it in accordance with the provisions of C&YPA 1969 s.1, it must be of the opinion that one of the following conditions is satisfied in respect of him:

"(a) his proper development is being avoidably prevented or neglected or his health is being avoidably impaired or neglected or he is being ill-treated; or

(b) it is probable that the condition set out above will be satisfied in his case, having regard to the fact that the court or another court has found that the condition is or was satisfied in the case of another child or young person who is or was a member of the household to which he belongs; or

(c) it is probable that the condition set out in paragraph (a) will be satisfied in his case, having regard to the fact that a person who has been convicted of an offence mentioned in C&YPA 1933 Sched. 1 is, or may become, a member of the same household as the child; or

(d) he is exposed to moral danger; or

(e) he is beyond the control of his parent or guardian; or

(f) he is of compulsory school age within the meaning of EA 1944 and is not receiving efficient full time education suitable for his age, ability and aptitude; or

(g) he is guilty of an offence excluding homicide,

and also that he is in need of care or control which he is unlikely to receive unless the court makes an order under this section in respect of him."

It is most important that those who contemplate bringing juveniles before the court under the provisions of C&YPA 1969 s.1 should fully understand that it is necessary to establish that both parts of the section are satisfied in respect of the relevant infant. It will not be enough to satisfy the court that he is beyond the control of his parent or guardian. If it cannot be shown that he is in need of care or control that he is unlikely to receive unless an order is made, the court will not be able to make the order sought.

2. Conflict of interests between relevant infant and parent or guardian

In certain proceedings brought before the court under the provisions of Part I C&YPA 1969 a situation can arise in which there is clearly a conflict of interests between the relevant infant and his parent or guardian. Provisions have, therefore, been included in the legislation to ensure that the court can deal satisfactorily with such a situation (C&YPA 1969 s.32A(1)). There are also special provisions in relation to certain unopposed applications in which the various interests may differ.

If before or in the course of proceedings in respect of a child or young person:

> (*a*) on an application under s.15(1) of the Act for the discharge of a relevant supervision order or a supervision order made under s.21(2) of the Act on the discharge of a relevant care order; or
>
> (*b*) on an application under s.21(2) of the Act for the discharge of a relevant care order or a care order made under s.15(1) of the Act on the discharge of a relevant supervision order,

it appears to the court that the application is unopposed, the court, unless satisfied that to do so is not necessary for safeguarding the interests of the relevant infant, shall order that in relation to proceedings on the application no parent or guardian of his shall be treated as representing him or otherwise authorised to act on his behalf ... Where the application in question was made by the parent or guardian on behalf of the relevant infant the order made under this section shall not invalidate the application (C&YPA 1969 s.32A(2)). See page 243 for a form of notice of such an order.

In any case in which the court makes an order under subs. (2) it must appoint a guardian *ad litem* of the relevant infant unless it is satisfied that it is not necessary to do so in order to safeguard his interests (C&YPA 1969 s.32B).

3. Appointment of guardian *ad litem*

An appointment of a guardian *ad litem* is made by order. The person to be appointed must be selected from the panel established by Regulations under CA 1975 s.103. (The Guardians Ad Litem and Reporting Officers (Panels) Regulations 1983 — reproduced in Appendix B, page 277). See page 243 for a form of notice of appointment of guardian *ad litem*. If it is not possible to make an appointment from this panel, the person appointed must be some other suitable person. The person appointed must not:

(a) be a member, officer or servant of a local authority or authorised person (within the meaning of s.1 C&YPA 1969) which is a party to the proceedings; or

(b) at any time have been a member, officer or servant of a local authority or a voluntary organisation (within the meaning of s.87(1) CCA 1980) who has been directly concerned in that capacity in arrangements relating to the care, accommodation or welfare of the relevant infant; or

(c) be a *serving* probation officer
(MCCR 1970 r.14A(2)).

The power to appoint a guardian *ad litem* or under s.32B(1) C&YPA 1969 and to give directions concerning legal representation of the infant in accordance with paragraph 6(c) of this rule may be exercised by a single justice or a justices' clerk. The power may be exercised before the hearing of the application to which the proceedings relate. A person exercising the power to appoint a guardian *ad litem* must at the same time consider whether the infant should be legally represented. He may direct the guardian appointed to instruct a solicitor to represent the infant (MCCR 1970 r.14A(4)).

4. Duties of guardian *ad litem*

The guardian *ad litem* appointed with a view to safeguarding the interests of the relevant infant before the court shall:

(a) so far as it is reasonably practicable, investigate all circumstances relevant to the proceedings and for that purpose shall interview such persons and inspect such records and obtain such professional assistance as he thinks appropriate. Paragraphs 34-40 of the *Guide for Guardians ad litem in the Juvenile Court*, reproduced in Appendix B (page 281), relate to the duty to inspect records;

(b) regard the need to safeguard and promote the infant's best interests until he achieves adulthood as paramount and take into account his wishes and feelings and ensure that they are made known to the court;

(c) unless it has already been decided that a solicitor be appointed to represent the infant, obtain the views of the court on the question of representation and, unless otherwise directed instruct a solicitor to represent him;

(d) consider, in conjunction with the solicitor, how the infant's case should be presented and instruct the solicitor, unless the solicitor feels that the infant wishes to and can give him instructions himself;

(e) seek the views of the court if difficulties arise in relation to the performance of his duties;

(f) as soon as practicable make a written report for the court for the purposes of r.20(1)(a); and

(g) perform such other duties as the court may direct (MCCR 1970 r.14A(6)).

When the court has finally disposed of the case the guardian *ad litem* shall consider whether it would be in the infant's best interests to appeal to the Crown Court and, if he considers that it would be, he shall give notice of appeal on behalf of the infant (MCCR 1970 r.14A(7)).

Any order made under C&YPA 1969 s.32B (appointment of guardian *ad litem*) also has effect for the purpose of any appeal to the Crown Court arising out of the proceedings (C&YPA 1969 s.32B(3)).

5. Assistance in conducting case

As a general rule, unless the relevant infant otherwise requests, the court must allow his parent or guardian to conduct the case on his behalf (MCCR 1970 r.17(1)).

If the court thinks it appropriate to do so it may, unless the relevant infant otherwise requests, or a guardian *ad litem* has been appointed, allow a relative or some other responsible person to conduct the case on the infant's behalf. Any person allowed to conduct the case in this way is to be referred to as 'his friend' (MCCR 1970 r.17(2)).

There are exceptions to the general rule. It does not apply in any case in which the relevant infant or his parent or guardian is legally represented. The general rule also ceases to apply if the proceedings have been brought under C&YPA 1969 s.1 (application for a care order) at the request of the parent or guardian on the grounds that the relevant infant is beyond his control (see page 14). The third exception is where the court has made an order under s.32A C&YPA 1969 that in relation to the proceedings his parent or guardian is not to be treated as representing the relevant infant or as otherwise authorised to act on his behalf.

6. Evidence in absence of relevant infant or parent or guardian

If the court is of the opinion that having regard to the grounds upon which proceedings have been brought under C&YPA 1969 s.1, or to the evidence that is likely to be given, it is in the interests of the relevant infant that the whole, or any part, of the evidence should not be given in his presence, it may, unless the relevant infant is conducting his own case, hear the whole or part of the evidence in his absence.

Any evidence relating to the character or conduct of the relevant infant shall be heard in his presence. This evidence includes any evidence that may be given during the course of proceedings brought under s.1 of the Act that the offence condition is satisfied (MCCR 1970 r.18(1)).

Should the court be satisfied that in the special circumstances it is appropriate to do so, it may require the parent or guardian of the relevant infant to withdraw from the court while the relevant infant makes a statement or gives evidence. Whenever a parent or guardian is required to withdraw the court must inform him of the substance of any allegation made against him by the relevant infant (MCCR 1970 r.18(2) and see page 49).

It is important to understand that the power to require a parent or guardian to withdraw does not apply when evidence is being given in proceedings brought under s.1 C&YPA 1969 on the ground that the offence condition is satisfied.

7. Explanation of nature of the proceedings

Unless the relevant infant is the applicant or the court has the power by virtue of any enactment to proceed in his absence, the court must inform him of the general nature of the proceedings and of the grounds on which they are brought. The explanation must be given in terms that are suitable having regard to his age and understanding. If because of the age and understanding of the relevant infant it is impracticable to give him proper explanations, the court must inform any parent or guardian of his who is present at the hearing that they have found this to be the case (MCCR 1970 r.16(1)).

If the proceedings before the court are care proceedings brought under C&YPA 1969 s.1 and it is alleged that the offence condition is satisfied, then, unless the case is one which falls to be remitted to another court because the relevant infant appears to reside in a petty sessional division other than the one for which the court acts and it does not appear to be appropriate to determine whether the offence conditon is satisfied before remitting the case, the court must:

(a) explain to the relevant infant the substance of the alleged offence in simple language suitable to his age and understanding and ask him whether or not he admits to being guilty of that offence and, before considering any matter relevant to the proceedings, shall consider and determine whether or not the offence condition is satisfied, and

(b) on determining whether or not the offence condition is satisfied, inform the relevant infant of their finding
(MCCR 1970 r.16(2)).

8. Procedure on hearing the application

(a) The oath

The evidence in support of the application and the evidence given by or on behalf of the relevant infant will normally be given under oath or upon the solemn affirmation of the witness. Everything that has been said in Chapter 5 in relation to the oath (see page 36) applies with equal force to the hearing of applications for orders under Part I of C&YPA 1969.

(b) Order of speeches

The general rule in care proceedings is that the order of speeches shall be that prescribed by MCR 1981 r.14 in relation to the hearing of a complaint (MCCR 1970 r.15(2)).

The complainant calls his evidence first but before doing so may address the court. At the conclusion of the evidence for the complainant, the defendant (relevant infant) may address the court, whether or not he afterwards calls evidence. At the conclusion of the evidence for the defence the defendant may address the court if he has not already done so.

Either party may address the court a second time, with the leave of the court, but where the court grants leave to one party it cannot refuse leave to the other party. Where the defendant obtains leave to address the court a second time his second address shall be made before the second address, if any, of the complainant (MCR 1981 r.14).

The order of speeches set out above does not apply when the court is hearing an application made under the provisions of C&YPA 1969 s.1 based partly upon an allegation that the offence condition is satisfied in the case of the child or young person subject of the application. In these circumstances the order of speeches recited in MCR r.13 applies (order of speeches on the hearing of an information) (MCCR 1970 r.16(2)(c)). The order of speeches contained in this rule is set out in detail at page 37 *et seq*.

These rules apply in such a case because, while care proceedings applications are usually civil proceedings, that is not the case when the application is based, in part, upon the offence condition.

When the court is hearing civil proceedings it cannot receive unsworn statements in evidence in the absence of agreement or some specific statutory provision. This being the case the defendant has no right to make a statement without taking the oath instead of giving evidence on oath or affirmation: *Aggas* v *Aggas* (1971).

(c) The evidence of the complainant

In care proceedings the burden of proof is upon the person who makes application for the order (the complainant). Before an order can be made the complainant must satisfy the court that the grounds for the application have been proved. The complainant must call evidence, under oath or affirmation, in support of the application.

The evidence given will be subject to cross examination by the relevant infant or by his legal representative or, if he is not represented, by his parent or guardian or any person acting as *his friend*, unless for one of the reasons set out at the beginning of the chapter they are precluded from conducting the case on his behalf.

At the end of the complainant's case the court must decide whether he has made out a *prima facie* case. If it is decided that the complainant has not made out his case, the application will be dismissed.

If the court should decide that there is a case for the defendant to answer it must tell him or the person conducting the case on his behalf that he may give evidence or make a statement and call witnesses (MCCR 1970 r.19).

(d) The evidence of the relevant infant

If the court decides that a *prima facie* case has been made out, the relevant infant may give evidence and call any witnesses that he may wish to call. The defendant may examine the witnesses himself or they may be examined by his legal representative. If the defendant is not legally represented then, unless he is precluded from conducting the case, his parent or guardian may examine the witnesses on his behalf.

9. Procedure after complainant's case has been proved

If, after hearing the evidence for both parties, the court concludes that the applicant has not proved his case, the application will be dismissed and the defendant will be allowed to leave court.

In any case in which the court finds that the applicant has proved his case the following procedure should be followed:

(a) where the guardian *ad litem* has made a written report to the court (see page 55), the court shall take it into consideration. It may be received and considered without being read aloud. A guardian *ad litem* is also entitled to make oral representations;

(b) the court shall take into consideration as much information relating to the relevant infant's general conduct, home surroundings, school record and medical history as may be necessary to enable it to deal with the case in his best interests. In particular, the court must take into consideration any information that is provided by the local authority in carrying out its obligations under the provisions of C&YPA 1969 s.9 (duty of local authority or education authority to carry out investigations and provide the court with information);

(c) if the information that is required is not fully available, the court must consider the desirability of adjourning the hearing in order that any inquiry that may be necessary may be made (see page 51);

(d) any written report of a probation officer, local authority, local education authority or registered medical practitioner may be received and considered by the court without being read aloud; and

(e) if the court considers it necessary in the interests of the relevant infant, it may require him or his parent or guardian, if present, to withdraw from the court (see page 46).
(MCCR 1970 r.20(1)).

If a report has been considered without being read aloud or if the relevant infant or his parent or guardian has been asked to withdraw from the court then:

(a) the relevant infant must be told the substance of any part of the information that has been given to the court which relates to his character and conduct and the court considers to be material to the manner in which the case should be dealt with. The court is under a duty to give this information unless it appears to it to be impracticable to do so having regard to the age and understanding of the relevant infant;

(b) the relevant infant's parent or guardian shall be told the substance of any part of the information which the court considers to be material to the manner in which the case should be dealt with and which has references to his character or conduct or to the character, conduct, home surroundings or health of the relevant infant.

Should the relevant infant or his parent or guardian wish to produce further evidence in the light of the information received about the content of the report, the court must adjourn the hearing to enable that evidence to be produced if it thinks the further evidence would be material (MCCR 1970 r.20(2)).

A form of offence condition finding is set out at page 236.

10. Explanation of proposed order

Before the court finally disposes of the case it must inform the relevant infant, any person conducting the case on his behalf and his parent or guardian, if present, of the manner in which it proposes to deal with the case and allow any of those persons to make representations. The court is only relieved of this obligation if it considers that it would be undesirable to give the information or, having regard to the age and understanding of the relevant infant it would be impracticable to give him the information (MCCR 1970 r.21(1)).

Finally, when the court has made its order, it is under a duty to explain the general nature and effect of it to the relevant infant unless it appears to be impracticable so to do having regard to his age and understanding or, in the case of an order requiring his parent or guardian to enter into a recognizance, it appears to be undesirable to do so (MCCR 1970 r.21(2)).

Chapter 7

Reports

1. The court's duty to receive and consider reports

In Chapters 5 and 6 reference has been made to the court's receiving and considering reports before finally disposing of the case before it. In criminal cases the court will receive and consider reports if they find the defendant guilty of the charge that has been preferred against him. In care proceedings reports will be received and considered after the complainant's case has been proved. It is necessary to consider in greater detail the extent of the court's duty in particular circumstances.

The Secretary of State has the authority to make Regulations requiring courts to receive and consider reports before using any sentencing option that may be specified in the Regulations. To date he has not used his powers. Adult courts are encouraged to consider reports before imposing imprisonment. In the juvenile court, justices are under a duty to receive and consider certain types of report if they are available.

In criminal cases the court must take into consideration such information as to the general conduct, home surroundings, school record and medical history of the defendant as may be necessary to enable it to deal with the case in his best interests. The court must pay particular regard to any such information contained in any report prepared by the local authority — social services department or education authority — in carrying out its duties under C&YPA 1969 s.9 (MCCR 1970 r.10(1)(b)).

In care proceedings the court's duty to receive and consider reports is expressed in identical terms (MCCR 1970 r.20(1)(b)).

Both rules go on to provide that if the information is not fully available to the court, the court must consider the desirability of adjourning the case to enable such enquiry as may be necessary to be made (MCCR 1970 r.10(1)(c) and r.20(1)(c)).

A defending solicitor may obtain reports on his own initiative for use in the defence or in mitigation, but the fees of the person preparing the report will then be the responsibility of that solicitor. This does not usually present a problem if the defendant is legally aided, as any fee incurred can be recovered from the legal aid fund.

In any case in which the court asks for a report to be prepared, the court will be responsible for payment of the fees incurred.

In many cases those representing defendants will not arrange for reports, as they will hope to persuade the court to do so. The danger in taking this course of action is that should the court not agree with the submission that a report is necessary, the chance to use such information as it might contain will be lost.

Probation officers and social workers will not usually produce reports unless they have been asked to do so by the court; but the defendant's solicitor may be able to persuade them to produce a pre-trial report if they agree that the court will ultimately require a report.

2. Who may supply reports?

Courts may receive reports from probation officers, local authorities (Social Services Department social workers), guardians *ad litem*, local authorities and registered medical practitioners.

Reports prepared by probation officers and other social workers will take the form of social inquiry reports. These reports will be comprehensive and will deal with many aspects of the subject's history and family background. The information will often be based upon interviews with the subject and his family, but they may also contain information obtained from other sources, eg family doctor or school headteacher.

Local education authority reports tend to be restricted to information about the subject's record of school attendance and about his academic and other achievements whilst at school. From time to time a member of the teaching staff at the defendant's school will feel that it would be helpful to prepare a report. These reports can be of great assistance to the court as they often contain more detailed information about the defendant's school record than ordinary school reports.

If the court is satisfied that the accused did the act or made the omission charged, but feels that an inquiry ought to be made into his physical or mental condition before the method of dealing with him is determined, it may ask for medical reports to be prepared. Medical reports may also be put before the court from time to time as part of the defence case. This course of action will be taken when those who represent the defendant are of the opinion that his physical or mental condition is relevant to the case before the court or the manner in which they would seek to persuade the court to deal with the case.

3. Who may see reports?

When reports are submitted to the adult court a copy must be given to the offender or to his counsel or solicitor. If a juvenile appears before an adult court and he is not represented by solicitor or counsel, then any report that may be submitted need not be given to him but shall be given to his parent or guardian if present in court (PCCA 1973 s.46).

This section is of no application in the juvenile court. The law relating to the receiving of reports in the juvenile court is contained in MCCR 1970 rr.10 and 20.

Reference has already been made (see pages 39 and 49) to the fact that reports may be received and considered, both in criminal cases and in care proceedings, without being read aloud. The rules also give the court the power to require the child or young person before the court, or his parent or guardian, to withdraw from the court if it considers it necessary in the interests of the child or young person. As a result it becomes possible for the court to receive and consider reports in the absence of the subject or in the absence of his parent or guardian.

This does not amount to enabling the court to receive information that remains a complete mystery to the child or young person concerned and to his parent or guardian. It simply gives the court the power to make an order in appropriate cases which may make it easier to receive reports and other information.

Once the report has been received and considered the court has a duty to make the subject of it and his parent or guardian aware of the substance of any part of the report that it considers material to the manner in which it proposes to deal with the case. Furthermore, if, having been told of the substance of any part of the report, the defendant or his parent or guardian wishes to produce further evidence, the court must adjourn the hearing for that purpose, if it is of the opinion that the further evidence would be material (MCCR 1970 rr.10(2) and 20(2)).

4. Confidentiality

It is necessary to give some consideration to the question of confidentiality of reports. Frequently those who produce reports for submission to the court misunderstand this aspect of the law.

In the paragraphs immediately preceding, reference was made to the court's duty to draw to the attention of the child or young person in question, and his parent or guardian, the substance of any part of a report that is material to the manner in which the court intends to deal with the case. This being so, a court cannot keep material information strictly between the author of the report in question and the court, however much it may have been urged to do so.

Even if courts were not required by rules to draw relevant information to the attention of the child or young person before the court and to his parent or guardian, principles of natural justice would demand that they do so. It would be quite wrong for a court to be able to receive information, which may well have great relevance to the eventual disposal of the case, if that information did not have to be made known to the persons that it would affect.

5. Special reports

(a) Reports on unruly persons

In Chapter 4 (page 32), reference was made to the court's power to remand a young person to a remand centre or to a prison if he is of so unruly a character that he cannot safely be committed to the care of the local authority. Before making such a remand, the court must also be satisfied, on the basis of a report from the appropriate local authority, that no suitable accommodation is available for him in a community home; or, if the court is remanding for the first time, that there has not been enough time to obtain such a report (CUC(C)O 1977).

It is important that the local authority submit a written report to the court if it is of the opinion that the young person in question is too unruly to be contained in a community home. The report should set out the grounds upon which the local authority has formed its opinion.

The court has also to be satisfied on the basis of the *written* report that no suitable accommodation can be found for him in a community home. The court cannot be satisfied that this is the case if it is only in possession of a document expressing the view that he cannot be accommodated without any reference being made to the facts upon which the opinion was based.

If the court is not satisfied that the young person in question cannot safely be committed to the care of the local authority it will have no choice in the matter; a commitment to the care of the local authority will follow.

(b) Guardian ad litem reports

A guardian *ad litem* appointed by a court with the object of safeguarding the interests of a relevant infant before the court must, if he thinks that it would assist the court, make a report in writing to the court (MCCR 1970 r.14A(6)(f)).

The court for its part is under a duty to take any report submitted into consideration. It may be received and considered without being read aloud (MCCR 1970 r.20(1)(a)).

(c) Antecedent history

In criminal proceedings the prosecution should prepare a document setting out the antecedent history of the child or young person before the court. It will not be used unless a finding of guilt is recorded. The document should contain information about the defendant, his home and family circumstances, and, if he has left school, about his work record.

If the defendant has appeared before the court on previous occasions the antecedent history should contain a record of the previous appearance or appearances. The information given should include the date of the finding of guilt, the date of sentence if different, the nature of the offence and the sentence or order that was passed or made. The justices should have the chance to see the full record as should the clerk of the court.

If the defendant is represented his lawyer will also be allowed to see the full record. The defendant or his advocate may challenge any information contained in the record of previous findings of guilt if it is in dispute. If the information cannot be agreed the court may wish to adjourn the hearing while the records are verified. The defendant or his legal representative may also wish to comment upon or explain the circumstances of any item shown on the record.

Juvenile liaison schemes have brought with them a substantial increase in the number of cases in which cautions are given to young offenders as an alternative to prosecution. Cautions are administered by senior police officers at a police station; the courts are not involved in the process at all.

A senior police officer considers the facts of the case and such other information as may be available, including information about the offender's previous record and other persons allegedly involved in the offence, and decides whether, in the light of all the circumstances, the offender should be prosecuted or cautioned.

A caution will not be given in any case in which the alleged offender denies the offence. If a young person has been cautioned it follows that he has admitted to the police officer considering his case that the offence in question was committed by him. Even so, the offender has not appeared before a court in connection with the offence and no finding of guilt has been recorded.

The statement of antecedents should contain information relating to cautions that have been given to the defendant but that information ought not to be included in the report under the heading 'previous findings of guilt'. The better practice is for this sort of information to be contained in the general antecedents. The list of previous findings of guilt should contain only the details of findings of guilt resulting from court appearances. Guidance on the citing of police cautions was given in Home Office Circular No 49/1978 (CS 9/1978), paragraph 3 of which reads:

> *Procedure for citing cautions*
> 3. Since the police are responsible for the decision to caution and for administering the caution, the Conference agreed that the most simple and direct method of citing the caution would be for the police to provide the information when reporting on the juvenile's antecedents. It was considered that the cautions should be separately reported or listed so that there could be no possibility of confusion between a caution and a previous finding of guilt, and that only the fact of a caution and the offence should be mentioned. In order to avoid the unnecessary attendance at court of police officers it was hoped that courts would normally accept written notification of a previous caution unless the fact of the caution was challenged.

(d) Mental Health Act reports

Before making a hospital order or a guardianship order under the provisions of MHA 1983 s.37 the court must consider reports from two medical practitioners. At least one of those practitioners must be approved for the purposes of MHA 1983 s.12 by the Secretary of State, as having special experience in the diagnosis or treatment of mental disorders.

A written report purporting to be signed by a medical practitioner may be received in evidence without proof of the signature or qualifications of the practitioner. In any case, the court may require that the practitioner by whom a report was signed attend the court to give oral evidence.

If such a report is tendered in evidence otherwise than by or on behalf of the accused, a copy must be given to his counsel or solicitor if he is represented, or if he is not represented, the substance of the report must be disclosed to his parent or guardian, if present in court.

Except where the report relates only to arrangements for his admission to a hospital, the subject of the report may require the signatory of it to be called to give oral evidence, and evidence in rebuttal of the evidence in the report may be called by or on behalf of that person (MHA 1983 s.54).

Chapter 8

Sentences and orders available in criminal cases

1. Fines

Courts have the power to impose fines upon juveniles found guilty of criminal offences. The amount of the fine that can be ordered will be subject to the statutory maximum for that offence and also to the maximum that can be imposed upon a young person of the defendant's age.

(a) Children

In the case of an offender who has not attained the age of fourteen years the maximum fine that can be imposed for one offence is £100 (MCA 1980 s.36(2)). This subsection will cease to have effect if s.4 C&YPA 1969 comes into force. This will be so because that section will prohibit criminal proceedings against children. However, there appear to be no plans to bring this section into force in the foreseeable future.

(b) Young persons

The maximum fine that can be imposed upon a young person for a single offence is £400. This figure is, of course, subject to the maximum laid down by statute for the particular offence (MCA 1980 s.36(1)).

(c) Power to order parent or guardian to pay fine etc

Whenever a fine is imposed or an order made for payment of costs or compensation, the court is under a duty to order the parent or guardian of the child or young person before the court to pay instead of the child or young person himself, unless the court is satisfied:

   (i) that the parent or guardian cannot be found; or

   (ii) that it would be *unreasonable* to make an order for payment, having regard to the circumstances of the case.

An order may be made against a parent or guardian who, having been required to attend, has failed to do so. Save in these circumstances no such order shall be made without giving the parent or guardian the opportunity of being heard.

A parent or guardian may appeal to the Crown Court against an order made under this section (C&YPA 1933 s.55 as substituted by CJA 1982 s.26).

A local authority into whose care a child or young person has been received is not his 'guardian' for the purposes of this section (*Leeds City Council* v *West Yorkshire Metropolitan Police* (1982).

2. Supervision orders

(a) General provisions

An offender found guilty by a juvenile court may be made the subject of a supervision order (C&YPA 1969 s.7(7)(b)). A supervision order has the effect of placing the offender under the supervision of a local authority designated in the order or of a probation officer (C&YPA 1969 s.11).

'A court shall not designate a local authority as supervisor unless the local authority agrees, or it appears to the court that the supervised person resides or will reside in the area of the authority' (C&YPA 1969 s.13(1)).

Children under the age of thirteen should generally be placed under the supervision of a local authority. A court must not place such a child under the supervision of a probation officer unless the local authority named or to be named in the order so requests and a probation officer is already exercising or has exercised, in relation to another member of the household to which that child belongs, duties imposed upon him by PCCA 1973 Sched. 3 para. 8 or by rules made under para. 18(1)(b) of that schedule (C&YPA 1969 s.13(2)).

The Secretary of State has made an order in accordance with powers vested in him under C&YPA 1969 s.34(1)(a) directing that for the purposes of C&YPA 1969 s.13(2), 'child' shall exclude any child who has attained the age of 13 (SIs 1970 No 1882, 1973 No 485 and 1974 No 1083).

Children over the age of thirteen and young persons who are found guilty of offences by a juvenile court may be placed under the supervision of a probation officer. In such a case, the supervisor shall be a probation officer appointed for or assigned to the petty sessions area named in the order (C&YPA 1969 s.13(3)).

While a supervision order remains in force it is the duty of the supervisor to advise, assist and befriend the supervised person (C&YPA 1969 s.14).

(b) Special requirements

A supervision order may include special requirements, for example, that the supervised person reside with an individual named in the order who agrees to the requirement (C&YPA 1969 s.12(1)).

If the court is satisfied that a scheme for intermediate treatment under the provisions of C&YPA 1969 s.19(6) is in force for the regional planning area in which the supervised person resides or is to reside, it may include in a supervision order a requirement that the supervised person comply with any of the following directions given by the supervisor:

(i) to live at a place or places specified in the directions for a period or periods so specified;

(ii) to present himself to a person or persons specified in the directions at a place or places and on a day or days so specified;

(iii) to participate in activities specified in the directions on a day or days so specified
(C&YPA 1969 s.12(2)).

The effect of these provisions is to enable the court to make an order that the supervised person, as part of his supervision, take part in such 'intermediate treatment' activities as his supervisor might direct. The supervisor must decide whether and to what extent he shall exercise the powers given to him by the court.

Intermediate treatment may take different forms in different areas. Childrens Regional Planning Areas were set up by the Department of Health and Social Security when the C&YPA 1969 came into force. Each area has a Regional Planning Committee which is responsible for establishing a network of public and private bodies (eg boys' clubs, cubs, guides, day training centres) willing and able to accept persons under supervision as participants in their activities.

If the court has ordered that there should be an intermediate treatment requirement in the order, the supervisor may, if he thinks the supervised person would derive benefit from taking part in a particular activity, direct that he takes part.

Solicitors and barristers may from time to time feel that some sort of involvement outside the home might be helpful to their client. It is in order to raise the question of intermediate treatment in such a case when addressing the court on the sentence to be passed or order to be made, but it is advisable to discuss the possibility with a probation officer first as some areas still have no effective scheme for intermediate treatment.

The periods specified in any directions given must be in accordance with the following provisions:

(a) the aggregate of the periods specified shall not exceed ninety days or such shorter period, if any, as may be specified in the order;

(b) for the purpose of calculating the period or periods in respect of which directions may be given in pursuance of the order the supervisor shall be entitled to disregard any day in respect of which directions previously given under the order were not complied with.

(C&YPA 1969 s.12(3)).

(c) Stipulated intermediate treatment

If a court decides to make a supervision order after finding a juvenile guilty of an offence or upon the discharge of a care order made in *criminal proceedings*, it may, instead of requiring him to comply with directions given by his supervisor, insert specific requirements into the order. They may require the juvenile to:

(i) do anything that a supervisor has power or would have power to direct him to do;

(ii) remain for specified periods between 6 p.m. and 6 a.m. at a specified place or at one of several specified places; and

(iii) refrain from participating in specified activities —
- on specified day(s) while the order is in force, or
- during the whole of a specified portion of that period.

(C&YPA 1969 s.12 (3C)).

The requirements imposed under s.12(3C) may not operate for more than 90 days in total (C&YPA 1969 s.12 (3E)).

Orders made restricting the movements of a juvenile between 6 p.m. and 6 a.m. are known as *night restriction orders*.

The court may only include requirements set out in s.12(3C) if:

(i) it has consulted the supervisor about the offender's circumstances and the feasibility of securing compliance with the requirements and is satisfied that it is feasible to secure that compliance;

(ii) it considers the requirements necessary for securing the supervised person's good conduct or preventing the repetition of the offence or the commission of further offences by the supervised person; and

(iii) it has the consent of the supervised person, or if he is a child, the consent of his parent or guardian.
(C&YPA 1969 s.12 (3F)).

The court may not include a requirement that involves the co-operation of a person other than the supervisor or the supervised person without that person's consent. The court may not require the supervised person to reside with a specified individual or to undergo medical treatment (C&YPA 1969 s.12 (3G)).

An order made under the provisions of s.12(3C) may not include any requirement that would involve the supervised person in being away from home for two consecutive nights nor for more than two nights in any week, or any requirement which, if he is of compulsory school age, would mean him participating in activities during school hours, unless the court is satisfied that the facilities to be used are for the time being specified in a scheme in force for the area in which the supervised person resides or will reside (C&YPA 1969 s.19(13)).

The restriction placed on participation in activities during school hours does not apply to activities carried out in accordance with arrangements made or approved by the local education authority in whose area the supervised person resides or will reside (C&YPA 1969 s.19(14)).

A night restriction order may not require a person to remain at a place for more than 10 hours in any one night. The place or one of the places specified in a night restriction order must be the place where the supervised person resides. No night restriction order may be imposed in relation to a day outside a period of three months from the day on which the order is made, and may not be imposed for more than 30 days in total. Persons required to remain at a place by virtue of a night restriction order may leave it if accompanied by a parent, guardian, the supervisor or some other person specified in the order (C&YPA 1969 s.12 (3H-M)).

For the purposes of s.12, a night restriction order imposed for a period beginning on one day and ending on the next shall be treated as imposed only in respect of the day on which the period begins (C&YPA 1969 s.12(3N)).

(d) Medical requirements

If a court is proposing to make a supervision order and is satisfied on the evidence of a properly approved medical practitioner that the mental condition of the person who is to be made subject of the order is such as requires and may be susceptible to treatment, but not such as to warrant his detention in pursuance of a hospital order, the court may include in the order a requirement that he shall submit to treatment of one of the following descriptions:

    (i) treatment by or under the supervision of a specified registered medical practitioner;

    (ii) treatment as a non-resident patient at a specified place; or

    (iii) treatment as a resident patient in a hospital or nursing home within the meaning of MHA 1983 but not a special hospital within the meaning of that Act.

    (C&YPA 1969 s.12(4)).

No requirement may be included in an order by virtue of s.12(4):

    (i) unless the court is satisfied that arrangements have been made or can be made for the treatment in question and, in the case of a resident patient, for his reception; and

    (ii) in the case of an order made in respect of a person who has attained the age of fourteen, unless he consents to the requirements being included in the order.

Any requirement that is included in a supervision order by virtue of s.12(4) ceases to have effect after the supervised person becomes eighteen (C&YPA 1969 s.12(5) as amended by CLA 1977 s.37 and Sched. 12).

(e) Failure to comply with requirements

If, while a supervision order is in force under these provisions, a juvenile court is satisfied, on the application of the supervisor, that the supervised person has failed to comply with a requirement of an order, it may:

    (i) fine him an amount not exceeding £100, or

    (ii) subject to C&YPA 1969 s.16(10), make an attendance centre order in respect of him.

    (C&YPA 1969 s.15(2A)).

A form of supervision order is printed at page 239.

3. Care orders

In any case in which imprisonment could be ordered if the defendant were an adult the court may make a care order (C&YPA 1969 s.7(7) as amended by MCA 1980 Sched.7). An order may be made even though the offender attained the age of seventeen before the order is made (C&YPA 1963 s.29 as amended by C&YPA 1969 Scheds. 5 and 6).

A court shall not make a care order under s.7(7) unless it is of the opinion that:

(a) a care order is appropriate because of the seriousness of the offence; *and*

(b) the child or young person is in need of care or control which he is unlikely to receive unless the court makes a care order. (C&YPA 1969 s.7(7A)).

A care order has the effect of placing the offender in the care of a local authority. The appropriate local authority shall be the authority in whose area it appears the offender resides or, if he does not appear to reside in the area of any local authority, the local authority in whose area it appears the offence was committed (C&YPA 1969 s.20(1) and (2)).

In deciding where any person lives for the purposes of s.20, any period during which, while in the care of the local authority, he resided outside the local authority's area shall be disregarded (C&YPA 1969 s.20(2A) included by virtue of HASSASSA 1983 Sched.2)

A care order made in respect of an offender who has attained the age of sixteen will usually cease to have effect when he attains the age of nineteen (C&YPA 1969 s.20(3)(a)). If, by the date on which the order is made, the offender has not attained the age of sixteen, the order will usually cease to have effect when he becomes eighteen (C&YPA 1969 s.20(3)(b)).

A form of care order is printed at page 236.

Where a care order is made following a finding that a person is guilty of an offence punishable with imprisonment in the case of a person over 21, the court may add to the order a condition that the power conferred by s.21(2) CCA 1980 — the power of a local authority to allow a parent, guardian, relative or friend charge and control — shall for a period not exceeding 6 months:

(a) not be exercisable; or

(b) not be exercisable except to allow the subject of the order to

be under the charge or control of a *specified* parent, guardian, relative or friend
(C&YPA 1969 s.20A(1)).

If the subject of an order is convicted or found guilty of another offence, punishable with imprisonment in the case of a person over 21, before the period specified in a condition under this section has expired, the court may replace that condition with another condition under the section (C&YPA 1969 s.20A(2)).

A court may not exercise the powers conferred by this section unless it is of the opinion that it is appropriate to do so because of the seriousness of the offence *and* that no other method of dealing with the person to whom the order relates is appropriate.

The power conferred by this section cannot be used if the defendant is not represented unless:

(a) he applied for legal aid and the application was refused on the ground that it did not appear that his means were such that he needed assistance; or

(b) having been informed of his right to apply for legal aid, he refused to do so or failed to do so.

Before adding a condition under this section the court must explain its effect to the subject of the care order.

At any time while a condition is in force, the person to whom the order relates, his parent or guardian or the local authority in whose care he is, may apply for the revocation or variation of the condition (C&YPA 1969 s.20A(3)−(6)).

Section 20A was inserted in C&YPA 1969 by CJA 1982 s.22.

4. Detention centre

A male offender between the ages of 14 and 17 who is found guilty of an offence which is punishable with imprisonment in the case of a person aged 21 or over, may be sent by a juvenile court to a detention centre for such period not exceeding four months as the court considers appropriate. Such a sentence may only be passed if the court considers:

(a) that the only appropriate method of dealing with him is to pass a custodial sentence on him; but

(b) that the term of such sentence should be no more than 4 months.

In a case in which the maximum term of imprisonment that could be imposed is less than four months, the maximum period of detention is restricted to that period. The court may not order detention in a detention centre for a period of less than 21 days except for an offence under s.15(11) CJA 1982 (breach of the conditions of a supervision order following release from detention or youth custody).

The court is precluded from making a detention centre order if the defendant's physical or mental condition makes him unsuitable for such a sentence, or if the defendant has ever served a sentence:

(a) of imprisonment;

(b) of detention for a grave crime (s.52 C&YPA 1933);

(c) of Borstal training;

(d) of youth custody (s.6 CJA 1982); or

(e) of custody for life (s.8 CJA 1982).

Exceptionally, a court may make a detention centre order in respect of a person who has served one of the sentences mentioned above if it appears that there are special circumstances (in relation to the offence or the offender) which warrant the making of such an order in his case (s.4 CJA 1982)

Consecutive orders for detention may be made provided that the effect is not that the offender is detained for more than four months at a time (s.5(1) CJA 1982). If a court makes an order in respect of an offender aged 15 or over that has the effect of sentencing to detention for more than four months, he shall be treated for all purposes as if he had been sentenced to a term of youth custody equal to the aggregate of the terms of detention ordered. If, on the other hand the offender is less than 15 years of age, any period of detention in excess of four months in aggregate shall be treated as remitted.

If an offender who has attained the age of 15 is serving a term of detention in a detention centre and he is convicted of another offence, if the court considers that the only appropriate method of dealing with him is to pass a custodial sentence on him and that the length of sentence to be passed would, taken together with the period of detention that he is already serving, exceed four months, the court should pass a youth custody sentence for whatever term it considers appropriate (see below). The court shall also direct that any detention centre order to which he is subject at the time of the conviction for which the youth custody sentence is imposed shall be treated for all purposes as if it had been a sentence of youth custody (s.5(2)-(6) CJA 1982).

5. Youth custody

Where a male person between the ages of 15 and 17 is found guilty by a juvenile court of an offence punishable in the case of a person aged 21 or over with imprisonment and the court considers that the only appropriate method of dealing with him is to pass a custodial sentence, and that it would be appropriate to sentence the offender to a term of more than four months or terms of more than four months in the aggregate, or that, though a sentence of less than four months would be appropriate, a detention centre order is precluded by s.4(5), it shall pass a sentence of youth custody upon him. In such a case the court must state in open court its reasons for finding that a custodial sentence is the only appropriate way of dealing with the offender (s.6 CJA 1982).

An offender who has not attained the age of 17 years shall not be sentenced to a term of youth custody which exceeds twelve months at a time. Subject to this restriction, the maximum sentence that can be imposed is the same as the maximum imprisonment that may be imposed for that offence in the case of a person who has attained the age of 21 years, and consecutive periods of youth custody may be ordered (s.7 CJA 1982).

6. Attendance centre orders

If the court would, but for the statutory restrictions upon imprisonment of youth offenders, have power to impose imprisonment in any case, it may have the power to order that the defendant attend an attendance centre. The court may only make such an order if it has been notified by the Secretary of State that an attendance centre is available for the reception from that court of persons of the defendant's class or description.

No order can be made in respect of an offender who has previously been sentenced to imprisonment, detention for a grave crime (s.53 C&YPA 1933), Borstal training, youth custody, custody for life (s.8 CJA 1982) or detention in a detention centre, unless it appears that there are special circumstances, relating to the offence or the offender, which warrant the making of such an order in his case. If the court is able to make an order it shall be for attendance at the centre specified in the order for such number of hours as shall be specified (CJA 1982 s.17 (1)–(3)).

The aggregate number of hours for which an order may require an offender to attend an attendance centre is:

    (a) not less than 12 hours (unless the offender is under 14 years of age and the court is of the opinion that 12 hours would be excessive);

(b) not more than 12 hours (except where the court is of the opinion that, having regard to all circumstances, 12 hours would be inadequate).

Where the court does consider 12 hours to be inadequate, it may not exceed 24 hours if the offender is under 17 years of age.

A court may make an attendance centre order even though a previous order in respect of the offender has not ceased to have effect. The hours specified in the new order may be determined without regard to:

(a) the number specified in the previous order; or

(b) the fact that that order is still in effect.
(CJA 1982 s.17(6)).

The times fixed for an offender to attend must be such as to avoid interference, so far as practicable, with his school hours or his working hours (CJA 1982 s.17(8)).

Attendance centres are usually staffed by police officers. They often operate on alternate Saturdays. An offender will be ordered to make his first appearance at the centre on a day on which the centre will be open and it will be left for the officer in charge to arrange future attendances. It is likely that for the duration of the order attendances will be made at fortnightly intervals and that the length of each session will be two hours. Working to this pattern an offender ordered to attend for twelve hours will make six attendances over a period of twelve weeks.

For a form of attendance centre order, see page 246.

7. Absolute or conditional discharges

The power to order absolute and conditional discharges contained in PCCA 1973 s.7 extends to the juvenile court as well as the adult courts. The power may be exercised when the court is of the opinion, having regard to the circumstances of the case under consideration, including the nature of the offence and the character of the offender, that it is inexpedient to inflict punishment and that a period of supervision would not be appropriate.

Any discharge so ordered may be absolute or subject to a condition that the offender does not commit another offence during such period not exceeding three years from the date of the order as may be specified therein (PCCA 1973 s.7(1)).

Before the court can make an order for conditional discharge, the court must explain to the offender, in ordinary language, that if he commits another offence during the period that the order remains in force he will be liable to be sentenced for the original offence (PCCA 1973 s.7(3)).

It is not proper for a court that is dealing with an offender for *one* offence to order a discharge and to impose a fine: *R* v *McClelland* (1951).

8. Bind over of parent or guardian

When any juvenile is found guilty of an offence the court may order his parent or guardian to enter into a recognizance to take proper care of him and exercise proper control over him (C&YPA 1969 s.7(7)(c)). No parent or guardian of any juvenile found guilty of an offence may be ordered to enter into such a recognizance without his consent.

For a form of order under this provision, see page 248.

9. Compensation

A court that finds a juvenile guilty of an offence may order that he pay compensation for any personal injury, loss or damage resulting from that offence or any other offence which is taken into consideration when sentence is determined. However, it is not possible to make an order for compensation for any loss suffered due to an accident arising out of the presence of a motor vehicle on a road, unless the offence was committed under TA 1968 and the damage was caused while the property in question was out of the possession of its owner.

Consequently, if a defendant commits an act of careless driving and in the course of that offence he causes damage to another vehicle, the court has no power to compensate the owner of the other vehicle for the loss suffered as a result of that damage. If, on the other hand, a defendant takes a motor vehicle without the consent of the owner and whilst that vehicle is out of its owner's possession it is damaged in a road traffic accident, the court can order the defendant to compensate the owner.

The maximum sum that can be ordered is £2,000. This is curious since the maximum fine that may be imposed for any one offence is £100 in the case of a child and £400 in the case of a young person. The anomaly exists because MCA 1980 s.150 provides that 'fine' includes compensation payable under a conviction (or finding of guilt) except for the purpose of any enactment imposing a limit on the amount of any fine.

This being so, the amount of compensation that may be ordered in a criminal case is restricted by the provisions of MCA 1980 s.40 only, which impose a limit of £2,000.

Thus, if a defendant is found guilty of two criminal offences and loss is sustained as a result of each offence, it is possible for the court to order up to £2,000 compensation in respect of each loss.

Compensation may also be ordered in respect of loss suffered as a result of an offence that has been taken into consideration, but only to the extent to which the maximum sums that can be ordered in relation to offences charged have not been used up. The effect of this provision is that the aggregate amount that may be ordered by way of compensation is £2,000 multiplied by the number of offences of which the defendant has been found guilty. Offences are not taken into consideration in care proceedings.

If a defendant is found guilty of two offences and the loss suffered in each case is £750 then, if that sum is ordered to be paid in each case, there will be a residue of £2,500 that can be used to provide compensation for any loss that has been caused by an offence or offences that the court has taken into consideration when dealing with the defendant (PCCA 1973 s.35).

The provisions of C&YPA 1933 s.55(1) apply to compensation. The court *must* order that the sum be paid by the parent or guardian of any defendant who has not attained the age of fourteen and *may* so order in the case of a defendant who has attained that age, unless the court is satisfied that the parent or guardian cannot be found or that he has not conduced to the commission of the offence by neglecting to exercise proper care or control of the child or young person.

A compensation order may be made as a sentence in its own right or in addition to some other sentence (PCCA 1973 s.35 as amended by CJA 1982 s.67).

If the question of whether or not compensation is payable at all by the defendant is raised, courts should normally refuse to make a compensation order (*R* v *Kneeshaw* (1974)).

10. Deferment of sentence

A court may defer passing sentence on an offender in order to take into account, in determining sentence, his conduct after the finding of guilt. In considering conduct after the finding of guilt the court may look particularly at any reparation that he may have made for his offence. The court may also defer sentence to enable any change in the offender's circumstances to be taken into account.

Sentence may be deferred only with the consent of the offender and may not be deferred for a period in excess of six months from the date on which the deferment is announced.

Sentence may be passed before the expiration of the period of deferment if during that period the offender is found guilty in Great Britain of any offence (PCCA 1973 s.1).

The court that deals with the offender after the deferment need not be composed of the same justices who found him guilty of the offence. However, if the court that sentences the offender is not composed of the same justices, it must be put into possession of sufficient of the facts of the case as to enable it to deal with the matter judicially (MCA 1980 s.121).

11. Community service

When dealing with an offender who has attained the age of 16 years a juvenile court may, if the offence is punishable in the case of an adult with imprisonment, make a community service order that requires him to carry out unpaid work for not less than 40 nor more than 120 hours. The period must be specified in the order.

The court must obtain the consent of the offender to the making of the order. No order may be made unless the court is satisfied that provision for the offender to perform work under such an order can be made and that the offender is a suitable person to perform such work.

Before making an order the court must consider a report by a probation officer or social services department social worker, and if it thinks it necessary hear evidence from that person.

If two or more orders are made at the same time they must not exceed 120 hours in the aggregate.

Before making an order the court must explain to the offender in ordinary language:

(a) the purpose and effect of the order;
(b) the consequences that may follow a failure to comply with any requirements;
(c) the court's powers to review the order upon application by the offender or the probation officer.

(PCCA 1973 s.14 as amended by CJA 1982 Scheds.12 and 16).

Though there is power to make a community service order in the case of a sixteen year old, the extent to which it is possible to use that power is very much dependent upon the resources available locally and the extent to which the community services officer has been able to find work for persons of that age.

Chapter 9

Orders that may be made in care proceedings

1. Recognizance of parent or guardian

In any case in which the court finds that an application for an order under C&YPA 1969 s.1 (see page 42) has been proved, it may make an order requiring the parent or guardian of the relevant infant to enter into a recognizance to take proper care of him and exercise proper control over him (C&YPA 1969 s.1(3)(a)).

It is not possible for an order to be made under this subsection unless the parent or guardian in question consents to it (C&YPA 1969 s.1(5)(a)).

If an order is made it shall not require the parent or guardian in question to enter into a recognizance in a sum exceeding £1,000. The order may not continue for a period in excess of three years or, if the relevant infant will become eighteen before three years has elapsed, such shorter period as will take the relevant infant to his eighteenth birthday (C&YPA 1969 s.2(13)).

2. Recognizance of defendant

In any care proceedings in which the court finds an offence condition satisfied, it may, if it thinks fit and if the relevant infant consents, order him to enter into recognizance in a sum not exceeding £50 for a period of not more than one year, to keep the peace or to be of good behaviour (C&YPA 1969 s.3(7)).

Where such an order is made it will be made instead of any order that might have been made under C&YPA 1969 s.1(3).

For a form of such an order, see page 242.

3. Supervision orders

(a) General provisions

If a court finds that an application under C&YPA 1969 s.1 has been proved in respect of a relevant infant it may place him under supervision (C&YPA 1969 s.1(3)(b)).

(b) Selection of supervisor

The order has the effect of placing the relevant infant under the supervision of a local authority designated by the order, or of a probation officer (C&YPA 1969 s.11).

The court may not designate a local authority as the supervisor unless the authority agrees, or it appears to the court that the supervised person resides or will reside in the area of the authority.

If the supervision order is made in respect of a child, the court may not insert a provision in the order placing him under the supervision of a probation officer unless the local authority asks for this to be done and a probation officer is already exercising or has exercised, in relation to another member of the household to which the child belongs, the duties of a probation officer. Where a provision of a supervision order places the relevant infant under the supervision of a probation officer, the supervisor shall be a probation officer appointed for or assigned to the petty sessions area named in the order.

If the probation officer selected dies, or is unable to carry out his duties, another probation officer shall be selected (C&YPA 1969 s.13 as amended by PCCA 1973 Sched. 5 and CLA 1977 Sched. 12).

(c) Duties of supervisor

While a supervision order continues to be in force it shall be the duty of the supervisor to advise, assist and befriend the supervised person (C&YPA 1969 s.14).

(d) Provisions of the order

A supervision order made pursuant to C&YPA 1969 s.1(3)(b) may not contain any of the requirements that could otherwise be contained in a supervision order by virtue of C&YPA 1969 s.12(3B), since the latter are relevant to orders made in criminal cases only.

A court may not make a supervision order unless it is satisfied that the supervised person resides or will reside in the area of a local authority (C&YPA 1969 s.18(1)).

A supervision order must name the area of the local authority and the petty sessions area in which it appears to the court making the order that the supervised person resides or will reside. A supervision order may contain such conditions as the court may consider appropriate for facilitating the performance by the supervisor of his functions. These provisions may include any prescribed provisions for required visits to be made by the supervised person to the supervisor (C&YPA 1969 s.18(2)).

The *intermediate treatment* requirements referred to in Chapter 8 (page 60) may also be added to a supervision order in care proceedings or on the discharge of a care order made in such proceedings (C&YPA 1969 s.12(2)).

There is no power to include stipulated intermediate treatment requirements (page 61) in a supervision order made in care proceedings or on the discharge of a care order made in such proceedings, since these provisions are only available in the case of a supervision order made after a *finding of guilt* or on the discharge of a care order that was made in *criminal* proceedings (C&YPA 1969 s.12(3A) and (3C)).

(e) Duration of order

Unless a supervision order has been previously discharged it shall cease to have effect on the expiration of the period specified in the order, beginning with the date on which the order was originally made. The maximum period that may be specified in an order is three years.

A supervision order made under the provisions of C&YPA 1969 s.1(3) or on the occasion of the discharge of a care order will cease to have effect when the supervised person attains the age of eighteen if that date is earlier than the expiration of any period specified in the order (C&YPA 1969 s.17).

For forms of supervision order, see page 239 *et seq.*

4. Care orders

(a) General provisions

Whenever care proceedings result in a finding that the applicant's case has been proved, the court may make a care order (C&YPA 1969 s.1(3)(c)). Any provision of the C&YPA 1969 authorising the making of a care order shall be construed as authorising the making of an order committing the subject of the order to the care of a local authority (C&YPA 1969 s.20(1)).

(b) Deciding upon appropriate local authority

The local authority to whose care the relevant infant is to be committed shall be the one in whose area it appears to the court making the order that the relevant infant resides. If he does not appear to reside in the area of a local authority, the defendant shall be placed in the care of the local authority in whose area it appears the events giving rise to the order arose (C&YPA 1969 s.20(2)).

In determining the place of residence of any person for the purposes of this section, any period during which, while in the care of a local authority (whether by virtue of a care order or not) he resided outside the local authority's area shall be disregarded (C&YPA 1969 s.20(2A) included by virtue of HASSASSA 1983 Sched. 2).

(c) Duties of local authority

The duties of local authorities in relation to a person committed to care by virtue of a care order are to be found in CCA 1980 s.10 as amended by CJA 1982 Sched.14 and HASSASSA 1983 Scheds. 2 and 10. The section provides that the local authority to whose care a person is committed by virtue of a care order, shall receive him into their care and keep him in their care while the order continues to be in force (CCA 1980 s.10(1)).

The local authority shall have the same powers and duties in respect of persons in their care as their parents or guardians would have, apart from the order (CCA 1980 s.10(2)). However, s.10 does not give the local authority the right to consent or refuse to consent to the making of an adoption order, or to agree or refuse to agree to the making of an adoption order (CCA 1980 s.10(5)).

The authority must not cause a person in its care to be brought up in any religious creed other than that in which he would have been brought up but for the order (CCA 1980 s.10(3)).

If a person subject to a care order has attained the age of five years and has not been allowed to leave the community home or other establishment in which he has been accommodated for the preceding three months so that he could attend an educational establishment or at work, the local authority has a duty to appoint an independent person to be his visitor if:

   (i) communication between the person in care and his parent or guardian has been so infrequent that it is appropriate to appoint a visitor; or

    (ii) he has not lived with or visited or been visited by either of his parents or his guardian during the preceding twelve months.

A person appointed as an independent visitor shall:

    (i) visit, advise and befriend the person to whom the care order relates; and

    (ii) be entitled to exercise on behalf of that person his powers under C&YPA 1969 s.21(2) (the power to apply for the discharge of the order, see page 84) (CCA 1980 s.11(1)).

(d) Duration of care orders

Unless a care order is discharged in accordance with the provisions of C&YPA 1969 s.21, it ceases to have effect:

    (i) if the person to whom it relates had attained the age of sixteen when the order was made, when he attains the age of nineteen; and

    (ii) in any other case, when that person attains the age of eighteen.
    (C&YPA 1969 s.20(3)).

For a form of care order, see page 236.

5. Hospital orders

If a court finds that a juvenile before it is in need of care or control and is satisfied on the evidence of two registered medical practitioners that the offender is suffering from mental illness, psychopathic disorder, severe mental impairment or mental impairment, and that the mental disorder is severe enough to warrant it, it may make an order for his detention in hospital for medical treatment in accordance with the provisions of MHA 1983 s.37 (C&YPA 1969 s.1(3)(d)).

If the court is to be able to make a hospital order, at least one of the medical practitioners whose evidence is to be taken into account must be a practitioner approved by the Secretary of State for the purposes of MHA 1983 s.12. The practitioner in question will have special experience in the diagnosis or treatment of mental disorders (MHA 1983 s.54). Generally, the court may receive in evidence a written report that purports to be signed by a medical practitioner without proof of the signature or qualifications of that practitioner. However, in any case the court may require the attendance before it of the practitioner by whom any report was signed, in order that he may give oral evidence (MHA 1983 s.54(2)).

The expression 'mental disorder' is defined in MHA 1983 s.1 as follows:

> "In this act 'mental disorder' means mental illness, arrested or incomplete development of mind, psychopathic disorder and any other disorder or disability of mind."

The section goes on to define other expressions used in MHA 1983 s.37:

> *Severe mental impairment:* a state of arrested or incomplete development of mind which includes severe impairment of intelligence and social functioning and is associated with abnormally aggressive or seriously irresponsible conduct on the part of the person concerned.
> *Mental impairment:* a state of arrested or incomplete development of mind (not amounting to severe mental impairment) which includes significant impairment of intelligence and social functioning and is associated with abnormally aggressive or seriously irresponsible conduct on the part of the person concerned.
> *Psychopathic disorder:* a persistent disorder or disability of mind (whether or not including subnormality of intelligence) which results in abnormally aggressive or seriously irresponsible conduct on the part of the person concerned.

An order made under the provisions of MHA 1983 s.37 is sufficient authority:

(a) for a constable, approved social worker or any other person directed to do so by the court to convey the patient to the hospital specified in the order within a period of twenty-eight days; and

(b) for the managers of the hospital to admit him at any time within that period and thereafter to detain him in accordance with the provisions of the Act

(MHA 1983 s.40).

Any order made must specify the hospital to which the patient is to be admitted (MHA 1983 s.37(1)).

No court may make a hospital order in respect of a child or young person before it unless satisfied that arrangements have been made for him to be admitted to the hospital specified in the order within a period of twenty-eight days beginning with the date on which the order is made.

The court by which a hospital order is made may give such directions

77

as it thinks fit for the conveyance of the patient to a place of safety and for his detention therein pending his admission to the hospital (MHA 1983 s.37(4)).

See page 244 for a form of hospital order.

6. Guardianship orders

If a court finds that a child or young person before it is in need of care or control and is satisfied on the evidence of two medical practitioners that he is suffering from mental illness, psychopathic disorder, severe mental impairment or mental impairment and that the disorder is sufficiently severe to justify the making of an order, it may make an order placing him under the guardianship of a local health authority or any other person who is willing to receive him into guardianship (C&YPA 1969 s.1(3)(e)).

One of the two medical practitioners whose evidence is given to the court must be approved for the purposes of MHA 1983 s.12 by the Secretary of State as having special experience in the diagnosis or treatment of mental disorders.

The court is given the power to make guardianship orders as an alternative to hospital orders. The conditions that must be satisfied before the court may make a hospital order (above) must also be satisfied before the court can make a guardianship order.

Any order made must specify the local health authority or approved person into whose guardianship the child or young person in question is to be received (MHA 1983 s.37(1)). The court may not make a guardianship order unless it is satisfied that the authority or person in question is willing to receive the subject of the order into guardianship (MHA 1983 s.37(6)).

7. General restriction on the making of orders in care proceedings

None of the orders that may be made by virtue of the provisions of C&YPA 1969 s.1(3) may be made if the young person before the court has attained the age of sixteen years and is or has been married (C&YPA 1969 s.1(5)(c)).

It has been held that for the purpose of deciding the status of a child or young person in care proceedings, a polygamous marriage would be recognised by English law (*Mohamed* v *Knott* (1968)).

Chapter 10

Variation and discharge of supervision orders and care orders

Supervision orders and care orders, whether made following a finding of guilt or on the basis of a finding that the child or young person in question was in need of care or control, may be varied, and may also be discharged before the date on which they would normally cease to have effect.

In the case of a supervision order the order for variation or discharge may be made on the application of either the supervisor or the supervised person.

Orders for the variation or discharge of care orders may be made on the application of the local authority to whose care the relevant infant is committed, or on the application of the relevant infant or of his parent or guardian.

In either case, application for variation or discharge is made by complaint.

1. Supervision orders

(a) Powers to vary or discharge

If, while a supervision order is in force in respect of a supervised person who has not attained the age of eighteen, it appears to a juvenile court, on the application of the supervisor or the supervised person, that it is appropriate to make an order, the court may make an order discharging the supervision order or varying it.

In any case in which it is appropriate the supervision order may be varied by:

    (i) cancelling any requirement included in it in pursuance of C&YPA 1969 s.12 or 18(2)(b); or

    (ii) inserting in it (either in addition to or in substitution for any of its provisions) any provision which could have been included in the order if the court had then the power to make it and were exercising the power.

No requirement that the supervised person submit to medical treatment may be added to an order by way of variation after a period of 3 months has elapsed from the date on which the order was made, unless the order made on variation merely substitutes one requirement for another which was included in the original order (C&YPA 1969 s.15(1)).

On discharging a supervision order the court may make an order (see page 237) placing the supervised person in the care of a local authority (C&YPA 1969 s.15(1)).

If, on the application of the supervisor, a juvenile court is satisfied that the supervised person (not having attained 18) has failed to comply with a requirement in a supervision order made under C&YPA 1969 s.7 (on a finding of guilt for an offence punishable in the case of an adult with imprisonment) or on the discharge of a care order under s.21(2), it may fine the supervised person or make an attendance centre order in respect of him (see page 251). This power to deal with failures to comply with requirements of orders may be exercised at the same time that an order is made under C&YPA 1969 s.15(1) (C&YPA 1969 s.15(2A)).

(b) Powers of courts after attainment of age by supervised person

Magistrates' courts other than juvenile courts have the power, by virtue of C&YPA 1969 s.15(3) and (4), to deal with applications for the variation of any supervision order made in respect of a supervised person who has since attained the age of eighteen.

Juvenile courts are given the same powers when dealing with applications in relation to a supervision order made in respect of a person who has since attained the age of seventeen (C&YPA 1969 s.15(2)).

The effect of these provisions is that juvenile courts may, on the application of a supervisor or supervised person, make an order varying the provisions of the relevant supervision order even though the supervised person has attained the age of seventeen and is, therefore, no longer a juvenile. The court may also discharge a supervision order in the same circumstances.

In exercising its powers under the section a juvenile court may vary the relevant supervision order in any of the following ways:

(i) by inserting in it a provision specifying the duration of the order or altering or cancelling any such provison; or

(ii) by altering any provision of the order by virtue of which the supervisor is designated or selected; or

(iii) by altering the name of the local authority or petty sessions area as the case may be, in which it appears to the court the supervised person resides or will reside; or

(iv) by cancelling any provision that was inserted in the order for the purpose of facilitating the performance by the supervisor of his functions or inserting any such provision; or

(v) by cancelling any requirement included in the order which required the supervised person to reside with a named individual or required him to comply with any of the directions given to him by the supervisor in accordance with C&YPA 1969 s.12(2), that is to say:

● to live at a place or places specified in the directions for a period or periods so specified;

● to present himself to a person or persons specified in the directions at a place or places and on a day or days so specified;

● to participate in activities specified in the directions on a day or days so specified.

If, on the application of the supervisor, it is proved to the satisfaction of the magistrates' court that a person who has attained the age of *eighteen* has failed to comply with the requirements of a supervision order, it may, whether or not it makes an order under s.15(3) varying or cancelling and requirements of the order:

(i) order him to pay a fine not exceeding £100, or, subject to the provisions of s.15(10), make an attendance centre order in respect of him; or

(ii) if it discharges the supervision order, make an order imposing any punishment which it could have imposed on him if it had then had the power to try him for the offence in relation to which the supervision order was made
(C&YPA 1969 s.15(4)).

The powers given to a magistrates' court under s.15(4) may be exercised by a juvenile court in a case where the supervised person has attained the age of *seventeen* (C&YPA 1969 s.15(2)).

However, the power granted to the juvenile court by virtue of s.15(2) may only be exercised where the supervision order in question was made in criminal proceedings.

(c) Discharge or variation of requirement for treatment

In any case in which the supervised person is being treated for his mental condition in pursuance of a requirement included in the order by virtue of C&YPA s.12(4), the court may cancel or vary that requirement. The power to do so exists in any case in which a medical practitioner by whom or under whose direction a supervised person is being treated is unwilling to continue to treat or direct the treatment of him or is of the opinion that:

(i) the treatment should be continued beyond the period specified in the order; or

(ii) the supervised person needs different treatment; or

(iii) he is not susceptible to the treatment; or

(iv) he does not require further treatment.

If any medical practitioner responsible for the treatment of a person subject of a supervision order believes that an order varying or cancelling the requirement is necessary he must make a report in writing to that effect to the supervisor. On receiving such a report the supervisor must refer it to a juvenile court. The court may then exercise its powers of variation or cancellation (C&YPA 1969 s.15(5)).

If the supervised person has attained the age of fourteen, a court may not make an order which varies the order placing him under supervision by inserting a requirement that he undergoes medical treatment or by altering any such requirement already in the order without his consent, unless the alteration removes the requirement or reduces its duration (C&YPA 1969 s.16(7)).

(d) Securing attendance of supervised person

As a general rule the court may not make an order varying or discharging a supervision order unless the supervised person is present before the court. Where the supervisor makes an application or reference to the court he may bring the supervised person before the court (C&YPA 1969 s.16(1)).

Subject to the restrictions on the court's power to issue warrants to secure the attendance of persons before the court contained in MCA 1980, s.55(3) (see page 30), the court to which an application for variation or discharge of a supervision order is made may issue a summons or a warrant to secure the attendance at court of the supervised person (C&YPA 1969 s.16(2)).

If a supervised person is arrested by authority of a warrant issued to secure his attendance and he cannot be brought before the court immediately, the person who has the custody of him:

(i) may make arrangements for his detention in a place of safety for a period of not more than seventy-two hours from the time of the arrest; and

(ii) shall within that period bring him before a justice unless he has been brought before the court within that period.

Whenever a supervised person who has been arrested in accordance with the procedure set out in the last paragraph is brought before a justice, the justice shall order that he be released forthwith or:

(i) if he has not attained the age of eighteen, make an interim order in respect of him;

(ii) if he has attained that age, remand him.
(C&YPA 1969 s.16(3)).

If the supervised person is brought before the court under a warrant issued to secure his attendance before the court or under the provisions of an interim order made by virtue of C&YPA 1969 s.16(3), or the court considers that it is likely to use its powers under that subsection to make an order in respect of the supervised person, but before deciding whether to do so, seeks information with respect to him which it considers is unlikely to be obtained unless an interim order is made in respect of him, the court may make such an interim order (C&YPA 1969 s.16(4)). For the form of such an order, see page 233.

The court may make an order varying or discharging a supervision order in the absence of the supervised person if the effect of the order is confined to one or more of the following matters:

(i) discharging the supervision order;

(ii) cancelling a provision included in the supervision order in pursuance of s.12 or s.18(2)(b) of the Act;

(iii) reducing the duration of the supervision order itself or of any provision included in it in pursuance of C&YPA 1969 s.12;

(iv) altering the name of any area included in the order;

(v) changing the supervisor.
(C&YPA 1969 s.16(5)).

A form of order for variation or discharge of a supervision order is shown on page 241.

2. Care orders

(a) Extension

If it appears to a juvenile court, upon the application of a local authority having the care of a person by virtue of a care order that would cease to have effect by virtue of C&YPA 1969 s.20(3)(b) (attainment of age 18):

(i) that the person in question is accommodated in a community home or in a home provided by the Secretary of State; and

(ii) that by reason of his mental condition or behaviour it is in his interest or the public interest for him to continue to be so accommodated after he attains the age of eighteen,

the court may order that the care order shall continue in force until he attains the age of nineteen. The court may not make an order under this subsection unless the person in question is present before the court (C&YPA 1969 s.21(1)).

For a form of order extending or discharging a care order, see page 238.

(b) Discharge

A juvenile court may discharge a care order on the application of the local authority to whose care a person is committed by virtue of the order, or upon the application of that person, if it thinks it appropriate to do so. On discharging the care order the court may make a supervision order (for form, see page 240), unless the order discharged was an interim order or the person to whom the discharged order related has attained the age of eighteen (C&YPA 1969 s.21(2)).

The juvenile court must not discharge a care order, or make a supervision order after discharging a care order, in the case of a person who has not attained the age of eighteen and appears to the court to be in need of care or control, unless the court is satisfied that, whether through the making of the supervision order or otherwise, he will receive that care or control (C&YPA 1969 s.21(2A)).

If an application for the discharge of a care order is dismissed, no further application for discharge may be made by any person during the period of three months beginning with the date on which the application is dismissed (C&YPA 1969 s.21(3)(b)).

If the application is for the discharge of an interim order and it is dismissed, no further application for its discharge shall be made without the consent of the juvenile court (C&YPA 1969 s.21(3)(a)).

For a form of discharge or extension of a care order, see page 238.

(c) Cessation

If an adoption order is made in respect of a person who has been made the subject of a care order, the care order ceases to have effect.

Any order that is made in respect of a person who has been made the subject of a care order, in accordance with the provisions of CA 1975 s.14 (an order freeing a child for adoption), shall also bring the care order to an end.

A care order ceases to have effect if an order is made in respect of the person who is the subject of that order in accordance with the provisions of AA 1958 s.53 (an order for provisional adoption by persons domiciled outside the United Kingdom) (C&YPA 1969 s.21A).

When CA 1975 s.18 is brought into force, provisional adoption orders granted to persons domiciled outside the United Kingdom will become the subject of CA 1975 s.25.

Chapter 11

Appeals

1. Criminal case

(a) Appeal to Crown Court

A juvenile may appeal to the Crown Court against any finding of guilt and/or sentence recorded in a juvenile court if he denied the charge to which that finding of guilt and sentence relates. He may appeal against any sentence imposed, but not against the finding of guilt, in any case in which he admitted the offence to which the sentence relates (MCA 1980 s.108). An order for conditional discharge is not a sentence for the purposes of the section, and for that reason there is no right of appeal against such an order.

When appropriate: An appeal to the Crown Court will be the appropriate remedy for an aggrieved defendant whenever the issue that the higher court is to be asked to decide is one of fact.

Time limits: An appeal is commenced by the appellant's giving notice in writing to the clerk of the juvenile court and to any other party to the appeal that he is aggrieved by the decision. The notice must be given within 21 days of the day on which the decision that gave rise to the appeal was given. If the date upon which sentence was passed and the date upon which the finding of guilt was announced are not the same date, the period allowed for service of the notice of appeal begins operating from the date of sentence.

Extension of time limits: The time for giving notice of appeal may be extended either before or after it expires, by the Crown Court, on an application submitted to the Chief Clerk of the Crown Court in writing. The notice must state the grounds of the application. If the Crown Court extends the time for giving notice of appeal, the appropriate officer of the Crown Court must give notice of the extension to the appellant and to the Clerk of the court from whose decision the appeal is brought. It is for the appellant to give notice of the extension to any other party to the appeal (CCR 1982 r.7).

Appeal by parent or guardian: A parent or guardian who is aggrieved by a decision that he should pay the fine, compensation or costs imposed on or ordered against his child, may appeal to the Crown Court against that order. The time limits for service of notice of appeal are the same as for an appeal by a defendant, and the other provisions of CCR 1982 r.7 also apply.

Form of notice: A notice of appeal must state whether the appeal is against the finding of guilt or against sentence or both. For a form of notice of appeal, see page 260.

Abandonment: If an appellant fails to prosecute his appeal or gives notice of abandonment of appeal, the court against whose decision the appeal was brought may issue process for enforcing that decision. On application of the other party to the appeal, the court may order the appellant to pay to that party such costs as appear to the court to be just and reasonable in respect of the expenses properly incurred by that party in connection with the appeal before notice of abandonment of the appeal was given to him (MCA 1980 s.109).

(b) Appeal by way of case stated

When appropriate: Any person who was a party to proceedings before a juvenile court or is aggrieved by the decision of the court, may question the proceeding on the ground that it is wrong in law or is in excess of jurisdiction. The appeal takes the form of an application to the justices composing the court that made the decision to state a case for the opinion of the High Court on the question of law or jurisdiction involved (MCA 1980 s.111(1)).

Section 111(1) refers to persons who are aggrieved by the conviction, order, determination or other proceeding of the court. It is, therefore, possible for a person to make application for the justices to state a case even though they were not a party to the proceeding before the juvenile court.

In a criminal case a person who has suffered a loss as a result of the defendant's actions might make application for the justices to state a case if he is aggrieved by any part of the court's order and is of the opinion that the justices have erred in law or jurisdiction. Such a person might, for example, be aggrieved by the justice's decision not to award compensation, or as to the amount of any compensation awarded, for the loss suffered.

Time limits: An application for the justices to state a case must be made within twenty-one days of the date on which the decision of the court was given. If the court has adjourned the trial of an information after a finding of guilt has been recorded, the date on which the court sentences or otherwise deals with the offender is the date from which the period for service of the notice of appeal must be calculated (MCA 1980 s.111(2) and (3)).

Loss of right of appeal to Crown Court: In any case in which an application is made for the justices to state a case for the opinion of the High Court, any right that the applicant might have had to appeal to the Crown Court against the finding or decision ceases (MCA 1980 s.111(4)).

Refusal to state case: If the justices are of the opinion that an application for them to state a case for the opinion of the High Court is frivolous, they may refuse to state a case and, if the applicant so requires, shall give him a certificate stating that the application has been refused. The justices cannot refuse to state a case if the application is made by or under the direction of the Attorney General (MCA 1980 s.111(5)).

In any case in which justices have refused to state a case, the High Court may, on the application of the person who applied for the case to be stated, make an order of *mandamus* requiring the justices to state a case (MCA 1980 s.111(6)).

Procedure for stating case: Once an application for the justices to state a case has been received, strict time limits are applied to each of the following stages of the procedure. At each stage 21 days is allowed for completion of that part of the appeal process.

Within 21 days after the receipt of the application the clerk of the court whose decision is questioned must send a draft case, in which are stated the matters required, to the applicant or his solicitor and to the respondent or his solicitor (MCR 1981 r.77(1)).

If the applicant was not a party to the proceedings before the juvenile court, both the prosecutor and the defendant in those proceedings would be respondents to the appeal. The clerk of the court must, in such circumstances, take great care to ensure that both are served with a copy of the draft case and given the opportunity to make representations.

Within 21 days after receiving the draft case from the clerk, each party may make representations thereon. The representations must be made in writing and must be signed by or on behalf of the party making them. The representations must be sent to the clerk of the court whose decision is questioned (MCR 1981 r.77(2)).

Within the 21 days after the last day on which representations may be made, the justices whose decision is the subject of the appeal must make any adjustments to the draft case that may be necessary. They must then state and sign the case.

A case may be stated on behalf of the justices whose decision is questioned by any two or more of them and may be signed on their behalf by their clerk if they so direct.

Once the case has been stated and signed, the clerk of the court shall send it to the applicant or his solicitor forthwith (MCR 1981 r.78).

Extension of time limits: The time limits that are applied to each stage of the procedure can be extended. If, after receiving the application, the clerk of the court is unable to send the draft case to the parties within 21 days, he must send it as soon as practicable after that time. The remaining provisions of the rule still apply.

In any case in which the draft case is despatched after the time limit laid down in the rules has elapsed, the clerk must attach to the draft case, and to the final case when it is despatched, a statement of the delay and the reason for it (MCR 1981 r.79(1)).

If, for any reason, the parties to the appeal or either one of them is unable to make representations in relation to the draft case within 21 days of its receipt, they must apply to the clerk of the court, in writing, for an extension of time. The application must include details of the reasons for the application.

Upon receipt of an application for an extension of time in which to make representations, the clerk may, by notice in writing to the parties to the appeal, extend the time limit. In any case in which the clerk does extend the time limit in this way he must, when he despatches the final case, attach to it a statement of the extension and the reason for it (MCR 1981 r.79(2)).

If, having received the representations of the parties to the appeal, the justices are unable to state a case within the time laid down in the rules, they must do so as soon as practicable thereafter. If the justices do state the final case after the usual time limit has expired, the clerk must, when he sends the case to the parties to the appeal, send with it a statement of the delay and the reasons for it (MCR 1981 r.79(3)).

2. Care proceedings

(a) Appeal to Crown Court

When appropriate: A relevant infant can appeal to the Crown Court against any order made in respect of him by virtue of C&YPA 1969 s.1(3) (see Chapter 9), except an order requiring his parent or guardian to enter into a recognizance to take proper care of him (where the parent or guardian would have consented as a precondition to the making of the order) (C&YPA 1969 s.2(12)). The relevant infant's parents may appeal to the Crown Court on his behalf: *B* v *Gloucestershire County Council* (1980).

The right of appeal to the Crown Court enjoyed by the relevant infant extends to any case in which the justices find the offence condition satisfied where the offence was not admitted. In these circumstances the relevant infant may appeal to the Crown Court against the finding if:

(i) the finding is made in pursuance of C&YPA 1969 s.3(5) (which allows courts dealing with a case which appears to fall to be remitted to another court, to determine whether the offence condition is satisfied before remitting it) (see page 101) and the court to which the case is remitted decides not to make any order under C&YPA 1969 s.1 in respect of him; or

(ii) the finding is made in a case which does not appear to fall to be remitted to another court and the court determines not to make any order under C&YPA 1969 s.1 in respect of the relevant infant

(C&YPA 1969 s.3(8)).

No appeal may be brought if a court finds the offence condition satisfied with respect to a relevant infant who is a young person but decides, instead of making any of the orders that may be made by virtue of C&YPA 1969 s.1(3), to order him to enter into a recognizance to keep the peace or to be of good behaviour (C&YPA 1969 s.3(7)). Again, the right of appeal is denied because the consent of the relevant infant is required before the order can be made.

A person to whom a relevant care order relates or related may appeal to the Crown Court against any order that extends the duration of the order beyond his eighteenth birthday, if it would have ceased to have effect when the relevant infant attained the age of eighteen.

If a court discharges a care order and makes a supervision order in respect of the person who was the subject of that order, he may appeal to the Crown Court against the making of that supervision order.

Similarly, the person to whom a care order relates may appeal to the Crown Court against the dismissal of an application for the discharge of that order (C&YPA 1969 s.21(4)).

Time limits: The provisions of CCR 1982 r.7 apply to appeals arising out of care proceedings. Notice of appeal must be given in writing within 21 days after the date of the order or finding that gives rise to the appeal. Applications for extension of time for giving notice of appeal may be made in writing to the chief clerk of the Crown Court.

Appointment of guardian ad litem: In any case in which the juvenile court has ordered that the parent or guardian of the relevant infant shall not be treated as representing him due to the conflict of interest between that person and the relevant infant (an order made under the provisions of C&YPA 1969 s.32A; see page 43) that order has effect for the purposes of the appeal. The Crown Court must appoint a guardian *ad litem* of the relevant child or young person for the purposes of the appeal if it appears to the court that it is in his interest to do so (CCR 1982 r.9(2)).

The Crown Court must also make an order appointing a guardian *ad litem* of the relevant child or young person in any case in which the Crown Court itself makes an order that his parent or guardian shall not be treated as representing him due to the conflict of interest between that person and the relevant child or young person (CCR 1982 r.9(1)).

If an order has been made that the parent or guardian of a relevant infant shall not be treated as representing him and a guardian *ad litem* is appointed for the purposes of the appeal to the Crown Court, the parent or guardian of the relevant infant shall be entitled:

(i) to meet any allegations made against him in the course of the proceedings on the appeal by cross examining any witness for the appellant or respondent and giving or calling evidence; and

(ii) to make representations to the court
(CCR 1982 r.10(1)).

(b) Appeal by way of case stated

When appropriate: As with criminal proceedings, it is appropriate for a person who was a party to any proceedings before a juvenile court to appeal to the High Court, if they are aggrieved by the decision of the court, either because they believe that it was wrong in law or that it was a matter decided in excess of jurisdiction (MCA 1980 s.111(1)).

Time limits: The time limits for applications for case stated in criminal cases (see page 88) apply also to applications following care proceedings in the juvenile court. Notice of application must be made within twenty-one days of the date on which the decision of the court was given (MCA 1980 s.111(2)).

Refusal to state a case: Justices who are of the opinion that an application for them to state a case is frivolous may refuse to do so. If justices do decide to refuse to state a case for the consideration of the High Court, they must, if the applicant so requests, give him a certificate stating that the application has been refused.

Again, justices may not refuse to state a case if the application is made by or under the direction of the Attorney General (MCA 1980 s.111(5)).

The High Court may make an order of *mandamus* in any case in which the justices have refused to state a case, requiring them to do so (MCA 1980 s.111(6)).

Procedure for stating case: Upon receipt of an application for the justices to state a case the clerk to the justices must follow the procedure described earlier in this chapter (page 88). The same time limits apply.

It is only necessary to add that when considering the question of service of the draft case, justices' clerks must remember that in care proceedings cases there might be a number of persons who ought to be regarded as respondents to the appeal. It might, for example, be necessary to serve a copy of the draft case upon a parent who was separately represented in the proceedings as well as upon the applicant and respondent.

Extension of time limits: The law relating to extension of time limits laid down for completing the various stages of the procedure in an appeal by way of case stated is to be found in MCR 1981 r.79. The provisions of the rule are set out earlier in the chapter (page 89) and apply with equal force to applications that relate to care proceedings.

3. Recognizance to prosecute appeal

In any case in which justices are asked to state a case for the consideration of the High Court, whether the application relates to a criminal case or to care proceedings, they cannot be required to state the case until the applicant has entered into a recognizance to prosecute the appeal. The recognizance shall be taken before the magistrates' court and may be taken with or without sureties. The recognizance must be taken subject to the condition that the applicant prosecute his appeal without delay, submit to the judgment of the High Court and pay such costs as that court may award.

If the appeal relates to proceedings other than criminal proceedings, the clerk of the court is not obliged to deliver the case to the applicant until he has paid the fees payable for the case and for the recognizance (MCA 1980 s.114).

The fees that may be charged in connection with the case and the recognizance are set out in MCA 1980 Sched. 6.

Chapter 12

Enforcement of fines and orders

1. Fine enforcement

Special rules apply to the enforcement of fines imposed upon juveniles. They apply until the defaulter attains the age of seventeen. After that time the court may use its powers for enforcing payment by an adult defaulter. Generally, the rules apply to sums adjudged to be paid by a conviction and references to fines in the following paragraphs should be taken to include references to costs and compensation.

(a) Remission

On inquiring into the means of a juvenile who has made default in the payment of a fine, the court may remit the whole or any part of the outstanding sum if it thinks it just to do so having regard to any change in his circumstances since the conviction. However, this power extends to outstanding *fines* alone; the court may not remit any other sum adjudged to be paid on conviction (MCA 1980 s.85).

(b) Payment by instalments

A court that makes an order for the payment of a fine and any court that deals with a person who has made default in payment of a fine may allow time for the payment to be made or make an order for the outstanding sum to be paid by instalments. If time has been allowed for payment, the court can extend the time allowed, on application by or on behalf of the person liable to make the payment. When dealing with an application for the extension of time allowed for payment the court may also order payment by instalments.

If an order for payment by instalments has been made and the person liable to make the payments defaults in the payment of any one of those instalments, enforcement proceedings may be taken as though default had been made in the payment of all the instalments then unpaid (MCA 1980 s.75).

The power to allow further time for payment and to order payment of outstanding sums by instalments may be exercised by the justices' clerk as well as by the court (JCR 1970 para. 6 of Sched.).

(c) Money payment supervision

If a juvenile adjudged to pay a fine does not make payment forthwith, the court imposing the fine and any court that is called upon to deal with the default subsequently, may order that he be placed under the supervision of such person as the court may from time to time appoint. If a money payment supervision order has been made, the court should obtain and consider a report from the supervisor before making any further order in respect of the default (MCA 1980 s.88).

(d) Order for payment by parent or guardian

In any case in which the court would have the power to commit a juvenile to prison for non-payment of a fine, were it not for the restrictions placed by statute upon the imprisonment of young offenders, an order may be made directing that any sum that remains unpaid be paid by the defaulter's parent or guardian instead of by the defaulter (MCA 1980 s.81(1)(b)). No order may be made under this subsection unless the court has, on at least one occasion, inquired into the defaulter's means in his presence (MCA 1980 s.81(3)).

No order may be made for an outstanding sum to be paid by the defaulter's parent or guardian unless the court is satisfied that the defaulter has, or has had since the date on which the sum in question was adjudged to be paid, the means to pay the sum or any instalment on which he has defaulted, and refuses or neglects or has refused or neglected to make the payment (MCA 1980 s.81(4)).

Before a parent or guardian of a defaulter is ordered to make payment of a sum outstanding he must be given the opportunity of being heard. The court may only make the order without hearing from the parent or guardian in question if he has been required to attend but has failed to do so (MCA 1980 s.81(5)).

(e) Recognizance of parent or guardian

A court that would, but for the restrictions placed by statute upon the imprisonment of young offenders, have the power to commit a juvenile to prison for non payment of a fine, may make an order requiring the defaulter's parent or guardian to enter into a recognizance to ensure that he pays so much of the sum as remains unpaid (MCA 1980 s.81(1)(a)).

An order may only be made under this subsection if, on at least one occasion, the court has inquired into the means of the defaulter in his presence (MCA 1980 s.81(3)).

Before an order can be made requiring the parent or guardian of a defaulter to enter into a recognizance he must consent to the making of such an order (MCA 1980 s.81(2)(a)).

(f) Attachment of earnings

If in any case the defaulter is in employment, the court may make an order directing his employer to make weekly payments in respect of the outstanding fine from the defaulter's earnings (AEA 1971 s.1(3)).

'Earnings' includes any sums payable to a person by way of wages or salary, including fees, bonus, commission, overtime pay or other emoluments payable under a contract of service in addition to wages or salary. Pay or allowances paid to a debtor as a member of Her Majesty's Forces are not to be treated as earnings (AEA 1971 s.24).

An attachment of earnings order must specify the whole amount payable under the adjudication or so much of the sum as remains unpaid at the time the order is made. The order must contain a normal deduction rate, which will be the amount that the defaulter can reasonably pay each week in meeting his liability for the debt. The court must also fix a sum below which the earnings actually paid to the defaulter should not fall. This sum shall be the defaulter's 'protected earnings' (AEA 1971 s.6(4) and (5)).

In determining the protected earnings rate the court must have regard to the debtor's resources and needs (AEA 1971 s.6(5)(b)). Regard should also be paid to the needs of any other person for whom the debtor must, or reasonably may, provide (AEA 1971 s.25(3)). In most cases it would be unreasonable to fix protected earnings below the scale rate of the Supplementary Benefits Commission (*Billington* v *Billington* (1974)).

If the wages earned by the defaulter should fall below the level of his protected earnings no deduction may be made by his employer from his earnings. If his earnings in any week are low and the full amount of the deduction cannot be made, any arrears that accrue may be collected in any week in which his earnings are sufficiently high to enable both the protected earnings to be paid to the defaulter and the normal deduction to be made and to leave a balance that would normally be paid to the defaulter (AEA 1971 Sched. 3).

Whenever there is an attachment of earnings order in force both the employer and the defaulter are under an obligation to advise the clerk to the justices responsible for collecting the outstanding fine of any changes in his employment or earnings.

The debtor shall notify the clerk in writing of every occasion on which he leaves any employment, or becomes unemployed or re-employed, within seven days from the date on which he did so (AEA 1971 s.15(a)). The notice must also contain particulars of the debtor's earnings and anticipated earnings if he has become employed or re-employed (AEA 1971 s.15(b)).

An employer who has been subject to a direction in an attachment of earnings order to deduct payments from the earnings of a debtor must notify the court if the debtor does not work for him or ceases to work for him. The notice must be given within ten days of the service of the order or of the date on which the debtor left employment (AEA 1971 s.7(2)).

Any new employer, if he is aware of the existence of an attachment of earnings order, must notify the court in writing within seven days of the commencement of employment that he is the debtor's employer. The notice given must include a statement of the debtor's earnings and anticipated earnings (AEA 1971 s.15(c)).

The court has the power to transfer an attachment of earnings order to any new employer if the defaulter changes his employment (AEA 1971 s.9(4)).

In any case in which an attachment of earnings order has been made, the employer shall, if he has been served with the order, comply with it. He may not, however, be liable for any non compliance with the order before seven days have elapsed after the service of the order upon him (AEA 1971 s.7(1)). Should the employer fail to comply with the order served upon him or to notify the court that the debtor has ceased to be employed by him, he commits an offence (AEA 1971 s.23(2)).

(g) *Attendance centre order*

A court dealing with a juvenile for the non payment of fines that have been imposed upon him may order that he attend an attendance centre in lieu of payment, if it has received notice from the Secretary of State that an attendance centre is available for the reception from that court of persons of his class or description. The power to make such an order arises because the court would have the power to impose imprisonment on the defaulter were it not for the restrictions placed upon the imprisonment of young offenders (CJA 1982 s.17(1)).

The court may not order that a defaulter attend an attendance centre if he has on an earlier occasion been sentenced to:

   (i) imprisonment;
  (ii) detention under s.53 C&YPA 1933;
 (iii) Borstal training;
 (iv) youth custody or custody for life under CJA 1982;
  (v) detention in a detention centre,

unless it appears that there are special circumstances that warrant the making of such an order in his case (CJA 1982 s.17(3)).

The section provides that whenever an attendance centre order is made the defaulter shall attend at the centre for the number of hours specified in the order. The number of hours specified is usually twelve (see page 67) since the order may not be for less than twelve (unless it relates to a child and the court is of the opinion that twelve hours would be excessive); nor more than twelve save in cases in which the court is of the opinion that twelve hours would be inadequate. In the case of a debtor under the age of seventeen the order may not be for more than twenty-four hours (CJA 1982 s.17(5)).

The court may not make an order that a juvenile attend an attendance centre in lieu of payment of a fine unless it has inquired into his means, in his presence, on at least one occasion since the date on which the fine was imposed (MCA 1980 s.81(3)).

If full payment is made in respect of the outstanding fines after an attendance centre order has been made, the order shall cease to have effect. If, after the order is made the defaulter makes payment of part of the outstanding sum, the total number of hours for which he was required to attend the centre must be reduced in proportion (CJA 1982 s.17(13)).

2. Enforcement of orders not involving the payment of money

(a) Attendance centre order

If it appears to a justice acting for the petty sessions area in which an attendance centre is situated that a person who has been made the subject of an attendance centre order has failed to attend the centre without a reasonable excuse, or has broken the rules of the centre whilst in attendance in a way which makes it impossible for the breach to be dealt with under those rules, he may authorise the issue of a summons or warrant requiring him to be brought before the court. If it is proved to the satisfaction of the court that the offender has failed to appear at the centre without reasonable excuse, or has broken the rules of the centre, it may deal with him in any way in which he could have been dealt with by the court that made the order if the order had not been made (CJA 1982 s.19). Jurisdiction is vested in the court for the area in which the attendance centre is situated, or the court that made the order (CJA 1982 s.19(2)).

(*b*) *Supervision order*

If while a supervision order is in force in relation to a juvenile, it is proved to the satisfaction of a juvenile court, on the application of the supervisor, that he has failed to comply with any requirement included in the order, the court may order him to pay a fine not exceeding £100 or make an attendance centre order in respect of him. These powers may be used whether or not the court makes an order under C&YPA 1969 s.15(1) discharging or varying the supervision order in question (C&YPA 1969 s.15(2A)).

(*c*) *Recognizance of young person or of parent or guardian*

If a young person is found to be in breach of a recognizance entered into following a finding that an offence condition is satisfied in respect of him (C&YPA 1969 s.3(7)), it may order that he forfeit all or part of the sum that was pledged by way of recognizance.

Similarly, if a court is satisfied that a parent or guardian is in breach of the conditions of a recognizance entered into under the provisions of C&YPA 1969 s.1(3)(a), he may be ordered to forfeit all or part of the sum pledged by way of recognizance.

Chapter 13

Miscellaneous procedures

1. Remission of cases between courts

A number of situations can arise in which a court dealing with a juvenile may make an order remitting the case to another court to be further dealt with or for sentencing.

(a) Remission by adult court before finding of guilt

In Chapter 1, page 8, mention is made of the circumstances in which a juvenile may be tried in an adult court. As a general rule the jurisdiction in question is based upon the juvenile's involvement with an adult.

If a juvenile appears with an adult defendant and that older defendant pleads guilty but the juvenile denies the allegation made, the court may remit the juvenile to be tried by a juvenile court acting for the same area, or to a juvenile court for the area in which the juvenile habitually resides. Similarly, if the court inquires into the information as examining justices in the case of the older accused and commits him for trial or discharges him and proceeds to the summary trial of the information of the juvenile, then, if he denies the allegation the court may remit him to a juvenile court before any evidence is called in his case (MCA 1980 s.29(2)).

This section makes it possible for an adult court to send a juvenile to the juvenile court to be tried once his connection with the adult has come to an end, even though the juvenile has not been found guilty. The court will usually exercise this power in view of the sentencing restrictions mentioned below.

Whenever a juvenile is so remitted he does not have any right of appeal against the order of remission. The court that remits him may give whatever directions appear to be necessary with regard to his custody or release on bail until he can be brought before the juvenile court (MCA 1980 s.29(4)).

(b) Remission by adult court following finding of guilt

Under the last heading attention was focused upon orders for remission *before* there has been any finding as to the guilt of the accused. In any case in which an adult court finds that a juvenile before it is guilty of an offence charged, it must, save in the most exceptional circumstances, make an order remitting him to a juvenile court for sentence.

A magistrates' court must remit any juvenile found guilty of an offence to the juvenile court acting for the same area or to the juvenile court acting for the area in which he habitually resides, unless it is satisfied that it would be undesirable to do so.

Where any case is so remitted, the offender must be brought before the juvenile court and that court may deal with him in any way in which it might have dealt with him if he had been tried and found guilty by that court (C&YPA 1933 s.56(1)).

A magistrates' court can only sentence a juvenile in those cases in which it decides that the appropriate sentence is a fine or an order for absolute or conditional discharge, or an order requiring his parent or guardian to enter into a recognizance to take proper care of him and exercise proper control over him. Since the sentencing options available to an adult court in relation to a juvenile offender are therefore extremely limited, it does not happen very frequently (save perhaps in motoring cases) that an adult court is satisfied that it is undesirable to remit a juvenile to a juvenile court to be sentenced.

If the court is satisfied that it *can* deal with the defendant in one of the ways mentioned in the last paragraph it may, when sentencing the offender, make any of the other orders that it has the power to make at the same time. It may, therefore, make orders for compensation, restitution, forfeiture, disqualification or endorsement (C&YPA 1969 s.7(8) as amended by MCA 1980 Sched. 7).

Whenever a case is remitted by an adult court to a juvenile court, the offender has the same right of appeal against any order that is made by the court to which the case is remitted as if he had been found guilty by that court. The offender may not appeal against the order remitting the case to the juvenile court (C&YPA 1933 s.56(2)).

(c) Remission by a juvenile court following a finding of guilt

The provisions of C&YPA 1933 s.56 not only require a magistrates' court to remit a juvenile to a juvenile court to be sentenced, save in exceptional cases, but also allow a juvenile court that has found an offender guilty of an offence to remit him to another juvenile court for sentence whenever it is appropriate to do so (C&YPA 1933 s.56(1) as amended by C&YPA 1963 Sched. 3).

This provision is of the greatest assistance to courts when they have before them offenders who, though arrested in the area for which the court acts, live in an area some way distant. The section is enormously helpful in any case in which it is felt that social inquiry or other reports should be obtained before sentence is passed. In these circumstancs it is possible to pass the question of sentence over to the offender's local juvenile court, so obviating the need for offender, parents, probation officer or social worker to make another, perhaps lengthy, journey to court.

Once again, in any case which has been remitted to a local juvenile court for sentence, the offender has the same right of appeal against any order of the court sentencing him that he would have had if that court had found him guilty of the offence. He may not, however, appeal against the order remitting him to the other juvenile court (C&YPA 1933 s.56(2)).

Any juvenile court that remits an offender to another court for sentence may make any directions necessary with respect to his custody or release on bail until he can be brought before the court to which he is remitted (C&YPA 1933 s.56(3)).

(d) Remission by a juvenile court in a care proceedings case

If in a care proceedings case it appears to the court that the relevant infant resides in a petty sessions area other than the one for which it acts, it must direct that he be brought before a juvenile court acting for the petty sessions area in which he does reside, unless it dismisses the application (C&YPA 1969 s.2(11)).

The provisions of this subsection do not apply if the relevant infant is brought before the court in accordance with the provisions of C&YPA 1969 s.2(5), ie within seventy-two hours of arrest on a warrant issued under the provisions of C&YPA 1969 s.2(4) (see page 29). In such a case the court must, unless it releases the relevant infant forthwith, make an interim order in respect of him.

The court has no discretion if the relevant infant does not live in its area. It is obliged to direct that he be brought before the court for the area in which he lives, unless the proceedings are dismissed.

Despite the lack of discretion the court must hear the application so that it can come to a decision on whether to dismiss it or to make a direction under the subsection.

For a form of remittal order, see page 242.

2. Place of safety applications

Any person who believes that any of the conditions of C&YPA 1969 s.1(2)(a) – (e) (see page 42) is satisfied in respect of a child or young person may apply to a justice for an order authorising the applicant to take him to a place of safety and detain him there for 28 days or for such shorter period as the order may authorise.

If any person believes that an appropriate court would find the conditions set out in C&YPA 1969 s.1 (2)(b) (see page 42) satisfied in respect of a child or young person he may also apply for an order.

An application for an order may also be made if a child or young person is about to leave the United Kingdom in contravention of C&YPA 1933 s.25 – a section that regulates the sending abroad of juvenile entertainers.

Any application for a place of safety order may be made to a justice and may be made to a justice who is not a member of the juvenile court panel for the petty sessions area in question. If the justice is satisfied that the belief of the applicant is reasonably held, he may grant the application (C&YPA 1969 s.28(1)).

This type of application is frequently made before a justice at his home and often outside the normal working hours of the court staff. It is most frequently made by a local authority social worker who has reason to believe that the child in question is at risk of suffering a non-accidental injury. The application is made *ex parte* and if it is granted can result in a child or young person being taken from his home to a place of safety and detained there for a period of up to twenty-eight days, without his parent or guardian having any opportunity to appear before a court or to be heard.

The provisions of this section do, whenever they are exercised, affect the liberty of the subject in a very real way. It is most important, therefore, that applications under the section are only made when it is absolutely necessary, and that the procedure laid down is adhered to strictly. Justices take their responsibilities under this section extremely seriously and most courts have a system in operation that ensures that the advice of the justices' clerk or one of his assistant clerks is available to any justice called upon to hear an application, even though they may be asked to do so at a time at which the court is usually closed.

It is important to remember that the police have statutory powers enabling them to detain a child or young person if they have reasonable cause to believe that any of the conditions set out in C&YPA 1969 s.1(2)(a)–(d) is satisfied (C&YPA 1969 s.28(2)). This power may be exercised without reference to a court or justice. In urgent cases social services officers and others concerned for the safety of a child should contact police to see if they are able to use their statutory powers. The power given to police to detain a child or young person in these circumstances is retained notwithstanding the restrictions imposed generally in PACEA 1984 (PACEA 1984 s.26 and Sched. 2).

If it is necessary for the social services department to seek an order under C&YPA 1969 s.28(1), regard must be paid to the fact that the justice, if satisfied that an order should be made, may authorise the detention of the child or young person for twenty-eight days *or* for such shorter period as appears to him to be appropriate. Applicants for place of safety orders sometimes claim an entitlement to a twenty-eight day order. There is no such entitlement. The order should be only for as long as is necessary to enable an application to be made to a juvenile court for an order under the provisions of C&YPA 1969 s.1(3) (see page 72). In deciding how long an applicant might reasonably be allowed in which to bring the detainee before the court, the justice should have in mind all that has been said in preceding paragraphs about the liberty of the subject and the lack of opportunity for parent or guardian to make representations when the order is applied for.

In any case in which an order is granted the child or young person may be kept in a 'place of safety' until he is brought before the court. A place of safety is 'a community home provided by a local authority or a controlled community home, any police station or any hospital, surgery or other suitable place, the occupier of which is willing temporarily to receive a child or young person'. (C&YPA 1933 s.107 as amended by C&YPA 1969 Sched. 5).

For a form or order under these provisions, see page 231.

3. Review of care orders

In any case in which a child or young person is placed in the care of a local authority, the authority is under a duty to review the case of each child in its care in accordance with any Regulations that may be made by the Secretary of State (CCA 1980 s.20).

The Regulations may make provision as to:

    (a) the manner in which cases are to be reviewed;

(b) the considerations to which the local authority are to have regard in reviewing cases; and

(c) the time when a child's case is first to be reviewed and the frequency of subsequent reviews.

4. Interim orders

Any court that has the power to make a care order in respect of a child or young person before it may, if it is not in a position to decide whether to make a care order, make an interim order in respect of him.

Generally, an interim order is a care order containing a provision that it is to expire after a period of twenty-eight days has elapsed from the date on which it was made, or on such earlier date as may be specified in the order. In the case of an order made by a single justice the twenty-eight day period begins with the date on which the person subject of it was first in legal custody in relation to the matter (C&YPA 1969 s.20(1)).

A person made subject of an interim care order shall be committed for the duration of the order to the care of the local authority for the area in which he lives, or, if it does not appear to the court that he resides in the area of a particular local authority, to the local authority in whose area it appears the offence was committed or the circumstances in consequence of which the order was made arose (C&YPA 1969 s.20(2)).

No interim order may be made in respect of a person who is not present before the court or justice unless the justice or court dealing with the application is satisfied that he is under five years of age or cannot be present due to illness or accident (C&YPA 1969 s.22 (1)).

An interim order shall require the local authority to bring the relevant infant before the juvenile court on the expiration of the order or on such earlier occasion as the court may require (C&YPA 1969 s.22(2)).

A juvenile court acting for the same area as the justice or court that made an interim order may, before the expiration of the order, make a further interim order (C&YPA 1969 s.22(3)).

Forms of interim care order are set out at page 231 *et seq.*

5. Secure accommodation applications

Very strict controls are placed upon local authorities in relation to the use of accommodation within community homes for restricting the liberty of children in their care. These are discussed in detail in Chapter 24.

Generally, a child to whom the Secure Accommodation (No 2) Regulations 1983 apply may not be kept in secure accommodation for more than 72 hours, whether consecutively or in aggregate, in any period of 28 consecutive days, without the authority of a juvenile court.

If any authority wishes to keep a child in accommodation for restricting liberty for a longer period than is allowed under the regulations, they must make application to a juvenile court under CCA 1980 s.21A for an order authorising the keeping of the child in secure accommodation for an extended period.

On hearing an application under s.21A, the juvenile court must determine whether any relevant criteria (see page 178) for keeping a child in accommodation provided for the purpose of restricting liberty are satisfied in his case. If the court does find that such criteria are satisfied it shall make an order authorising the child to be kept in such accommodation. The order shall specify the maximum period for which he may be so kept (CCA 1980 s.21A(3)).

If a juvenile court adjourns an application under subs.3, it may make an interim order permitting the keeping of the child in accommodation provided for the purpose of restricting liberty for the period of the adjournment (CCA 1980 s.21A(4)).

A juvenile court may not exercise the powers conferred by the section in relation to an unrepresented child unless:

(a) he applied for legal aid and the application was refused on the ground that it did not appear his means were such that he required assistance; or

(b) having been informed of his right to apply for legal aid and having had the opportunity to do so, he refused or failed to apply. (CCA 1980 s.21A(6)).

A person who is aggrieved by a determination under s.21A(3) may appeal to the Crown Court (CCA 1980 s.21A(5)).

An order authorising extended use of secure accommodation is printed at page 265. The Secure Accommodation (No 2) Regulations 1983 are reproduced at page 270.

Part II

OFFENCES
IN RELATION TO MINORS

Chapter 14

Sexual offences involving girls

The Sexual Offences Act 1956 contains numerous provisions designed to protect girls from any form of sexual abuse. Many other provisions apply with equal force to girls as they do to older females. In this chapter attention is concentrated on offences in which the age of the victim is of particular relevance.

1. Intercourse with a girl under thirteen

It is an offence for a man to have unlawful sexual intercourse with a girl under the age of *thirteen* (SOA 1956 s.5). Trial is on indictment. The consent of the girl is no defence to a charge under this section (*R* v *Beale* (1865)).

'Unlawful' means outside the bonds of marriage (illicit) (*R* v *Chapman* (1958)).

It is not necessary for the prosecutor to prove the completion of intercourse by the emission of seed in order to prove the offence. Intercourse is deemed to be complete upon proof of penetration (SOA 1956 s.44).

The age of a girl can be proved by a certified copy of an entry in the register of births, signed by the officer having the custody of the book (*R* v *Weaver* (1873)) but there must also be some positive proof of the identity of the girl (*R* v *Rogers* (1914)).

On conviction a defendant is liable to imprisonment for life (SOA 1956 Sched.2).

2. Intercourse with a girl under sixteen

It is an offence for a man to have unlawful sexual intercourse with a girl under the age of *sixteen*. However, in the case of a girl under the age of sixteen but over the age of thirteen, trial may be summary or on indictment.

A man who is under the age of twenty-four will have a defence to a charge under this section if he has not been charged with a like offence before and he believes the girl in question to be sixteen or over and he has reasonable cause for the belief.

In any case in which a marriage is invalid under MA 1949 s.2 or AMA 1929 s.1, the invalidity does not make the husband guilty of an offence under this section by virtue of having had sexual intercourse with her, if he believes her to be his wife and has reasonable cause for that belief (SOA 1956 s.6).

A husband who is validly married under foreign law to a wife who is under the age of sixteen should not be charged with an offence under this section (*Mohamed* v *Knott* (1968)).

On summary conviction a defendant will be liable to a fine not exceeding Level 5 on the standard scale or to imprisonment for a term not exceeding six months or to both. On conviction on indictment a defendant will be liable to an unlimited fine or to imprisonment for a term not exceeding two years or to both (SOA 1956 Sched. 2).

3. Abduction of an unmarried girl with intention that she shall have unlawful sexual intercourse

If any person takes an unmarried girl under the age of *eighteen* out of the possession of her parent or guardian against his will, with the intention that she shall have unlawful sexual intercourse with men or with a particular man, they commit an offence. Trial is on indictment.

A person is not guilty of an offence under the section if he believes the girl to be eighteen or over and he has reasonable cause for the belief (SOA 1956 s.19).

There must be some persuasion, inducement or blandishment on the part of the man to constitute 'taking' (*R* v *Kauffman* (1904)).

The reference in s.19 to a *person* must be taken as an indication that the offence is capable of being committed by a female. The same word is used in s.15 (a section concerned with indecent assaults upon men) and it has been held that a woman may be convicted of that offence (*R* v *Hare* (1934)). In other sections of the statute it is clear that the offence under consideration can only be committed by a man.

On conviction a defendant is liable to an unlimited fine or to imprisonment for a term not exceeding two years or to both (SOA 1956 Sched.2).

4. Abduction of an unmarried girl under sixteen

Any person who, without lawful authority or excuse, takes an unmarried girl under the age of *sixteen* out of the possession of her parent or guardian against his will is guilty of an offence. Such offence is triable only on indictment, and upon conviction the defendant is liable to an unlimited fine or to imprisonment for a term not exceeding two years or to both (SOA 1956 s.20 and Sched. 2).

While in the case of an abduction under s.19 it is necessary to prove that there was an intention that the girl should have unlawful sexual intercourse with men or with a particular man, it is not necessary to prove any such intention in the case of a prosecution under this section. It is, however, necessary for the prosecutor to prove *mens rea*.

A plea that the defendant was told and reasonably believed that the girl was over the age of sixteen will not afford him a defence if in fact she was under that age (*R* v *Prince* (1875)).

5. Procuring a girl under twenty-one for sexual intercourse

It is an offence for any person to procure a girl under the age of twenty-one to have unlawful sexual intercourse in any part of the world with a third person.

No charge should be brought under this section if intercourse does not take place. The proper charge then would be one of attempting to commit the offence (*R* v *Johnson* (1963)).

A person shall not be convicted on the evidence of one person unless that person is corroborated in some material particular by evidence that implicates the accused (SOA 1956 s.23).

Offences under this section, and attempts to commit such an offence, are triable on indictment. On conviction the defendant is liable to an unlimited fine or to imprisonment for a term of two years or to both (SOA 1956 Sched.2).

6. Permitting a girl under thirteen to use premises for intercourse

If the owner or occupier of any premises, or any person who has, or acts or assists in, the management or control of any premises, induces or knowingly suffers a girl under the age of *thirteen* to resort to or to be on those premises for the purpose of having unlawful sexual intercourse with men or with a particular man, they are guilty of an offence (SOA 1956 s.25). Such an offence is triable on indictment, and on conviction the defendant will be liable to imprisonment for life (SOA 1956 Sched.2).

This section will apply to a mother who permits her daughter's prostitution in her own home (*R* v *Webster* (1885)).

7. Permitting a girl under sixteen to use premises for intercourse

If any of the persons referred to in s.25 (see above) induces or knowingly allows a girl under *sixteen* to use premises for the purpose of having unlawful sexual intercourse with men or with a particular man they are guilty of an offence (SOA 1956 s.26).

An offence under this section is triable summarily or on indictment. On conviction before a magistrates' court, the defendant will be liable to a fine not exceeding Level 5 on the standard scale or to a term of imprisonment not exceeding six months or to both. On indictment, the defendant is liable to an unlimited fine or to a term of imprisonment not exceeding two years or to both.

Again, this offence can be committed by a mother who permits her daughter's prostitution in her own home (*R* v *Webster*, above).

8. Causing or encouraging prostitution of, indecent assault on, or intercourse with, a girl under sixteen

If any person causes or encourages the prostitution of, or the commission of unlawful sexual intercourse with, or an indecent assault upon a girl under the age of *sixteen* for whom he is responsible, he is guilty of an offence (SOA 1956 s.28).

Offences charged under this section are triable on indictment and on conviction a defendant is liable to an unlimited fine or to imprisonment for a term not exceeding two years or to both (SOA 1956 Sched.2).

In certain circumstances a failure to prevent unlawful sexual intercourse taking place may constitute 'causing or encouraging' for the purposes of this section (*R* v *Ralphs* (1913)).

If a girl has become a prostitute, or has had unlawful sexual intercourse or has been indecently assaulted, a person shall be deemed to have caused or encouraged it, if he knowingly allowed her to consort with, or to enter or to continue in the employment of, any prostitute or person of known immoral character (SOA 1956 s.28(2)). Negligence alone is not sufficient to constitute 'knowingly allowing' for the purposes of this subsection. There must have been such permission as would be deemed to be 'causing or encouraging' (*R* v *Chainey* (1914); *R* v *Drury* (1975)).

For the purposes of s.28 the following persons are to be treated as being responsible for a girl:

(a) her parent or legal guardian; and

(b) any person who has actual control of her, or to whose charge she has been committed by her parent or legal guardian or by a person having the legal custody of her; and

(c) any other person who has the custody, charge or care of her.

'Parent' does not include a person deprived of her custody by a court of competent jurisdiction, but otherwise, in the case of an illegitimate girl does include her mother and any person who has been adjudged to be her putative father. 'Legal guardian' means, in relation to any girl, any person who is for the time being her guardian, having been appointed according to law by deed or Will, or by order of any court of competent jurisdiction (SOA 1956 s.28(3) and (4)).

In dealing with any offence under this section, if the girl in question appears to the court to have been under the age of sixteen at the time of the offence charged, she shall be presumed to have been so, unless the contrary is proved (SOA 1956 s.28(5) as amended by CA 1975 Sch.4).

9. General provisions

In all cases of offences referred to in this chapter, the wife or husband of the accused person may be called to give evidence by the prosecution or by the defence (PACEA 1984 s.80).

In all cases relating to unlawful sexual intercourse, 'unlawful' means illicit; outside the bond of marriage (*R* v *Chapman* (1958)).

Chapter 15

Abduction, kidnapping, false imprisonment and harbouring

The Child Abduction Act 1984 is designed to prevent the abduction of children whether by a parent or by any other person. It deals with the difficult situations that can arise when one parent takes a child out of the care and control of the other parent without proper consent, and where strangers take children from the control of those who have lawful control, or detain them unlawfully.

Kidnapping is a common law offence, as is false imprisonment.

1. Abduction

(a) *Abduction by a connected person*

Persons who are connected with a child under the age of *sixteen* may not take or send that child out of the United Kingdom without the appropriate consent. The consent required is:

  (i) the consent of each person who is a parent or guardian of the child or to whom custody of the child has been awarded by an order of a court in the United Kingdom; or
 (ii) the consent of the court that made the order if the child is the subject of a custody order; or
(iii) the leave of the court granted on an application for a direction under GMA 1971 s.7 or GA 1973 s.1(3).

A custody order made by a magistrates' court falls within (ii) above, and any magistrates' court acting for the same petty sessions area as the court that made the order may give consent for the purposes of this section (CAA 1984 s.1(3) and (4)).

The following persons are 'persons connected with a child':

  (i) parents or guardians of the child; or

(ii) persons who have been awarded custody, solely or jointly with another person, by order of a court in the United Kingdom; or

(iii) any person who is believed, on reasonable grounds, to be the father of an illegitimate child.

If any person connected with a child does take or send the child out of the United Kingdom without the appropriate consent they are guilty of an offence and will be liable to a sentence of imprisonment not exceeding seven years if convicted in the Crown Court, and a fine not exceeding Level 5 on the standard scale or to a term of imprisonment not exceeding six months or both on conviction in a magistrates' court.

No offence is committed if the person connected with the child acts in the belief that the other person has consented to the action he is taking or would have consented if aware of all the relevant circumstances. Similarly, no offence is committed if all reasonable steps have been taken to communicate with the other person concerned but communication has not been possible or the consent of the other person has been refused unreasonably (CAA 1984 s.1(5)). An unreasonable refusal to consent cannot be pleaded in cases in which the child in question is the subject of a custody order made by a court in the United Kingdom, or where the action that has been taken by the person connected with the child is in breach of a direction under GMA 1971 s.7 or GA 1973 s.1(3).

If in any proceedings taken under this section there is sufficient evidence to raise an issue referred to in the last paragraph, it is for the prosecutor to prove that the defences do not apply. (CAA 1984 s.1(1)–(6)as amended by FLA 1986 s.65).

For the purposes of s.1, 'guardian' means a person appointed by deed or Will or by order of a court of competent jurisdiction to be the guardian of the child. References to custody orders and orders awarding custody include orders awarding legal custody and orders awarding care and control (CAA 1984 s.1(7)).

In the case of a child who is in the care of a local authority or voluntary organisation or who is committed to a place of safety or is the subject of custodianship proceedings or an order relating to adoption, s.1 is modified by the provisions of the Schedule to the Act. It provides that in any of those cases subss.(3) to (6) are to be omitted. It further provides that references to appropriate consent in subs.1 shall have the following meanings:

(i) In the case of children who are in the care of a local authority or a voluntary organisation – the consent of the local authority or voluntary organisation in question;

(ii) In the case of children in places of safety — the leave of any magistrates' court acting for the area in which the place of safety is situated;

(iii) In the case of children who are subject to orders in connection with adoption — the consent of the adoption agency involved or the leave of the court to which an application has been made or by which an order has been made (depending upon the stage in the proceedings that has been reached by the time the consent is sought) (CAA 1984 s.1(8)).

Before any proceedings can be taken under the provisions of s.1 it is necessary for the consent of the DPP or Crown Prosecutor to have been obtained (CAA 1984 s.4(2)).

(b) Abduction by other persons

It is an offence for any person who is not a parent or guardian of a child or a person who has been awarded custody of a child (solely or jointly with another person) to take or detain a child under the age of *sixteen*, without lawful authority or reasonable excuse, so as to:

(i) remove him from the lawful control of any person having lawful control of him; or

(ii) keep him out of the lawful control of any person who has lawful control of him (CAA 1984 s.2(1)).

If proceedings have been taken under s.2(1), it is a defence for the defendant to show that at the time of the alleged offence he believed that the child had attained the age of sixteen, or, in the case of an illegitimate child, he had reasonable grounds for believing himself to be the child's father (CAA 1984 s.2(2)).

An offence under s.2 of the Act is triable either way and the penalties that may be imposed are the same as set out in *(a)* above.

The Child Abduction and Custody Act 1985 came into force on 1 August 1986. It enables the United Kingdom to ratify two international Conventions, one of which relates to civil aspects of international child abduction, the other to the recognition and enforcement of custody decisions.

In England, Wales and Northern Ireland, jurisdiction to entertain applications under either of the Conventions — the *Hague Convention on the Civil Aspects of International Child Abduction* and the *European Convention on Recognition and Enforcement of Decisions concerning Custody of Children* — is vested in the High Court. Custody applications in the magistrates' court may be stayed upon receipt of notice from the High Court that an application in respect of the child has been made under the Hague Convention.

Procedures in relation to these matters are set out in the Magistrates' Courts (Child Abduction and Custody) Rules 1986 (SI 1986 No 1141). The rules are reproduced at page 279.

(c) 'Taking' 'sending' and 'detaining'

For the purposes of Part I of the Statute a person who causes or induces a child to accompany him or any other person, or who causes a child to be taken, is to be regarded as having taken the child. A person who causes a child to be sent is to be regarded as having sent the child. Similarly, if a person causes a child to be detained or induces a child to remain with him or with another person, he is to be regarded as having detained the child (CAA 1984 s.3).

2. Kidnapping

(a) The offence

Kidnapping is a common law offence. It involves the deprivation of a person's liberty and a carrying away of that person against his will. A parent can commit the offence if he takes and carries away his own unmarried child under the age of *eighteen*, by fraud or force, without the consent of the child and without lawful excuse. The absence of consent is material. In the case of a child of tender years an absence of consent may be inferred from the age of the child. In the case of an older child, the jury must decide as a matter of fact whether the child in question has sufficient understanding and intelligence to be able to give his consent. If the jury decides that the child is of sufficient understanding and intelligence it must then go on to decide whether he did, in fact, consent (*R* v *D* (1984); *R* v *Rahman* (1985) should also be considered).

Offences of kidnapping are triable only on indictment and are punishable by fine or by imprisonment.

(b) Authority to prosecute

A prosecution for the alleged offence of kidnapping may only be instituted with the consent of the DPP or a Crown Prosecutor if the offence was committed against a child under the age of *sixteen* and by a person connected with that child (within the meaning of s.1 CAA 1984, see page 114) (CAA 1984 s.5).

3. False imprisonment

False imprisonment is also a common law offence. It involves un-lawful detention, compulsion, restraint of personal liberty (*Mee* v *Cruikshank* (1902); *R* v *Linsberg and Leies* (1905)). A parent who acts outside the bounds of reasonable parental discipline may be guilty of the offence in relation to his child (*R* v *Rahman* (1985)).

The offence is triable only on indictment and is punishable by fine or imprisonment.

4. Harbouring

The Child Care Act 1980 contains provisions designed to prevent persons from taking children away from the care of a local authority; assisting children to run away from the care of the local authority; harbouring or concealing a child who has run away or been taken away from the care of a local authority; or preventing the return of a child to the care of the local authority.

Section 13 provides that any person who:

(a) knowingly assists or induces or persistently attempts to induce a child in the care of a local authority under s.2 of the Act to run away; or

(b) without lawful authority takes such a child away; or

(c) knowingly harbours or conceals such a child who has run away or been taken away or prevents him from returning,

is guilty of an offence.

In any case in which a local authority, having allowed any person to take charge of a child with respect to whom a resolution under s.3 (assumption of parental rights and duties − see page 187) is in force, has given written notice requiring that person to return the child at a time specified in the notice, any person who harbours or conceals the child after that time or prevents him from returning as required by the notice shall be guilty of an offence. (CCA 1980 s.14)

A person convicted of an offence under s.13 is liable on summary conviction to a fine not exceeding Level 5 on the standard scale or to a term of imprisonment not exceeding three months or to both. On being convicted in a magistrates' court of an offence under s.14 a defendant will be liable to a fine not exceeding Level 3 on the standard scale or to a term of imprisonment not exceeding two months or to both.

Chapter 16

Cruelty and conduct that exposes minors to danger

Other chapters of this Part of the book have dealt with specific kinds of conduct, sexual conduct for example, likely to result in minors being exposed to danger. This chapter concentrates on provisions in C&YPA 1933 and various other statutes designed to provide additional safeguards.

1. Cruelty

(a) The offence

Section 1 of the Act of 1933 makes it an offence for any person over the age of sixteen who has the custody, charge or care of any child or young person under that age to act in a way that is likely to cause him unnecessary suffering or injury to health. For the purposes of the section 'injury to health' includes injury to or loss of sight, hearing, limb or organ of the body, and any mental derangement.

The offence is committed if the defendant wilfully assaults, ill treats, neglects, abandons or exposes the child or young person, or causes or procures him to be assaulted, ill-treated, neglected, abandoned or exposed in a manner likely to cause him unnecessary suffering or injury.

An offence under the section is triable either way. On conviction on indictment the defendant will be liable to a term of imprisonment not exceeding two years. On conviction in a magistrates' court he will be liable to a fine not exceeding Level 5 on the standard scale or to a term of imprisonment not exceeding six months or to both (C&YPA 1933 s.1(1)).

(b) Interpretation

Any parent or guardian of a child or young person and any person

119

legally liable to maintain him is presumed to have the custody of him. A father shall not be deemed to have ceased to have the custody of the child or young person by reason only that he has deserted, or otherwise does not reside with, the mother and the child or young person.

Any person to whom the charge of a child or young person is committed by any person who has the custody of him shall be presumed to have charge of him, and any other person having the actual possession or control of a child or young person shall be presumed to have the care of him (C&YPA 1933 s.17).

The father of an illegitimate child in respect of whom no affiliation order has been made is not a parent for the purposes of the section (*Butler* v *Gregory* (1902)). However, the fact that a mother is the lawful custodian of a child does not prevent the father from having custody, charge or care of the child within the meaning of s.1(1) if the mother, father and child are living together. This is so even though the mother has not obtained an affiliation order (*Liverpool Society for the Prevention of Cruelty to Children* v *Jones* (1914)).

It is not possible for a father, by virtue of a voluntary agreement giving custody to his wife, to oust the legal presumption under s.17 that he has his custody, but if he has been deprived of the custody of the child by a competent court, the presumption is rebutted (*Brooks* v *Blount* (1923)).

To prove an offence under s.1(1) a prosecutor must establish a deliberate or reckless act or failure, since offences under the section are not strict liability offences. The offence is not to be judged by the objective test of what a reasonable parent would have done (*R* v *Sheppard* (1981)).

It has been held that 'ill-treats' covers most, if not all, forms of neglect, and that the words, 'assaults, ill-treats, neglects, abandons or exposes' do not create separate, watertight offences (*R* v *Hayles* (1969)).

In making any decision as to whether a refusal to allow an operation constitutes neglect, justices must consider the nature of the operation and the reasonableness of the refusal (*Oakey* v *Jackson* (1914)).

To 'abandon' a child means to leave it to its fate (*R* v *Boulden* (1957)). It has been held that a child who had been carefully packed and sent by train to his father's address had been 'abandoned' even though he suffered no actual injury (*R* v *Falkingham* (1870)); and a father was convicted of 'abandoning' a child where, knowing that he had been left on his doorstep, he left him there for six hours on an October night (*R* v *White* (1871)).

'Exposure' does not necessarily consist of the physical placing of a child somewhere with the intention to injure it (*R* v *Williams* (1910)).

(c) Statutory presumptions

A parent or other person legally liable to maintain a child or young person shall be deemed to have neglected him in a manner likely to cause injury to his health if he has failed to provide adequate food, clothing, medical aid or lodging for him or, being unable to provide it, has failed to procure its provision under relevant enactments (eg Social Security Acts).

If it is proved that the death of an infant under *three* years of age was due to suffocation while in bed with a person over the age of sixteen who went to bed under the influence of drink, that other person shall be deemed to have neglected the infant in a manner likely to cause injury to its health. This presumption is not made, however, if the suffocation was a result of disease or the presence of any foreign body in the infant's throat or air passages (C&YPA 1933 s.1(2)).

(d) Miscellaneous provisions

A person may be convicted of an offence under s.1 even though the action of a third person prevented actual suffering or injury to health or the likelihood of such suffering or injury. A person may also be convicted of a s.1 offence even though the child or young person in question dies (C&YPA 1933 s.1(3)).

If it is proved that a person convicted of a s.1 offence had a direct or indirect interest in any money accruing or payable in the event of the death of the child or young person, and that he knew that the sum would accrue or become payable, the maximum penalty on conviction on indictment is increased to five years imprisonment. On conviction in a magistrates' court the court must take the defendant's knowledge of his interest into account in determining the sentence to be imposed (C&YPA 1933 s.1(5)).

For the purposes of subs.5, a person shall be deemed to be directly or indirectly interested in a sum of money if he has any share in or any benefit from the payment of that money, notwithstanding that he may not be a person to whom it is legally payable. A copy of a policy of insurance, certified to be a true copy by an officer or agent of the insurance company granting the policy, shall be evidence that the child or young person stated therein to be insured has in fact been so insured, and that the person in whose favour the policy has been granted is the person to whom the money thereby insured is legally payable (C&YPA 1933 s.1(6)).

Nothing in s.1 is to be treated as affecting in any way a right of a parent, a teacher, or any other person having the lawful control of a child or young person to administer punishment to him (C&YPA 1933 s.1(7)).

2. Minors in brothels

Any person who, having the custody, charge or care of a child or young person who has attained the age of *four* years and is under the age of *sixteen* years, allows that child or young person to reside in or to frequent a brothel commits an offence. The offence is triable in a magistrates' court only, and on conviction the defendant is liable to a fine not exceeding Level 2 on the standard scale or to a term of imprisonment not exceeding six months, or to both (C&YPA 1933 s.3).

A 'brothel' is a place where people of opposite sexes are allowed to resort for illicit intercourse (SOA 1956 s.33). This is so whether or not the women are common prostitutes (*Winter* v *Woolfe* (1931)). A house that is occupied by one woman and used only by her for prostitution is not a brothel (*Singleton* v *Ellison* (1895)).

3. Sex establishments

If the holder of a licence for a sex establishment:

(a) without reasonable excuse knowingly permits a person under the age of *eighteen* years to enter the establishment; or

(b) employs a person known to him to be under *eighteen* years of age in the business of the establishment,

he is guilty of an offence. The offence is triable in the magistrates' court only, and the maximum penalty that can be imposed is a fine not exceeding £20,000 (LG(MP)A 1982 Sched. 3 para. 23).

A constable may enter and inspect any sex establishment, at any reasonable time, with a view to seeing whether any person under the age of eighteen is in the establishment or employed in the business of the establishment (LG(MP)A 1982 Sched. 3 para.25). He may also enter such an establishment and inspect it if he has reason to suspect that an offence under para. 23 of the Schedule has been, is being or is about to be committed (LG(MP)A Sched. 3 para. 25(2)).

If a person, without reasonable excuse, refuses to permit a constable to exercise his powers of entry and inspection, he will be guilty of an offence punishable on conviction in a magistrates' court by a fine not exceeding Level 5 on the standard scale (LG(MP)A 1982 Sched. 3 para. 25(6)).

4. Exposure to risk of burning

It is an offence if any person who has attained the age of sixteen, having the custody, charge or care of a child under the age of *twelve* years, allows the child to be in any room containing an open fire, grate or any heating appliance liable to cause injury to a person by contact with it and it is not sufficiently protected to guard against the risk of his being burnt or scalded, without taking reasonable precautions against that risk, and as a result the child is killed or suffers serious injury. On conviction in a magistrates' court, a fine not exceeding Level 1 on the standard scale may be imposed (C&YPA 1933 s.11). Proceedings taken under s.11 will not affect any liability of any person to be proceeded against by indictment for any indictable offence.

5. Tattooing

Except where a tattoo is performed for medical reasons by a qualified medical practitioner, or by a person working under his direction, it is an offence for any person to tattoo a person under the age of *eighteen* years.

It is a defence to a charge under this Act for a person charged to show that at the time the tattoo was performed, he had reasonable cause to believe that the person tattooed was over the age of eighteen and did in fact so believe (TMA 1969 s.1).

A person convicted of an offence under s.1 of the statute is liable, on conviction in a magistrates' court, to a fine not exceeding Level 3 on the standard scale (TMA 1969 s.2).

A 'tattoo' is an insertion into the skin of any colouring material designed to leave a permanent mark.

6. Neglect of apprentices

A master who is bound to provide food, clothing, medical aid or lodging for an apprentice, by virtue of the articles of apprenticeship, commits an offence if, wilfully and without lawful excuse, he refuses or neglects to provide the same, and as a result the health of the apprentice is or is likely to be seriously or permanently injured. The offence is triable in the magistrates' court only, and is punishable by a fine not exceeding Level 2 on the standard scale, or by a term of imprisonment not exceeding six months (CPPA 1875 s.6).

7. Minors used for begging

Any person who causes or procures any child or young person under the age of *sixteen* years or, having the custody, charge or care of such a child or young person, allows him to be in any street, premises or place for the purpose of begging or receiving alms, or of inducing the giving of alms, is guilty of an offence and liable on conviction in a magistrates' court to a fine not exceeding Level 2 on the standard scale, or to a term of imprisonment not exceeding three months, or to both (C&YPA 1933 s.4(1)).

If it is proved that a child or young person was in a street, premises or place for any purpose mentioned in s.4(1) and that the person having the custody, charge or care of him allowed him to be in that street, premises or place, he shall be presumed to have allowed him to be there for that purpose unless the contrary is proved (C&YPA 1933 s.4(2)). If a person has with him, while singing, playing, performing or offering anything for sale in a street or public place, a child who has been lent or hired out to him, the child shall, for the purposes of s.4, be deemed to be in that street or place for the purpose of inducing the giving of alms (C&YPA 1933 s.4(3)).

A 'street' includes any highway, public bridge, road, lane, footway, square, court, alley or passage, whether a thoroughfare or not. 'Public place' includes any public park, garden, sea beach, railway station and any other ground to which the public for the time being have or are permitted to have access, whether on payment or otherwise (C&YPA 1933 s.107).

8. Drunkenness while in charge of a minor

If any person is found drunk in any highway or public place, whether a building or not, or on any licensed premises, while having the charge of a child apparently under the age of *seven* years, he may be apprehended, and if the child is under that age he shall be guilty of an offence and liable on conviction in a magistrates' court to a fine not exceeding Level 2 on the standard scale or to imprisonment for a term not exceeding one month (LA 1902 s.2(1)).

For the purposes of s.2 a 'public place' includes any place to which the public have access, whether on payment or otherwise (LA 1902 s.8).

In proceedings under s.2, if the child appears to the court to be under the age of seven, the child shall be deemed for the purposes of the section to be under that age unless the contrary is proved (LA 1902 s.2(2)).

9. Publications harmful to minors

It is an offence to print, publish, sell or let on hire any work that, as a whole, would tend to corrupt a child or young person into whose hands it might fall. The works to which the statute (C&YP(HP)A 1955) applies are any book, magazine or other like work of a kind likely to fall into the hands of children or young persons, and which consist wholly or mainly of stories told in pictures (with or without additional written matter) being stories portraying:

(a) the commission of crimes; or

(b) acts of violence or cruelty; or

(c) incidents of a repulsive or horrible nature,

in such a way that the work as a whole would tend to corrupt a child or young person into whose hands it might fall (C&YP(HP)A 1955 ss.1 and 2).

An offence under s.2 is triable in the magistrates' court only and on conviction a defendant is liable to a fine not exceeding Level 3 on the standard scale or to a term of imprisonment not exceeding four months or to both.

It shall be a defence for a defendant to prove that he had not examined the contents of the work and had no reasonable cause to suspect that it was one to which the Act applies.

No prosecution shall be instituted under the section (in England or Wales) without the consent of the Attorney-General (C&YPA (HP)A 1955 s.2). If the office of Attorney-General is vacant or he is unable to act owing to illness or absence the functions of the Attorney-General under this Act may be carried out by the Solicitor-General (Law Officers Act 1944 s.1).

10. Indecent photographs

The Protection of Children Act 1978 prohibits the taking of indecent photographs of children and the publishing and distribution of such photographs. The statute also makes it an offence for a person to be in possession of indecent photographs of children. The Act provides that it is an offence for a person:

(a) to take, or permit to be taken, any indecent photograph of a child; or

(b) to distribute or to show such indecent photographs; or

(c) to have such indecent photographs in his possession with a view to their being shown or distributed by himself or others; or

(d) to publish or cause to be published any advertisement likely to be understood as conveying that the advertiser distributes or shows such indecent photographs, or intends to do so (PCA 1978 s.1(1)).

For the purposes of the statute 'child' means persons under the age of *sixteen*.

A person is to be regarded as 'distributing' an indecent photograph if he parts with possession of it to, or offers it for acquisition by another person (PCA 1978 s.1(2)).

It is a defence for a person charged to prove:

(a) that he had a legitimate reason for distributing or showing the photographs or having them in his possession; or

(b) that he had not seen the photographs himself and did not know, nor had any cause to suspect, them to be indecent (PCA 1978 s.1(4)).

If a justice of the peace is satisfied by information on oath, laid by a constable or on behalf of the Director of Public Prosecutions, that there is ground for suspecting that, in any premises in the petty sessions area for which he acts, there are indecent photographs of children and that they:

(a) are or have been taken there; or

(b) are or have been shown there, or are kept there with a view to their being distributed or shown,

he may issue a warrant authorising any constable to enter and search the premises within fourteen days (by force if necessary) and to seize and remove any articles which he believes, with reasonable cause, to be or include indecent photographs of children taken or shown on the premises, or kept there with a view to their being distributed or shown (PCA 1978 s.4(1) and (2)).

Articles seized under s.4 shall, if they are not returned to the occupier of the premises, be brought before a justice acting for the same petty sessions area as the justice who issued the warrant (PCA 1978 s.4(3)).

The justice before whom seized articles are brought may issue a summons against the occupier of the premises requiring him to attend to show cause why they should not be forfeited. If the court is satisfied that the articles are in fact indecent photographs of children, taken on the premises or shown there or kept with a view to their being distributed or shown, the court shall order them to be forfeited. If the occupier does not attend the hearing no forfeiture order may be made unless the court is satisfied that the summons has been served upon him (PCA 1978 s.5).

Proceedings under s.1 may only be instituted with the consent of the Director of Public Prosecutions (PCA 1978 s.1(3)).

An offence under the statute is triable either way. On conviction on indictment a defendant is liable to imprisonment for a term not exceeding three years, or to a fine or both. On conviction in a magistrates' court a defendant will be liable to a fine not exceeding Level 5 on the standard scale or to imprisonment for a term not exceeding six months or to both (PCA 1978 s.6).

For the purposes of the Act, an indecent film, a copy of an indecent photograph or film, and an indecent photograph comprised in a film are to be regarded as indecent photographs. If photographs show children and they are indecent, they shall be treated for all purposes of the Act as indecent photographs of children. References to photographs include the negative as well as the positive version. A 'film' includes any form of video recording (PCA 1978 s.7).

11. Search for children at risk

A justice who is satisfied that a child has been or is being ill-treated, assaulted or neglected, may issue a warrant authorising a constable to search for the child and, if found, to remove him to a place of safety. The warrant must be based on an information confirmed on oath or affirmation (C&YPA 1933 s.40). See page 261 for a form of information and warrant.

Chapter 17

Education and employment of minors

1. Education

The principal statute controlling the education of minors is the
Education Act 1944. It provides that a person who is aged between
five years and sixteen years shall be deemed to be of 'compulsory
school age' (EA 1944 s.35 as amended by the Raising of the School
Leaving Age Order 1972).

(a) The duty of parents to secure their children's education

Any parent of a child of compulsory school age is under a duty to
cause him to receive efficient full-time education suitable for his
age, ability and aptitude and to any special educational needs he
may have. The education in question may be secured by regular
attendance at school or in some other way (EA 1944 s.36 as amended
by EA 1971 s.17).

In any case in which it is not practicable for a parent to arrange for
his child to become a registered pupil at a school because a school
term has already begun, he is not subject to the duty imposed by EA
1944 s.36 (Education (Miscellaneous Provisions) Act 1948 s.4).

(b) Education authorities' powers to require school attendance

Should it appear to an education authority that the parent of any
child of compulsory school age in its area is failing to carry out the
duty to secure that child's education, the authority must serve a
notice on that parent requiring him, within such time as may be
specified in the notice, to satisfy the authority that the child is
receiving efficient full-time education suitable to his age, ability and
aptitude and to any special educational needs he may have. The time
specified in any such notice may not be less than *fourteen days*.

If a parent who has been served with a notice fails, within the time allowed, to satisfy the education authority that his child is receiving the requisite education, then, if in the opinion of the authority it is expedient that he should attend school, the authority shall serve an order upon the parent requiring him to cause the child to become a registered pupil at a school named in the order. The order is referred to as a 'school attendance order' (EA 1944 s.37 (1) and (2)). Orders may be amended on application (EA 1980 s.11).

Before serving a school attendance order on a parent the education authority must serve upon him a written notice of its intention to serve the order in accordance with EA 1980 s.10.

(c) A parent's duty to comply with school attendance orders

Any parent who has a school attendance order served upon him is under a duty to comply with it, and if he fails to do so, he will be guilty of an offence punishable by a fine not exceeding Level 3 on the standard scale or imprisonment for a term not exceeding one month, unless he proves that he is causing the child to receive, otherwise than at school, efficient full-time education suitable to his age, ability and aptitude and to any special educational needs he may have (EA 1944 ss.37(5) and 40).

(d) The duty of parents to secure attendance of registered pupils

The parent of any child of compulsory school age who is a registered pupil at a school is under a duty to ensure that the child attends the school regularly. Any parent who fails to ensure the regular attendance of his child at school is guilty of an offence and liable to a fine not exceeding Level 3 on the standard scale or to imprisonment for a term not exceeding one month (EA 1944 ss.39(1) and 40).

In any proceedings taken under this section a child is not to be deemed to have failed to attend school regularly if he has been:

(a) absent from the school with leave, or

(b) prevented from attending by reason of sickness or any unavoidable cause, or

(c) absent on any day exclusively set apart for religious observance by the religious body to which his parents belong.

A child shall not be deemed to have failed to attend school regularly if his parent proves that the school at which the child is a registered pupil is not within walking distance of the child's home and that no suitable arrangements have been made by the local education authority either for his transport to and from the school or for boarding accommodation for him at the school or for him to become a registered pupil at a school nearer to his home (EA 1944 s.39(2)).

For the purposes of s.39(2) 'unavoidable cause' is not to be equated with 'reasonable cause' (*Jarman* v *Mid-Glamorgan Education Authority* (1985)). The chronic illness of a parent, or other family responsibilities or duties are not 'unavoidable causes' (*Jenkins* v *Howells* (1949)).

Under the provisions of C&YPA 1963 s.37, a licence may be granted which enables a child of compulsory school age to be absent from school for the purpose of taking part in public entertainments. A child shall not be deemed to have failed to attend school regularly for the purpose of proceedings under EA 1944 s.39 merely by virtue of absences at times authorised by a licence granted under C&YPA 1963 s.37.

(e) Vagrants preventing children from receiving education

Any person who is an habitual wanderer from place to place and who takes with him any child of compulsory school age will, on conviction by a magistrates' court be liable to a fine not exceeding Level 1 on the standard scale. He will not be guilty of an offence if he proves that the child in question is not prevented from receiving efficient full-time education suitable to his age, ability and aptitude, and to any special educational needs he may have as a result of being taken from place to place with him.

Proceedings may only be instituted by the local education authority. If in any case in which proceedings are brought it is proved that the parent or guardian of the child in question is engaged in any trade or business of such nature as to require him to travel from place to place, the person against whom the proceedings were brought shall be acquitted if it is proved that the child has attended at the school at which he is a registered pupil as regularly as the nature of the trade or business of the parent or guardian permits, and, in the case of a child who has attained the age of *six years* he made at least two hundred attendances during the period of twelve months ending with the date on which the proceedings were instituted (C&YPA 1933 s.10 as amended).

2. Employment

General provisions relating to the employment of minors are

contained in C&YPA 1933 Part II. Some of the provisions of the statute will be replaced by ECA 1973 when that Act is brought into force.

(a) General restrictions upon employment

No child of compulsory school age may be employed:

   (i) so long as he is under the age of *thirteen years*; or

  (ii) before the close of school hours on any day on which he is required to attend school; or

 (iii) before seven o'clock in the morning or after seven o'clock in the evening on any day; or

  (iv) for more than two hours on any day on which he is required to attend school; or

   (v) for more than two hours on any Sunday, or

  (vi) to lift, carry or move anything so heavy as to be likely to cause injury to him
(C&YPA 1933 s.18(1)).

In addition to the general statutory control set out above, there is power for local authorities to make byelaws (which require the confirmation of the Secretary of State) in relation to the employment of children. Any byelaws made may distinguish between children of different ages and sexes and between different localities, trades, occupations and circumstances and may contain provisions:

   (i) authorising—

     ● the employment of children under the age of *thirteen* years by their parents or guardians in light agricultural work, or

     ● the employment of children for not more than one hour before the commencement of school hours on any day on which they are required to attend school;

  (ii) prohibiting absolutely the employment of children in any specified occupation;

 (iii) prescribing—

     ● the age below which children are not to be employed,

     ● the number of hours in each day, or in each week, for which, and the times of day at which, they may be employed,

     ● the intervals to be allowed to them for meals and rest,

     ● the holidays and half-holidays to be allowed to them,

     ● any other conditions to be observed in relation to their employment

(C&YPA 1933 s.18(2)). Section 18 will be replaced by the Employment of Children Act 1973 when that Act is in force.

Nothing in the general prohibition or in byelaws made by a local authority shall prevent a child from taking part in a peformance that is authorised by a licence granted under Part II of the statute, or in any case where, by virtue of C&YPA 1963 s.37(3), the child may take part in the performance without a licence granted under that section (see page 130).

(b) Restrictions on employment of persons under eighteen other than children

The C&YPA 1933 contains provisions designed to enable local authorities to make byelaws in relation to the employment of persons who have reached the upper limit of compulsory school age but have not attained the age of eighteen. The provisions in question are set out in s.19. The section has not yet been brought into force since no order has been made by the Secretary of State in pursuance of subs.(3), a prerequisite of the powers vesting in local authorities. It now seems unlikely that the provisions of s.19 will ever come into operation since they will be repealed by ECA 1973 s.3 and Sched.2 when that is brought into force. At the time of going to press no commencement date has been fixed for that section or Schedule, and so local authority powers remain restricted to children who have not reached the upper limit of compulsory school age.

(c) Restrictions on the involvement of minors with street trading

There is a general prohibition on persons under the age of *seventeen* years being engaged or employed in street trading unless that person is employed in street trading by his parents (C&YPA 1933 s.20(1)).

The section gives local authorities powers to make byelaws regulating or prohibiting street trading by persons under the age of *eighteen* years. As with other byelaws relating to the employment of minors, any byelaws made may distinguish between persons of different ages and sexes and between different localities. They may also contain provisions:

(i) forbidding any such person engaging or being employed in street trading unless he holds a licence granted by the authority, and regulating the conditions on which such licences may be granted, suspended or revoked;

(ii) determining the days and hours during which, and the places at which such persons may engage or be employed in street trading;

(iii) requiring such persons so engaged or employed to wear badges;

(iv) regulating in any other respect the conduct of such persons while so engaged or employed
(C&YPA 1933 s.20(2)).

No person under the age of *eighteen* years may engage or be employed in street trading on a Sunday if the nature of that trading is such that the provisions of SA 1950 s.58 do not apply to it. (This section extends certain provisions to any place where a retail trade or business is carried on) (C&YPA 1933 s.20(3)).

(d) Penalties relating to the employment of minors

Any person who is employed in contravention of the provisions of Part II, any person who employs a minor in contravention of Part II and any person (other than the employed person) to whose act or default any such contravention may be attributed, is guilty of an offence and is liable to a fine not exceeding Level 3 on the standard scale.

A person under the age of eighteen who engages in street trading in contravention of s.20 or any byelaws made thereunder is guilty of an offence and liable to a fine not exceeding Level 1 on the standard scale (C&YPA 1933 s.21 as amended).

(e) Restrictions on the employment of children in industry and at sea

The restrictions imposed on the employment of minors by C&YPA 1933 are in addition to the general restrictions contained in the Employment of Women, Young Persons and Children Act 1920, which is concerned with the employment of young persons and children in industrial undertakings and ships.

For the purposes of this statute 'child' has the meaning given to it by EA 1944 s.58, ie a person who is not over compulsory school age. However, in Part IV of the Schedule to the Act, which is concerned with the employment of children at sea, the general restriction relates to children under the age of *fourteen*: art.2).

The Act gives effect to certain Conventions adopted at general conferences of the Industrial Labour Organisation of the League of Nations and also makes further provisions as to the conditions under which young persons are to be employed in factories and workshops.

Industrial undertakings: No child may be employed in an industrial undertaking (s.1(1)). In the Act 'industrial undertaking' specifically includes:

(i) mines, quarries and other works for the extraction of minerals from the earth;

(ii) industries in which articles are manufactured, altered, cleaned, repaired, ornamented, finished, adapted for sale, broken up, or demolished, or in which materials are transformed; including shipbuilding, and the generation, transformation, and transmission of electricity and motive power of any kind;

(iii) construction, reconstruction, maintenance, repair, alteration, or demolition of any building, railway, tramway, harbour, dock, pier, canal, inland waterway, road, tunnel, bridge, viaduct, sewer, drain, well, telegraphic or telephone installation, electrical undertaking, gaswork, waterwork, or other work of construction, as well as the preparation for or laying the foundations of any such work or structure;

(iv) transport of passengers or goods by road or rail or inland waterway, including the handling of goods at docks, quays, wharves, and warehouses, but excluding transport by hand.

The competent authority in each country is responsible for defining the line of division between industry, commerce and agriculture (EWYP&CA 1920 Sched. Pt.I, art.1).

Children under the age of *fourteen* shall not be employed or work in any public or private industrial undertaking, or in any branch thereof, other than an undertaking in which only members of the same family are employed. These provisions do not apply to work done by children in technical schools, provided that such work is approved and supervised by public authority (EWYP&CA 1920 Sched. Pt.I, arts.2 and 3).

To facilitate the enforcement of the provisions of the Schedule all employers in any industrial undertaking are required to keep a register of all persons under the age of *sixteen* employed by him, and the dates of their birth (EWYP&CA 1920 Sched. Pt.I, art.4).

The Education (Work Experience) Act 1973 does enable children who are in the last year of compulsory schooling to gain work experience through arrangements made by local education authorities. The provisions of that statute do not, however, permit the employment of any person in contravention of the provisions of EWYP&CA 1920.

Ships: No child under the age of *fourteen* may be employed in any ship other than a ship upon which only members of the same family are employed (EWYP&CA 1920 Sched. Pt.IV, art.2), but the provisions of the article do not apply to work done on school ships or training ships, provided such work is approved and supervised by public authority.

For the purposes of the statute 'ship' means any sea-going ship or boat of any description which is registered in the United Kingdom as a British ship and includes any British fishing boat entered in the fishing boat register (EWYP&CA 1920 s.4). However, for the purposes of the convention embodied in the statute the term 'vessel' is used and is defined as including all ships and boats, of any nature whatsoever, engaged in maritime navigation, whether publicly or privately owned (but excluding ships of war) (EWYP&CA 1920 Sched. Pt.IV, art.1).

(f) Restrictions on the employment of young persons

No young person under the age of eighteen shall be employed at night in any industrial undertaking except an undertaking in which only members of the same family are employed, save that young persons over the age of *sixteen* may be employed during the night in certain undertakings on work which by reason of the nature of the process, is required to be carried on continuously day and night. The undertakings in question are:

   (i) manufacture of iron and steel, processes in which rever-beratory or regenerative furnaces are used and galvanising of sheet metal or wire (except the pickling process);

  (ii) glass works;

 (iii) manufacture of paper;

 (iv) manufacture of raw sugar; and

  (v) gold mining reduction work
    EWYP&CA 1920 Sched. Pt. II. art.2).

'Night' signifies a period of at least eleven consecutive hours, including the interval between ten o'clock in the evening and five o'clock in the morning (EWYP&CA 1920 Sched. Pt.II, art.3).

In coal and lignite mines work may be carried on in the interval between ten o'clock at night and five o'clock in the morning, if an interval of ordinarily fifteen, and in no case less than thirteen, hours separates two periods of work. Where in the baking industry night work is prohibited for all workers, the interval between nine o'clock in the evening and four o'clock in the morning may be substituted for the interval between ten o'clock in the evening and five o'clock in the morning (EWYP&CA 1920 Sched. Pt.II, art.3).

The restrictions imposed by arts.2 and 3 do not apply to the night work of a young person between the ages of sixteen and eighteen in cases of emergencies which could not have been controlled or foreseen, which are not of a periodical character, and which interfere with the normal working of an industrial undertaking (EWYP&CA 1920 Sched. Pt.II, art.4).

Where a young person is employed in an industrial undertaking, a register of the young persons so employed, and of the dates of their birth, and of the dates on which they enter or leave the service of their employer, shall be kept and shall be open to inspection at all times (EWYP&CA 1920 s.1(4)).

(g) Mines and quarries

The provisions of s.1 EWYP&CA 1920 are applied to employment subject to the Mines and Quarries Act 1954. In particular, any provision in M&QA 1954 relating to registers to be kept, applies to registers that are to be kept under EWYP&CA 1920. In addition to the restrictions imported into the M&QA 1954 from the 1920 statute, there are further restrictions on the employment of minors in M&QA 1954 itself.

No male person under the age of sixteen may be employed below ground in a mine except for the purpose of receiving instruction of such description as may be prescribed. Descriptions of the types of instruction that may be given in coal mines have been prescribed in Mines (Employment of Young Persons) (Appointed Day) Order 1957 (SI 1957 No 1093) and Coal Mines (Training) Regulations 1967 (SI 1967 No 82 as amended by SI 1978 No 1648). There is a total prohibition on the employment of females underground (M&QA 1954 s.124).

The hours worked and the intervals to be allowed for meals and rest for young persons employed above ground at a mine or in a quarry must comply with the following conditions:

(i) the total hours worked, exclusive of intervals allowed for meals and rest, shall neither exceed nine in any day nor exceed forty-eight in any week and, except in the case of a male young person who has attained the age of sixteen, shall not exceed eight hours in any day unless the intervals allowed for meals and rest between spells amount to not less than one and a half hours;

(ii) a young person shall not be employed continuously for a spell of more than four and a half hours without an interval of at least half an hour for a meal or rest, so, however, that where an interval of not less than ten minutes is allowed in the course of a spell, the spell may be increased to five hours.

The total hours worked by a young person employed below ground at a mine other than coal, stratified ironstone, shale or fireclay (including intervals allowed for meals and rest, the period between the time at which he is required to attend for the purpose of going below ground and the time at which he leaves his working place and the period between the time at which he leaves his working place and the time at which he returns to the surface) shall neither exceed nine in any day nor exceed forty-eight in any week (M&QA 1954 s.125).

No female young person may work at a mine or quarry before 6 a.m. or after 9 p.m. on a weekday, or before 6 a.m. or after 2 p.m. on a Saturday. There must be an interval of at least twelve hours between periods of work.

A male who has not attained the age of sixteen may only work between 6 a.m. and 9 p.m. on a weekday and between 6 a.m. and 9 p.m. on a Saturday if employed above ground in a mine or quarry; and between 6 a.m. and 10 p.m. on a weekday and between 6 a.m. and 2 p.m. on a Saturday if employed below ground at a mine. Again, there must be an interval of a least twelve hours between periods of employment. (M&QA 1954 s.126(2), (3) and (4)).

A male young person over sixteen years may only work in a mine (whether above or below ground) or in a quarry between 6 a.m. and 10 p.m. on a weekday and between 6 a.m. and 2 p.m. on a Saturday. However, he may do surveying, measuring, repair or maintenance work after 2 p.m. on Saturday or on Sunday if such work requires to be done at that time. (M&QA 1954 s.127(1)).

A responsible person at a mine or quarry may, if authorised, post a notice there substituting 5 a.m. and 11 p.m. as earliest and latest working times for young males who have attained the age of sixteen. The authority must by given by the Minister if it is to be a general authorisation for all mines and quarries, or by an inspector in the case of a particular mine or quarry. (M&QA 1954 s.127(2)).

There must always be an interval of twelve hours between the periods worked by young persons, and should any young person work after 2 p.m. on a Saturday, he must be allowed to finish work by 2 p.m. on one of the days between that day and the next following Saturday (M&QA 1954 s.127).

The responsible person is under a duty to fix notices specifying the hours that may be worked by young persons and the intervals to be allowed to them for meals and rest (M&QA 1954 s.128).

'Responsible person' means the owner in the case of a quarry, and the manager in the case of a mine (M&QA s.182(1)).

The responsible person is also under a duty to keep a register at the office of the mine or quarry or at such other place as may be approved by the inspector containing the name, date of birth, residence and date of first employment of all young persons employed there. The register must indicate which of the male young persons are employed below ground. The responsible person must, if requested, produce the register to an officer of the local education authority.

Before a male young person is employed below ground in a mine his employer (if he is not the owner of the mine) must inform the manager that the young person is to be so employed (M&QA 1954 s.131).

The persons who may be guilty of offences under the Act are set out in s.152. The section also contains certain available defences to charges preferred. Any person convicted of an offence under the statute shall be liable on summary conviction to a fine not exceeding Level 5 on the standard scale. Offences under the Act are triable either way (H&SWA 1974 s.33).

(h) Factories

The provisions of s.1 EWYP&CA 1920 are applied to factories within the meaning of the Factories Act 1961, and any provisions of that Act as to the registers that must be kept apply with equal force to registers to be kept under EWYP&CA 1920.

The FA 1961 also contains provisions designed to control the working hours and conditions of young persons employed in factories. They are to be found in Part VI, which consists of ss.86-119.

There are restrictions on the hours that may be worked and periods of employment and requirements as to intervals for meals and rest. Generally, they must conform with the following conditions:

(i) the total hours worked, exclusive of intervals for meals and rest, may not exceed nine in a day or forty-eight in a week;

(ii) the period of employment shall not exceed eleven hours in any day and, in the case of a person who has not attained the age of sixteen, shall not begin earlier than 7 a.m. nor end later than 6 p.m. In the case of a young person of the age of sixteen it shall not begin before 7 a.m. but it may go on until 8 p.m. On Saturdays it must end by 1 p.m.;

(iii) employment may not continue for a spell of more than 4½ hours without an interval of at least half an hour for a meal or a rest unless there is an interval of not less then ten minutes in the course of the spell of work, in which case the period that may be worked before the half hour minimum break is required becomes five hours;

(iv) no young person may be employed during an interval allowed for meals or rest

(FA 1961 ss.86 and 87).

The occupier of any factory must fix the periods of employment each day of the week for young persons employed in the factory and the intervals that are allowed for meals and rest for those young persons. They must be specified in a notice in the prescribed form and posted in the factory. Subject to provisions of the Act that permit overtime in certain circumstances, young persons may not work outside the hours fixed. Different periods of employment and different intervals may be fixed for different days of the week, always providing they are within the general restrictions in ss.86 and 87. An occupier must give notice to the factories inspector for the district if he wishes to change the periods and intervals fixed (FA 1961 s.88).

There is a provision in the Act for the working of limited overtime by young persons who have attained the age of sixteen if pressure of work requires them to do so. The total hours worked, exclusive of intervals for rest and for meals may not exceed ten on any day and the period of employment may not exceed twelve hours in any day. The Minister may make regulations prohibiting overtime working by young persons if he is satisfied that it will prejudicially affect their health (FA 1961 s.89).

Sunday working is prohibited in the case of young persons (FA 1961 s.93). Normally, the occupier of a factory must allow Christmas Day, Good Friday and every bank holiday as holidays for young persons. It is possible for the occupier to substitute other days in certain circumstances, but if he wishes to do so he must post notice of the changes in the factory for not less than three weeks before any of the days to be changed. At least half of the days that are to be allowed to a young person as holiday must be allowed between the 15 March and 1 October (FA 1961 s.94).

Shift working by young persons who have attained the age of sixteen may be authorised by the Minister on the application of the occupier of a factory. Employment may then be between the times specified in the authorisation (FA 1961 s.97).

Section 97 sets out the procedures to be followed by persons wishing to apply for authorisations for shift working by young persons and deals with conditions that the Minister may impose.

Certain shift working by male young persons who have attained the age of sixteen is permitted without ministerial authorisation if the employment is on work which, because of the process used, must be carried on continuously, day and night. The Minister may make regulations for the purpose of safeguarding the welfare and interests of young persons employed on shift working in such employments and they and the conditions laid down in subs.(3) of the relevant section must be complied with. Subsection (3) provides:

    (i) that the number of turns worked by any young person shall not exceed six in any week;

   (ii) that the intervals between successive turns must not be less than fourteen hours; and

  (iii) that no young person may be employed between midnight and 6 a.m. in two consecutive weeks.

The Minister may modify the provisions of subs.(3) as respects young persons employed on a four shift system and young persons employed in the glass industry (FA 1961 s.99).

Sections 100-114 of the Act deal with exceptions to the general restrictions. Some relate to particular types of work, others to particular industries and some relate to particular days, eg Saturdays and Sundays in Jewish factories.

If any occupier wishes to avail himself of any exception he must serve notice on the factories inspector for the district and post a notice in his factory. The notice must be in the prescribed form. It must state the intention and specify the date from which it is to operate and it must be kept posted while the occupier continues to avail himself of the exception. The Minister may by order direct that occupiers availing themselves of exceptions enter in a prescribed register such particulars as may be specified respecting the employment of young persons in pursuance of the exception and report them to the inspector for the district (FA 1961 s.115).

Special regulations apply to particular occupations and they are contained in s.116. The employer of any young person to whom Regulations made under the section apply may give notice to the inspector for the district that he wishes to substitute the foregoing provisions of Part VI of the Act for the provisions of s.116 and those provisions then apply unless and until they are withdrawn by further notice (FA 1961 s.116).

Young persons may not work in any factory for more than 7 days unless they have been examined by the factory doctor and he has certified that they are fit for the employment (FA 1961 s.118).

Factory inspectors may, if of the opinion that the employment of a young person in a factory is prejudicial to his health or to the health of another person, serve notice on the occupier of the factory requiring that the employment of that young person in the factory, or on a process or kind of work, be discontinued after the period named in the notice, unless the appointed factory doctor has, after the service of the notice, personally examined the young person and certified that he is fit for employment in the factory or in the process or kind of work in question (FA 1961 s.119).

Any person guilty of an offence under Part VI of the Act is liable on summary conviction to a fine not exceeding Level 5 on the standard scale. This penalty is provided by s.33 H&SWA 1974, subs.(3) of which applies the penalties set out in the section to 'existing statutory provisions'. By virtue of Sched.1 FA 1961 is included.

(i) Merchant ships

The provisions of s.1 EWYP&CA 1920, in so far as they relate to employment in a ship, have effect as if they formed part of the Merchant Shipping Acts 1894 to 1920 (EWYP&CA 1920 s.1(6)).

At the present time the employment of young persons on merchant ships is controlled by the Merchant Shipping (International Labour Conventions) Act 1925. This Act will be repealed by MSA 1970 s.100(3) and Sched.5 when in force, but at the time of going to press no commencement date has been fixed.

The statute provides, *inter alia*, that:

   (i) no young person under the age of eighteen may be employed as a stoker or a trimmer in any ship (s.5);

  (ii) in every agreement with the crew, a list of young persons, with their dates of birth, and a summary of this section, shall be included, or, if there is no such agreement, the master shall keep a register of such persons (s.2); and

 (iii) no young person is to be employed, unless a medical certificate (in force for twelve months or until the end of the voyage in question) is delivered to the master (s.3).

The exception to the prohibition on the employment of young persons as stokers or trimmers is approved work in a school ship or training ship or on a ship mainly propelled otherwise than by steam. The restriction on the employment of young persons who do not hand to the master medical certificates valid for twelve months or to the end of the voyage does not apply if only members of the same family are employed on the ship or if the consent of a superintendent or consular official as to the employment of the young person until the next port of call has been obtained on the ground of urgency.

Persons guilty of offences under these sections are liable on summary conviction to fines not exceeding Level 2 on the standard scale.

A parent of a young person employed illegally is guilty of an offence if he produced or was privy to the production of a false or forged birth certificate, or if he made a false representation as a result of which the young person was illegally employed on a merchant ship. On summary conviction, such a parent is liable to a fine not exceeding Level 2 on the standard scale.

Chapter 18

Entertainment and performances by minors

The involvement of children in entertainments and public performances is controlled by both C&YPA 1933 and C&YPA 1963. Part II of the earlier Act is concerned with performances of a dangerous nature and with employment abroad, while Part II of the later statute relates to the general restrictions upon children taking part in performances for profit and the licensing of such performances.

1. Performances endangering life or limb

There is a general prohibition upon a person under the age of *sixteen* taking part in performances to which C&YPA 1963 s.37 (see page 144) applies, and in which his life or limbs are endangered. Any person who causes or procures such a person, or, being his parent or guardian, allows such a person, to take part in such a performance is guilty of an offence. They are liable on conviction in a magistrates' court to a fine not exceeding Level 3 on the standard scale. Proceedings may only be taken by or with the consent of the chief officer of police (C&YPA 1933 s.23 as amended).

Performances of a dangerous nature are defined in s.30 and include all acrobatic performances and all performances as a contortionist.

In England and Wales 'chief officer of police' has the same meaning as in the Police Act 1964. 'Guardian' includes any person who, in the opinion of the court having cognizance of the case, has for the time being charge of or control over the child or young person (C&YPA 1933 s.107).

2. Training for dangerous performances

Persons under the age of *twelve* may not be trained to take part in dangerous performances and persons under the age of *sixteen* may only be trained for that purpose in strict accordance with the terms of a licence granted and in force under C&YPA 1933 s.24.

Any person who causes or procures a person, or, being his parent or guardian, allows such a person, to train in contravention of the section is guilty of an offence and is liable on conviction by a magistrates' court to a fine not exceeding Level 3 on the standard scale.

Local authorities may grant licences allowing persons who have attained the age of twelve but not sixteen years to train for dangerous performances. Any licence granted must specify the place or places at which the person is to be trained and shall embody such conditions as are, in the opinion of the authority, necessary for his protection. A licence shall not be refused by a local authority if it is satisfied that the person is fit and willing to be trained and that proper provision has been made to secure his health and kind treatment (C&YPA 1933 s.24).

When a person is charged with an offence under this Statute and it is alleged that the person in respect of whom the offence was committed was a child or young person or was under or had attained any specific age, and he appears to the court to have been a child or young person or to have been under or to have attained that age at the date of the commission of the alleged offence, he shall for the purposes of the Act be presumed to have been a child or young person or to have been under or to have attained that age at that date, unless the contrary is proved (C&YPA 1933 s.99).

The authority to grant licences is vested in the local authority for the area or one of the areas in which the training is to take place. The authority also has the power to vary or revoke a licence granted by it if any of the conditions embodied in it are contravened, or if it appears that the person to whom the licence relates is no longer fit and willing to be trained, or that proper provision is no longer being made to secure his health and kind treatment (C&YPA 1963 s.41(1) and (2)).

If an authority refuses an application for a licence or varies or revokes a licence it shall state the grounds for doing so in writing to the applicant or the holder of the licence, as the case may be, and the applicant or licence holder may appeal to the magistrates' court against the refusal, variation or revocation (C&YPA 1963 s.41(3)).

3. Restrictions on persons under sixteen taking part in public performances

(a) Circumstances in which a licence is needed

Certain types of public performance can only be given by a person under the age of *sixteen* with the authority of a licence granted by a local authority in whose area he resides or, if he does not reside in Great Britain, by the local authority in whose area the applicant or one of the applicants for the licence resides or has his place of business.

The performances in question are:

(a) performances in connection with which a charge is made (whether for admission or otherwise);

(b) performances in licensed premises or in registered clubs;

(c) any broadcasting performance;

(d) any performance included in a cable programme service;

(e) any performance recorded with a view to its use in a broadcast or such service or in a film intended for public exhibition.

A child is to be treated as taking part in a performance for the purposes of this piece of legislation if he takes the place of a performer in any rehearsal or in any preparation for the recording of the performance (C&YPA 1963 s.37(1) and (2)).

No licence is needed, however, if the child in question has not taken part in any other performance to which the section relates on more than three days in the preceding six months. No licence is needed if the child in question is taking part in a performance given under arrangements made by a school, or by a body of persons approved for the purposes of the section by the Secretary of State, or by the local authority in whose area the performance takes place, and no payment in respect of the child's taking part in the performance is made (whether to him or to any other person) except for defraying expenses (C&YPA 1963 s.37(3)). The Secretary of State has made Regulations prescribing conditions to be observed with respect to the hours of work, rest or meals of children taking part in performances other than those arranged by schools or other approved bodies of persons (Children (Performances) Regulations 1968, SI 1968 No 1728).

(b) Restrictions on the power to grant licences

The power given to local authorities to grant licences is subject to such restrictions and conditions as the Secretary of State may prescribe by statutory instrument. Local authorities may not grant a licence for a child to take part in a performance unless satisfied that he is fit to do so, that proper provision has been made to secure his health and kind treatment and that, having regard to such provision as has been or will be made therefor, his education will not suffer. If they are so satisfied, the local authority shall not refuse to grant an application for a licence (C&YPA 1963 s.37(4)).

A licence granted under this section must specify the times, if any, during which the child in respect of whom it is granted may be absent from school for the purposes authorised by it. For the purposes of the Education Act 1944 (see page 128), any absence from school in accordance with a licence granted under this section shall be deemed to be absence with leave granted by a person authorised in that behalf by the managers, governors or proprietors of the school (C&YPA 1963 s.37(7)).

(c) Restrictions on licences for performances by children under thirteen

Local authorities may not grant licences authorising public performances by children under the age of *thirteen* unless:

(i) the licence relates to acting and the application for it is accompanied by a declaration that the part in question can only be taken by a child of about his age;

(ii) the licence is in respect of ballet dancing in a performance which consists only of ballet or opera and the application is accompanied by a declaration that the part to be danced can only be taken by a child of about his age; or

(iii) the nature of the part to be taken by the child is wholly or mainly musical and either the nature of the performance is wholly or mainly musical or the performance consists only of opera and ballet

(C&YPA 1963 s.38(1)).

In England and Wales, on the coming into force of an Order in Council made under EA 1944 raising the compulsory school age to sixteen, the age restriction in this section will be raised to fourteen (C&YPA 1963 s.38(2)).

(d) Other provisions in relation to licences

Licences granted under s.37 can be varied on the application of the holder, or by the local authority that granted it, or the local authority in whose area the performance, or one of the performances, to which it relates is to take place. A local authority may vary a licence of its own volition, if any of the conditions attached to it are not observed, or if it is not satisfied as to the matters referred to in s.37(4) (see above). Local authorities can revoke licences as well as simply varying the conditions attached to them. In any case in which a local authority proposes to vary or revoke a licence, other than on the application of the licence holder, it must give such notice of its intention as may be practicable to the licence holder before taking that action (C&YPA 1963 s.39(1) and (2)).

If a local authority grants a licence authorising a child to take part in a performance in the area of another local authority, it shall send that other authority such particulars as the Secretary of State may prescribe. The Children (Performances) Regulations 1968 (SI 1968 No 1728) contain details of the particulars prescribed at the time of going to press. In any case in which a local authority varies or revokes a licence granted by another authority, or a licence relating to a performance in the area of another authority, it shall inform that other authority. If practicable, the authority proposing to vary or revoke a licence in these circumstances shall consult the other authority before doing so (C&YPA 1963 s.39(3) and (4)).

The holder of a licence granted under s.37 is under a duty to keep any records prescribed in Regulations made by the Secretary of State (see C(P)R 1968), and produce them on request to an officer of the authority that granted the licence, at any time not later than six months after the performance or last performance to which it relates (C&YPA 1963 s.39(5)).

In any case in which a local authority refuses to grant a licence, revokes a licence or varies the conditions of a licence, other than on the application of the licence holder, it shall state its grounds for doing so, in writing to the applicant or the holder of the licence as the case may be. That person may appeal against the decision to the magistrates' court. There is no right of appeal against a decision to impose a condition that the authority is required to impose (C&YPA 1963 s.39(6)).

(e) Offences in relation to licences under s.37

Any person who:

(i) causes or procures any child, or being his parent or guardian, allows him, to take part in any performance without a licence, or

(ii) fails to observe any condition of a licence granted under s.37, or

(iii) knowingly or recklessly makes any false statement in or in connection with an application for a licence under the section is guilty of an offence, and on conviction by a magistrates' court is liable to a fine not exceeding Level 3 on the standard scale or to a term of imprisonment not exceeding three months or to both. Any person who fails to keep or to produce any record which he is required to keep or produce by virtue of s.39 is liable, on conviction by a magistrates' court, to the same maximum penalties (C&YPA 1963 s.40(1) and (2)).

A court convicting a s.37 licence holder of an offence under s.39 may, in addition to imposing a penalty upon him, order the revocation of the licence (C&YPA 1963 s.40(3)).

In any case in which it is alleged that an offence has been committed by virtue of a performance without a licence, it shall be a defence to prove that the accused believed that the child had not, in the six months preceding the performance, taken part in other performances to which s.37 applies on more than three days (the condition contained in s.37(3)(a)) and that he had reasonable grounds for that belief (C&YPA 1963 s.40(4)).

4. Persons under eighteen performing abroad for profit: s.25 licences

(a) The requirement for a licence

No person who has the custody, charge or care of a person under the age of *eighteen* shall allow him to go abroad for the purpose of singing, playing, performing or being exhibited for profit unless a licence has been granted in respect of him. Neither shall any person cause or procure any person under that age to go abroad for such purposes unless a licence has been granted (C&YPA 1933 s.25). For the purposes of this section 'abroad' means outside Great Britain and Ireland (C&YPA 1933 s.30).

The authority to grant licences under this section is given to the chief magistrate of the metropolitan magistrates' courts, any magistrate of the metropolitan magistrates' court in Bow Street, or any stipendiary magistrate appointed by Order in Council to exercise such jurisdiction. Before any licence can be granted, the applicant must give notice to the chief officer of police for the area in which the young person resides or resided. Such conditions and restrictions as may appear necessary may be attached to any licence granted, and the applicant may be called upon to give security or to enter into a recognizance for the observance of the restrictions or conditions in question.

The provisions of s.25 do not apply to any case in which it is proved that the person under the age of eighteen was a temporary resident in the United Kingdom.

(b) Offences in relation to s.25

If any person acts in contravention of the provisions of s.25, he is guilty of an offence, and liable on conviction by a magistrates' court to a fine not exceeding Level 3 on the standard scale, or imprisonment for a term not exceeding three months, or both. If it is alleged that he procured the young person to go abroad by means of a false pretence or false representation, he will be liable on conviction on indictment to imprisonment for a term not exceeding two years (C&YPA 1933 s.26(1)).

If it is proved that a person caused, procured or allowed a person under the age of eighteen to go abroad, and that while that person was abroad he was singing, playing, performing, or being exhibited for profit, it shall be presumed that that person caused or allowed that under age person to go abroad *for that purpose*. The court may order the defendant to take such steps as it directs to secure the return of the under age person to the United Kingdom, or to enter into the recognizance to make such provision as the court may direct to secure his health, kind treatment and adequate supervision while abroad and his return to the United Kingdom at the expiration of such period as the court may think fit (C&YPA 1933 s.26(2)).

Any performance mentioned in C&YPA 1963 s.37(2)(c) and (d) is also subject to C&YPA 1933 ss. 25 and 26 (C&YPA 1963 s.42(1)).

(c) Section 25 licences in respect of persons under fourteen

A licence may be granted under the provisions of s.25 in relation to a young person who has not attained the age of *fourteen* only if:

(i) the engagement he is to fulfil is for acting and the application for the licence is accompanied by a declaration that the part he is to play cannot be taken except by a person of about his age; or

(ii) the engagement is for dancing in a ballet which does not form part of an entertainment in which anything other than ballet or opera also forms part and the application for the licence is accompanied by a declaration that the part he is to dance cannot be taken except by a child of about his age; or

(iii) the engagement is for taking part in a performance the nature of which is wholly or mainly musical or which consists only of opera and ballet and the nature of his part in the performance is wholly or mainly musical

(C&YPA 1963 s.42).

5. Power of entry for purpose of making enquiries

The 1933 statute contains provisions for courts, upon application by a constable or a local authority, to order that the constable or an officer of the local authority enter, at any reasonable time within forty-eight hours of the making of the order, any place in which it is believed that a young person who is under age is employed or is training or performing, and to make enquiries in those premises in respect of him.

Additionally, constables and authorised officers of local authorities may at any time enter places used as broadcasting studios, cable programme studios or film studios or premises used for the recording of a performance with a view to its use in a broadcast or in a cable programme or a film intended for public exhibition, and make enquiries as to any children taking part in performances to which s.37 applies.

Similarly, at any time during the currency of a licence granted under s.37 or under provisions of the Act relating to training for dangerous performances, constables and authorised officers of local authorities may enter into any place where the person to whom the licence relates is authorised by the licence to take part in a performance or be trained, and may make enquiries therein with respect to that person (C&YPA 1933 s.28).

If any person obstructs any officer or constable in the exercise of any powers conferred by s.28 or refuses to answer or falsely answers any enquiry authorised by or under the section, he is guilty of an offence and on conviction before a magistrates' court is liable to a fine not exceeding Level 2 on the standard scale in respect of each offence (C&YPA 1933 s.28(3)).

6. Duty to provide for safety of children

In addition to providing for the welfare of children taking part in performances and entertainments, the Act of 1933 also establishes a general duty on persons providing entertainment for children or an entertainment at which the majority of persons attending are children. They must station and keep stationed wherever necessary a sufficient number of adult attendants, properly instructed as to their duties, to prevent more children or other persons being admitted to the building, or any part of it, than the building or any part of it can properly accommodate; to control the movement of children and other persons admitted while entering or leaving the building or any part of it; and to take all other reasonable precautions for the safety of the children. The duty exists in any case in which the number of children to be present exceeds 100 (C&YPA 1933 s.12(1)).

If the occupier of any building permits it to be used for the purpose of an entertainment, for hire or reward, he must take reasonable steps to secure the observance of the provisions of subs.(1) (C&YPA 1933 s.12(2)).

If any person fails to fulfil any obligation imposed upon him by this section, he will be liable on conviction by a magistrates' court to a fine not exceeding Level 3 on the standard scale of penalties. In addition, if the building in use is licensed under any enactment for music and dancing or as a theatre, the licence shall be liable to be revoked by the authority that granted it (C&YPA 1933 s.12(3)).

A constable may enter any building in which he has reason to believe an entertainment of the type referred to in s.12 is being, or is about to be provided, with a view to seeing whether the provisions of the section are carried into effect. An officer authorised by an authority by whom licences of the type referred to in the above paragraph may be granted has the same power of entry (C&YPA 1933 s.12(4)).

If the entertainment giving rise to proceedings is in a building that is licensed as a theatre or for music and dancing, proceedings under s.12 must be instituted by the authority that granted the licence. In any other case proceedings should be instituted by the police authority (C&YPA 1933 s.12(5)).

Section 12 does not apply to entertainments given in a private dwelling.

Chapter 19

Betting and gaming

1. Betting

(a) The offences

The Betting, Gaming and Lotteries Act 1963 prohibits betting with young persons and employing young persons for betting transactions or in betting offices. It provides that any person who:

    (i) has any betting transaction with a young person; or

   (ii) employs a young person in the effecting of any betting transaction or in a licensed betting office; or

  (iii) receives or negotiates a bet through a young person,

shall be guilty of an offence (BG&LA s.21).

For the purposes of s.21 'young person' means a person under the age of *eighteen* years whom the person committing the offence knew or ought to have known to be under that age, or a person who is apparently under that age. In the case of any proceedings for an offence in respect of a person apparently under the age of eighteen, it is a defence to prove that at the time of the alleged offence he had in fact attained that age (BG&LA 1963 s.21(2)).

A person does not commit an offence under s.21 by reason of:

    (i) the employment of a young person in the effecting of a betting transaction by post; or

   (ii) the carriage by a young person of a communication relating to a betting transaction for the purposes of its conveyance by post

(BG&LA 1963 s.21(1)).

It is also an offence under the statute for a person to send or cause to be sent to a person whom he knows to be under the age of *eighteen* any circular, notice, advertisement, letter, telegram or other document which invites or may reasonably be implied to invite the recipient to make any bet, or to enter into or take any share or interest in any betting transaction, or to apply to any person or at any place with a view to obtaining information or advice for the purpose of any bet or for information as to any race, fight, game, sport or other contingency upon which betting is generally carried on. The prohibition is upon any person who does anything described above for the purpose of earning commission, reward or other profit (BG&LA 1963 s.22(1)).

If any person is named or referred to in any document that is sent to a young person as a person to whom any payment may be made, or from whom any information may be obtained, for the purpose of or in relation to betting, he shall be deemed to have sent that document or caused it to have been sent unless he proves that he had not consented to be so named and that he was not in any way a party to, and was wholly ignorant of, the sending of the document (BG&LA 1963 s.22(2)).

If any document is sent to a person at a university, college, school or other place of education and that person is under the age of eighteen, the person sending the document or causing it to be sent shall be deemed to have known that person to be under that age unless he proves that he had reasonable grounds for believing him to be of full age (BG&LA 1963 s.22(3)).

(b) Penalties

Offences under ss.21 and 22 are triable summarily only and on conviction a defendant will be liable to a fine not exceeding Level 5 on the standard scale or to a term of imprisonment not exceeding six months or to both (BG&LA 1963 s.52(2)).

2. Gaming

(a) The offences

The Gaming Act 1968 contains a number of provisions that relate to minors. Section 7 provides that no person under the age of *eighteen* shall take part in any gaming to which Part I of the Act applies in premises in respect of which a justices' on-licence is for the time being in force. The section also provides that neither the holder of the justices' licence nor any person employed by him shall knowingly allow a person under the age of eighteen to take part in any such gaming on the premises (GA 1968 s.7(2)). A person 'knowingly' allows another person to take part when, intending what is happening, he deliberately looks the other way (*Ross* v *Moss* (1965)).

Section 17 provides that no person under the age of *eighteen* shall be present in any room while gaming to which Part II of the Act applies is taking place in that room, except in the special circumstances set out in s.20 (special provisions in relation to bingo clubs which allow persons under eighteen to be present while bingo is being played as long as they are not taking part) and s.21 (special provisions which allow persons under the age of eighteen to be present while gaming for prizes takes place in a bingo club provided they do not take part as players).

If the provisions of s.17 are contravened, the holder of any licence for the time being in force under the Act, or every officer of the club or institute for the time being registered under the Act is guilty of an offence (GA 1968 s.23(1)).

It is a defence for any person charged with an offence as a result of a contravention of the provisions of s.17 to prove:

(i) that the contravention occurred without his knowledge, and

(ii) that he exercised all such care as was reasonable in the circumstances to secure that the provision in question would not be contravened.

(GA 1968 s.23(3)).

(b) Penalties

Any person who takes part in gaming on licensed premises in contravention of s.7(1) is liable on summary conviction to a fine not exceeding Level 1 on the standard scale (GA 1968 s.8(6)). Any person who allows a person under the age of eighteen to take part in gaming on licensed premises in contravention of s.7(2) will also be liable on summary conviction to a fine not exceeding Level 1 on the standard scale (GA 1968 s.8(7)).

A person convicted of an offence under s.23(1) as a result of a contravention of the requirements of s.17 shall be liable on summary conviction to a fine not exceeding Level 5 on the standard scale. On conviction on indictment, the defendant will be liable to a fine or to a term of imprisonment not exceeding two years or to both (GA 1968 s.23(4)).

Chapter 20

Liquor and tobacco

The Children and Young Persons Act 1933 and the Licensing Act 1964 are the statutes that control the supply of intoxicating liquor and tobacco to minors. Both statutes are designed to protect the young from the harmful effects of the substances in question. It is usually an offence for the minor to purchase the substance and an offence for others to supply it to them or obtain it for them. Often the age of the minor is relevant to the question of whether or not an offence has been committed, and the various age restrictions need to be kept clearly in mind.

1. Intoxicating liquor

(a) Supply generally

Even in the privacy of the home it is an offence to give intoxicating liquor to a child under the age of five years, unless the intoxicant is given on the order of a qualified medical practitioner, or in a case of sickness, apprehended sickness or for other urgent cause. A person who gives intoxicating liquor, or causes it to be given, to a child under the age of five years is guilty of an offence that carries a fine not exceeding Level 1 on the standard scale (C&YPA 1933 s.5).

For the purposes of this section intoxicating liquor is defined in the same way as in the Licensing Act 1964 (C&YPA 1933 s.107) as:

spirits, wine, beer, cider, and any other fermented, distilled or spiritous liquor, but it does not include:

(i) any liquor which, whether made on the premises of a brewer for sale or elsewhere, is found on analysis of a sample thereof at any time to be of an original gravity not exceeding 1016° and of a strength not exceeding 1.2 per cent;

(ii) perfumes;

(iii) flavouring essences recognised by the Commissioners as not being intended for consumption as or with dutiable alcoholic liquor;

(iv) spirits, wine or made-wine so medicated as to be, in the opinion of the Commissioners, intended for use as a medicine and not as a beverage

(LA 1964 s.201).

(b) Prohibition on children in licensed premises

Persons under the age of *fourteen* are not allowed to be in the bar of licensed premises during permitted hours. Any person who allows, causes, procures or attempts to cause or procure any person under the age of fourteen to be in a bar in contravention of this general restriction is guilty of an offence and subject to a fine not exceeding Level 1 on the standard scale (LA 1964 s.168(1) and (2)).

A licence holder is not guilty of an offence under this section if he can show:

(i) that he used due diligence to prevent the under age person from being in the bar; or

(ii) that the person in question had apparently attained the age of fourteen.

No offence is committed under the provisions of the section if the child in question is:

(i) the licence holder's child; or

(ii) a resident in the premises, but is not employed there; or

(iii) in the bar solely for the purpose of passing to or from some part of the premises which is not a bar and to or from which there is no other convenient means of access or egress.

No offence is committed under the provisions of the section if the bar in question is in any railway refreshment rooms or other premises constructed, fitted or intended to be used *bona fide* for any purpose to which the holding of a justices' licence is merely ancillary (LA 1964 s.168 (3), (4) and (5)).

'Bar' includes any place that is exclusively or mainly used for the sale and consumption of intoxicating liquor (LA 1964 s.201). However, it is a question of fact whether or not any place is so used. In a Scottish case (*Donoghue* v *M'Intyre* (1911)) it was held that a small area sectioned off from the rest of the bar by a low partition was not itself a bar, but in *Dominy* v *Miller* (1923) the High Court upheld a decision of a magistrates' court that a similar structure within a main bar was itself a 'bar'.

(c) Sales etc to persons under the age of eighteen

Licensees and their servants must take great care to ensure that they do not *knowingly* sell intoxicating liquor to persons under the age of eighteen, or *knowingly* allow a person under the age of eighteen to consume intoxicating liquor in a bar. The penalty upon conviction for such an offence is a fine not exceeding Level 2 on the standard scale (LA 1964 s.169). In the context *knowingly* relates to the age of the person buying or consuming the intoxicating liquor. If the licensee or his servant genuinely believed him to be over eighteen and that belief is reasonable he will have a defence to a charge under the section in question. The onus of proving that the defendant knew that the person to whom the intoxicating liquor was supplied was under age lies with the prosecutor (*Sherras* v *De Rutzen* (1895)).

(d) Prohibition on purchase by minor of intoxicating liquor

Just as it is an offence for a licensee to knowingly sell intoxicating liquor to a person under the age of eighteen, it is an offence for a person under that age to buy it or, attempt to buy it in licensed premises, or to consume it in a bar (LA 1964 s.169(2)). A person convicted of such an offence is liable to a penalty not exceeding Level 3 on the standard scale.

(e) Prohibition on purchases by others for consumption by minors

It is an offence for any person to buy or attempt to buy intoxicating liquor for consumption in a bar in licensed premises by persons under the age of eighteen. The maximum penalty for such an offence is a fine not exceeding Level 3 on the standard scale (LA 1964 s.169 (3)).

(f) The exception in relation to drinks taken with meals

Paragraphs (c), (d) and (e) above are concerned with a general prohibition upon sales, purchases and consumption of intoxicating liquor to, for or by persons under the age of *eighteen*. Exceptionally, intoxicating liquor may be sold to a person who has attained the age of *sixteen* and purchased for a person who has attained that age if it is to be consumed at a meal in a part of the licensed premises usually set apart for the service of meals which is not a bar. The exception relates to certain types of intoxicating liquor only. They are *beer, porter, cider and perry* (LA 1964 s.169(4)).

2. Tobacco

The law controlling the sale of tobacco to minors is contained in C&YPA 1933 s.7. The principal statute has been amended by s.1 of the Protection of Children (Tobacco) Act 1986 which came into force on 8 October 1986. The general prohibition is on sales to persons who have not attained the age of *sixteen*.

(a) General prohibition on sales

There is a general prohibition on the sale of tobacco or cigarette papers to persons under the age of *sixteen*. The prohibition exists whether the tobacco or cigarette papers in question are for the use of the purchaser or some other person, and so it is an offence to sell them to an under age purchaser notwithstanding that they are being purchased 'for my dad'. Any person convicted of an offence under this section is liable to a fine not exceeding Level 3 on the standard scale (C&YPA 1933 s.7(1)).

(b) Automatic vending machine sales

If a complaint is made to a magistrates' court that a vending machine kept on any premises for the purpose of selling tobacco is being used extensively by under age persons, the court shall order the owner of that machine, or the person on whose premises the machine is installed, to take such precautions as may be specified in the order to prevent the machine being so used, or, if necessary to remove the machine, within such time as may be specified in the order.

If any person who receives such an order fails to comply with it they will be liable to a fine not exceeding Level 3 on the standard scale and to a daily penalty of £10 for each day thereafter during which the offence continues (C&YPA 1933 s.7(2) as amended by PC(T)A 1986 s.1(1)(b)).

Any person who is aggrieved by the making of an order under this subsection may appeal to the Crown Court (C&YPA 1933 s.102).

(c) The duty of constables and park-keepers

Constables and, curiously perhaps, park-keepers, are under a duty to seize any tobacco or cigarette papers in the possession of any person apparently under the age of sixteen whom he finds smoking in a street or public place. Only constables and park-keepers who are in uniform may carry out the duty to seize tobacco and cigarette papers in this way. Tobacco and cigarette papers seized must be

157

disposed of, in the case of a constable, in such manner as the police authority may direct, and in the case of a park-keeper, in such manner as the authority by whom he was appointed may direct (C&YPA 1933 s.7(3)).

For the purposes of this subsection a public place includes any public park, garden, sea beach, or railway station, and any ground to which the public for the time being are permitted to have access, whether on payment or otherwise (C&YPA 1933 s.107).

(d) Exceptions to the general prohibition and duty of seizure

The general prohibition on sales to under age persons and the duty to seize tobacco and cigarette papers in the possession of such persons do not apply in certain exceptional circumstances. They do not apply if the under age person is employed at the time by a manufacturer of or dealer in tobacco (wholesale or retail) and the tobacco or cigarette papers in question are in his possession for the purposes of his business. Similarly, they do not apply in the case of a messenger in uniform in the employment of a messenger company and employed as such at the time (C&YPA 1933 s.7(4)).

For the purposes of s.7 of the principal statute the expression 'tobacco' includes cigarettes and any product containing tobacco and intended for oral or nasal use. The expression 'cigarettes' includes cut tobacco rolled up in paper, tobacco leaf, or other material in such form as to be capable of immediate use for smoking (C&YPA 1933 s.7(5) as amended by PC(T)A 1986 s.1(1)(c)).

Chapter 21

Firearms, fireworks and gunpowder

1. Firearms

It is an offence for a minor to acquire and to possess a firearm and it is also an offence for persons to supply firearms or ammunition to minors. The statute controlling the sale, supply and possession of firearms and ammunition is the Firearms Act 1968.

(a) Possession by minors

No person under the age of *seventeen* may purchase or hire any firearm or ammunition. No person under the age of *fourteen* may have any firearm or ammunition in his possession, save in the exceptional circumstances set out in s.11(1), (3) and (4) (FA 1968 s.22(1) and (2)).

For the purposes of the section 'firearm' means a lethal barrelled weapon of any description from which any shot, bullet or other missile can be discharged. It includes:

(i) any prohibited weapon (whether a lethal weapon or not); and

(ii) any component part of such a lethal or prohibited weapon; and

(iii) any accessory to any such weapon designed and adapted to diminish the noise or flash caused by firing the weapon.

'Ammunition' means ammunition for any firearm and includes grenades, bombs and other like missiles, whether capable of use with a firearm or not, and also includes prohibited ammunition (FA 1968 s.57).

The exceptional circumstances in s.11 relate to certain sports, athletics and other approved activities.

A person under the age of *fifteen* commits an offence if he has with him an assembled shotgun, except when he is under the supervision of a person who is over the age of twenty-one, or while the shotgun is covered with a securely fastened gun cover in such a way that it cannot be fired (FA 1968 s.22(3)).

For the purposes of the subsection a 'shotgun' means a smooth bore gun with a barrel not less than 24 inches in length which is not an air gun (FA 1968 s.1(3)(a)).

Generally, it is an offence for a person under the age of *fourteen* to have with him an air weapon or ammunition for an air weapon (FA 1968 s.22(4)). However, no offence is committed under the subsection if the person in question is under the supervision of a person who has attained the age of twenty-one; but if the supervised person has an air weapon with him on premises in circumstances in which he would be prohibited from having it with him but for the provisions of this subsection, it will be an offence:

(i) for him to use the air weapon for firing a missile beyond those premises; or

(ii) for the person under whose supervision he is to allow him so to use it

(FA 1968 s.23(1)).

No offence has been committed if the minor in question is a member of a rifle club or miniature rifle club, approved for the time being by the Secretary of State for the purposes of ss.23 or 11(3) of the statute, and he is engaged as such a member in or in connection with target practice, or he is using the weapon or ammunition at a shooting gallery where the only firearms used are either air weapons or miniature rifles not exceeding .23 inch calibre (FA 1968 s.23(2)).

Persons over the age of fourteen but under the age of *seventeen* are not subject to the general prohibition imposed by s.22(4) but they are prohibited from having an air weapon with them in a public place unless the weapon in question is an air gun or air rifle which is covered with a securely fastened gun cover which prevents it from being fired (FA 1968 s.22(5)). The defence available to a minor under the age of fourteen by virtue of s.23(2) (above) is also available to a person over fourteen but under seventeen (FA 1968 s.23(2)).

(b) Supply to minors

The Act prohibits the sale, letting or hiring of firearms or ammunition to any person under the age of *seventeen* (FA 1968 s.24(1)). In addition it is an offence for any person to make a gift of or lend any firearm or ammunition to which s.1 of the statute applies to a person under the age of *fourteen*, or to part with the possession of any such firearm or ammunition to a person under that age, except in the circumstances set out in s.11(1), (3) or (4) — the section that is concerned with sporting, athletic and other approved activities (FA 1968 s.24(2)).

'Firearm', 'ammunition' and 'shotgun' are defined above, pages 159-160.

It is also unlawful for any person to make a gift of a shotgun or ammunition for a shotgun to a person under the age of *fifteen* (FA 1968 s.24(3)). It is an offence for any person to make a gift of an air weapon or ammunition for an air weapon, or to part with the possession of such a weapon or ammunition to a person under the age of *fourteen*, except where, by virtue of s.23 of the Act (see page 160) the person in question is not prohibited from having such a weapon or ammunition with him (FA 1968 s.24(4)).

In any proceedings brought under s.24, it is a defence to prove that the person charged with the offence believed the other person to be of or over the age mentioned in that provision and had reasonable ground for that belief (FA 1968 s.24(5)).

An arrangement that possession of a firearm that has been sold shall remain with the seller will not avoid the prohibition on sale in s.24 (*Watts* v *Seymour* (1967)).

(c) Penalties

The penalties for the offences referred to above are set out in the 6th Schedule to the Act. All the offences in question are summary in nature. Offences under the following subsections:

   (i) 22(1)-person under 17 acquiring firearm;
  (ii) 22(2)-person under 14 having firearm in his possession without authority;
 (iii) 24(1)-selling, letting or hiring a firearm to a person under 17; and
  (iv) 24(2)-supplying a firearm or ammunition to which s.1 applies to a person under 14,

are punishable by a fine not exceeding Level 5 on the standard scale or by a term of imprisonment not exceeding 6 months or both.

Offences under the following subsections:

   (i) 22(3)-person under 15 having shotgun with him without adult supervision;

  (ii) 22(4)-person under 14 having with him an air weapon or ammunition therefor;

 (iii) 22(5)-person under 17 having with him an air weapon in a public place;

 (iv) 23(1)-person under 14 using air weapon improperly when under supervision or supervisor permitting improper use;

  (v) 24(3)-making a gift of a shot gun to person under 15; and

 (vi) 24(4)-supplying an air weapon to a person under 14.

are punishable by a fine not exceeding Level 3 on the standard scale.

The court by which a person is convicted of an offence under s.22(4) or (5), 23(1) or 24(4) of the Act may make whatever order it thinks fit as to the forfeiture and disposal of any air weapon or ammunition in respect of which the offence was committed (Sched.6 Pt.II para.7). The court convicting for an offence under s.22(3), (4) or (5), 23(1) or 24(4) may make such order as it thinks fit as to the forfeiture or disposal of any firearm or ammunition found in his possession (Sched.6 Pt.II para.8). Finally, a court which has convicted for an offence under s.24(3) of the Act may make any order that it thinks fit as to the forfeiture or disposal of any shotgun or ammunition in respect of which the offence was committed (Sched.6 Pt.II para.9).

2. Fireworks and gunpowder

(a) Prohibition on sale etc to children

The *sale* of explosives to children under the age of *sixteen* is prohibited (Explosives Act 1875 s.31 as amended by the Explosives (Age of Purchase) Act 1976). The prohibition is extended to explosives other than gunpowder (including fireworks) by s.39 of the Act.

The Secretary of State, using powers granted to him by s.1 Consumer Safety Act 1978, has made regulations which make it an offence for any person to *supply, offer to supply or agree to supply* any fireworks to any person apparently under the age of *sixteen* (Fireworks (Safety) Regulations 1986, reg.2).

(b) Penalties

On the repeal of s.91 of the Act the authority of magistrates' courts to try offences under s.31 Explosives Act 1875 was lost. Offences involving the *sale* of fireworks and gunpowder can, therefore, only be tried on indictment.

However, any offence that relates to the *supply* of fireworks under the Fireworks (Safety) Regulations is only triable in the magistrates' court. The maximum penalty, contained in s.2 Consumer Safety Act 1978, is a fine not exceeding Level 5 on the standard scale and/or imprisonment for a term not exceeding 3 months.

Part III

THE ROLE OF THE LOCAL AUTHORITIES

Chapter 22

The welfare and care of children

1. The general duty

Local authorities are under a general duty to make available advice, guidance and assistance with the object of reducing the need to receive children into, or to keep them in, care (CCA 1980 s.1(1)). In carrying out this duty, local authorities may make arrangements with voluntary organisations or other persons for the provision by them of the advice, guidance or assistance contemplated by subs.(1) (CCA 1980 s.1(2)).

If the provisions the local authority is required to make under subs.(1) have been made under some other enactment, whether by that local authority or some other local authority, it is not necessary for further provisions to be made (CCA 1980 s.1(3)).

For the purposes of s.1 'children' means persons under the age of *eighteen* (CCA 1980 s.1(4)).

2. Orphans and deserted children

(a) Duty to take into care

In addition to the general duty to promote the welfare of children, there is a particular duty placed upon local authorities to provide for children who are orphans or who have been deserted. In any case where it appears to a local authority that a child in their area, appearing to be under the age of *seventeen*:

(i) has neither parent nor guardian or has been and remains abandoned by his parents or guardian or is lost; or

(ii) has parents or guardians who are, for the time being or permanently, prevented by reason of mental or bodily disease or infirmity or other incapacity, or any other circumstances, from providing for his proper accommodation, maintenance and upbringing; and

167

(iii) that, in either case, the intervention of the local authority is necessary in the interests of the welfare of the child,

the local authority must receive the child into care. (CCA 1980 s.2(1)).

If a local authority has received a child into its care under subs.(1) it shall keep the child for so long as his welfare appears to require it and the child has not attained the age of eighteen (CCA 1980 s.2(2)).

(b) Transfer of care of child to a parent, guardian or other local authority

The section does not authorise an authority to keep a child in their care if any parent or guardian desires to take over the care of the child. In all cases in which it appears to be consistent with the welfare of the child to do so, the local authority must endeavour to secure that the care of the child is taken over either:

(i) by a parent or guardian of his; or

(ii) by a relative or friend of his, being, where possible, a person of the same religious persuasion as the child or a person who gives an undertaking to bring the child up in that religious persuasion.

(CCA 1980 s.2(3)).

The provisions of subs.(3) do not create an absolute statutory duty on a local authority to hand over the child to a parent (*Krishnan* v *London Borough of Sutton* (1969)). In any case in which the local authority was of the opinion that it would not be consistent with the welfare of the child to return it to the care of a parent, guardian, relative or friend, application might be made to a juvenile court for an order under s.1 C&YPA 1969 (see Chapter 6).

In relation to any child, 'relative' means a grand-parent, brother, sister, uncle or aunt, whether of the full blood, of the half blood, or by affinity and includes, where the child is illegitimate, the father of the child and any person who would be a relative of the child if he were the legitimate child of his mother and father (CCA 1980 s.87).

A local authority may receive into care a child who is ordinarily resident in the area of another local authority. Where it does so the other local authority may take over the care of the child at any time not later than three months after the ordinary residence of the child has been determined, with the agreement of the local authority that first received him into care. In such a case the authority that received the child into its care first may recover from the other authority any expenses duly incurred under Part III of the Act in respect of the child (CCA 1980 s.2(4)).

In determining the ordinary residence of a child, any period during which he resides in any place:

(i) as an inmate of a school or other institution; or

(ii) in accordance with a requirement of a supervision order or probation order or of a supervision requirement (see Chapter 8); or

(iii) in accordance with the conditions of a recognizance; or

(iv) while boarded out under CCA 1980 by a local authority or education authority,

is to be disregarded (CCA 1980 s.2(5)).

(c) Assumption of parental rights and duties

If a local authority has received a child into care under s.2 of the Statute and it appears that:

(i) his parents are dead and that he has no guardian or custodian; or

(ii) a parent has:

- abandoned him, or

- suffers from some permanent disability rendering him incapable of caring for the child, or

- suffers from some mental disorder within the meaning of the Mental Health Act 1983 which renders him unfit to have the care of the child, or

- is of such habits or mode of life as to be unfit to have the care of the child, or

- has so consistently failed without reasonable cause to discharge the obligations of a parent as to be unfit to have the care of the child; or

(iii) that a resolution under paragraph (b) of s.3(1) of the Act is in force in relation to one parent of the child who is, or is likely to become, a member of the household comprising the child and his other parent; or

(iv) that throughout the three years preceding the passing of the resolution the child has been in the care of the local authority under s.2 of the Act, or partly in the care of a local authority and partly in the care of a voluntary organisation,

the local authority may resolve that the parental rights and duties in respect of the child shall vest in them. If the rights and duties were vested in the parent on whose account the resolution was passed, jointly with another person, they shall likewise be vested in the local authority jointly with that other person (CCA 1980 s.3(1)).

The local authority must serve notice in writing of the passing of the resolution under subs.(1) upon the person whose parental rights and duties have vested in the authority as a result of the resolution unless they are unaware of his whereabouts (CCA 1980 s.3(2)). Any such notice served under subs.(2) must inform the recipient of his right to object to the resolution that has been made, and the effect of any objection that he might make (CCA 1980 s.3(3)).

If a person serves a notice of an objection to a resolution upon the local authority within one month after notice of the resolution has been served on him the resolution will lapse on the expiration of fourteen days from the service of that notice of objection (CCA 1980 s.3(4)). Within that fourteen day period, the local authority may complain to a juvenile court having jurisdiction in the area of the authority. If the complaint is made within that time, the resolution does not lapse until the complaint has been heard and determined (CCA 1980 s.3(5)). The juvenile court hearing the complaint may order that the resolution shall not lapse if it is satisfied that the grounds on which the authority made the resolution were made out, that at the time of the hearing there are still grounds on which a resolution could be founded *and* that it is in the interests of the child to do so (CCA 1980 s.3(6)).

If the whereabouts of a parent have remained unknown for twelve months from the date on which a child was received into care of a local authority under s.2 of the Act, he shall be deemed to have abandoned the child (CCA 1980 s.3(8)).

In s.3 'parent' includes a guardian or custodian. 'Parental rights and duties' do not include either the right to consent or to refuse to consent to the making of an application for an order freeing the minor for adoption or the right to agree or to refuse to agree to the making of an adoption order (CCA 1980 s.3(10)).

3. Powers and duties in relation to children in care

Whenever a child is in the care of a local authority as a result of being remanded or committed to care by order of a court, the authority is under a duty to receive him and keep him in their care, notwithstanding any claim made by his parent or guardian (CCA 1980 s.10(1)).

The powers and duties vested in the authority are those that the parent or guardian would have had but for the order of commitment or the warrant, except that the authority shall not cause the child to be brought up in any religious creed other than that which he would have been brought up in apart from the order. Further, the section does not give the authority the right to consent to or refuse to consent to the making of an application for an order freeing the child for adoption or the power to agree or to refuse to agree to the making of an adoption order (CCA 1980 s.10(3) and (5)).

4. Duties of parents of children in care

Whenever a child is in the care of a local authority on a voluntary basis, any parent or guardian of the child is under a duty to keep the authority advised of his address for the time being.

Local authorities are required to inform the parent or guardian that the care of the child has been taken over, and this is especially important where one authority takes over the care of a child from another authority. The duty of the parent or guardian is to maintain contact with the authority in whose care the child is at the time. If there is a change of authority having the care of the child the parent or guardian is under no duty to maintain contact with the new authority until he has been informed of the change.

If any parent or guardian of a child in care knowingly fails to comply with the requirement to keep in touch with the local authority, he will be guilty of an offence and liable on summary conviction to a fine not exceeding Level 1 on the standard scale. It is, however, a defence to proceedings taken under this section for the defendant to prove that he was residing at the same address as the child's other parent, and that he had reasonable cause to believe that the other parent had informed the authority that both parents were residing at that address (CCA 1980 s.9).

Proceedings under s.9 may be instituted by the local authority (CCA 1980 s.84).

Similar provisions exist in relation to children who are in care as a result of an order of a court although, curiously, the maximum penalty that can be imposed upon a parent or guardian who fails to maintain contact in these circumstances is only a fine of £10 (CCA 1980 s.12).

It appears that s.84 does not extend to the institution of proceedings for offences under s.12, and so it is difficult to determine who, if anybody, would be authorised to institite proceedings for such an offence.

Chapter 23

Access to children in care

1. Visitors

Local authorities must arrange for children in their care who have attained the age of *five* to receive visits from an independent visitor if they remain within the community home for long periods and are communicating only infrequently with parents.

In any case in which a child of five years or over is accommodated in a community home or other establishment which he has not been allowed to leave during the preceding three months to attend school or work, if it appears to the local authority that:

    (a) communication between him and his parent or guardian has been so infrequent that it is appropriate to appoint a visitor for him; or

    (b) he has not lived with or visited or been visited by either of his parents or his guardian during the preceding twelve months,

they must appoint an independent person to be his visitor. A person appointed as a visitor has the duty of visiting, advising and befriending the child and is entitled to make application on behalf of the child for an order discharging the care order that is the basis for his accommodation in the community home or other establishment. The visitor is able to recover from the authority expenses that he has reasonably incurred in carrying out his duties (CCA 1980 s.11(1)).

An appointment as a visitor will come to an end if the care order in question ceases to be in force, or the visitor may resign, or the authority may terminate the visitor's appointment. However, if the appointment is terminated and the care order continues in force, the authority will have a duty under s.1 to make a further appointment (CCA 1980 s.11(2)).

For the purposes of s.11, 'independent person' means a person who satisfies the conditions, prescribed with a view to securing that he is independent of the local authority, in the Children and Young Persons (Definition of Independent Persons) Regulations 1971, SI 1971 No 486 (reproduced at page 269).

2. Access

(a) Duty to allow access

As a general rule, parents, guardians and custodians of children in care are able to have access to them, and local authorities are required to make arrangements for such access. In certain circumstances authorities may refuse to make arrangements for access or make an order terminating access. The power to refuse access and to terminate access exists only in cases in which the child in question is in care in consequence of:

   (a) a care order or interim care order;

   (b) an order under s.2(1) of the Matrimonial Proceedings (Magistrates' Courts) Act 1960;

   (c) a committal on remand to the care of the authority under s.23(1) C&YPA 1969;

   (d) an order under s.2(2)(b) GA 1973;

   (e) an order under s.17(1)(b) CA 1975 or s.26(1)(b) AA 1976 — order on the refusal of an adoption order;

   (f) an order under s.36(2) or (3)(a) CA 1975 — an order made on the revocation of a custodianship order;

   (g) an order under s.10(1) of the Domestic Proceedings and Magistrates' Courts Act 1978; or

   (h) a resolution to assume parental rights under s.3 CCA 1980.

This part of the Act does not apply to children in care in consequence of High Court orders (CCA 1980 s.12A, inserted by HASSASSA 1983 Sched.1).

An authority that wishes to refuse access or terminate access arrangements must give notice of the termination or refusal to the parent, guardian or custodian in the form prescribed by the Secretary of State in the Access (Notice of Termination and Refusal) Order 1983, SI 1983 No 1860 (reproduced at page 276). A notice given for this purpose must state that access will be terminated from the date of the service of the notice, and that the recipient has a right to apply to a court for an access order. Any such notice may be delivered to or left for the parent, guardian or custodian at his last known address or by sending it to that address by post.

Local authorities are not to be taken to be terminating access in cases where they propose to substitute new access arrangements for existing arrangements, or where they postpone access for such reasonable period as appears to them to be necessary to enable them to consider what arrangements for access should be made. (CCA 1980 s.12B, inserted by HASSASSA 1983 Sched.1)

When considering what arrangements to make for access, it is reasonable for the decision to be reached in 14 days or, exceptionally, 21 days. However, in the initial stages of a care order where the matter being considered is whether to refuse access or not, a longer period may be necessary (*R* v *Bolton Metropolitan Borough, ex p B* (1985)).

(b) Access order

If any parent, guardian or custodian wishes to apply for an access order he should make a complaint to an appropriate juvenile court, ie the juvenile court for the area of the authority serving the notice under s.12B. If the court decides to make an order it shall be an order requiring the authority to allow the child's parent, guardian or custodian access to the child subject to such conditions as the order may specify with regard to commencement, frequency, duration and place of access, or to any other matter for which it appears to the court that provision ought to be made (CCA 1980 s.12C, inserted by HASSASSA 1983 Sched.1).

If adoption proceedings are pending at the time an application for an access order is made, the first decision should be whether access should be allowed between child and parent. Whether parental access is justified when adoption proceedings are pending will depend upon the circumstances emerging in evidence (*Southwark London Borough Council* v *H* (1985)).

The interests of the child are paramount and access should only be ordered if it is a desirable development in the interests of the child (*Hereford and Worcester County Council* v *JAH* (1985)).

A juvenile court making an access order can keep some control over the development of access by asking for further reports from the social services or the probation service (*Hereford and Worcester County Council* v *EH* (1985)).

Any appeal brought against the making of an access order will lie to the High Court (s.12C(5)).

The maximum period acceptable for the hearing of an appeal is 28 days. Consequently, a stay of execution should seldom be granted for more than 14 days (*Hereford and Worcester County Council* v *EH*, above).

The parent, guardian or custodian named in an access order, or the local authority, may apply to the court for the variation or discharge of an access order. Proceedings are brought by way of complaint to the appropriate juvenile court (CCA 1980 s.12D, inserted by HASSASSA 1983 Sched.1).

For forms of access order, and an order of variation or discharge, see pages 263 and 264.

(c) Emergency applications for suspension of access

If a justice of the peace who is a member of a juvenile court panel is satisfied that continued access to a child by its parent, guardian or custodian in accordance with the terms of an access order will put the child's welfare *seriously* at risk, he may make an order suspending the operation of the access order for 7 days beginning with the date of the order, or for such shorter period beginning with that date as shall be specified in the order. An application may be heard *ex parte*. A form of order is set out at page 264.

If during the period for which the operation of the access order is suspended the local authority makes an application for the variation or discharge of the access order, the operation of the order shall be suspended until the date on which the application for variation or discharge is determined or abandoned (CCA 1980 s.12E, inserted by HASSASSA 1983 Sched.1).

(d) Duty of courts dealing with access applications

A court dealing with an application for an access order or for any other order under Part IA CCA 1980 or with an appeal, is under a duty to regard the welfare of the child as the first and paramount consideration in determining the matter. Should the court consider it necessary, in order to safeguard the interests of the child, it may order that he be made a party to the proceedings. Whenever it does so it must appoint a guardian *ad litem* of the child for the purposes of the proceedings unless satisfied that such an appointment is not necessary for safeguarding the interests of the child.

A guardian *ad litem* appointed in pursuance of the section shall be under a duty to safeguard the interests of the child in the manner prescribed by Part IIIA Magistrates' Courts (Children etc) Rules 1970, SI 1970 No 1792, as amended by SI's 1976 No 1769, 1978 No 869, 1983 Nos 526 and 1793 and 1984 No 567 (CCA 1980 s.12F, inserted by HASSASSA 1983 Sched.1).

In any case in which justices hearing an application under this Part of the Act decline to accept advice received from the guardian *ad litem*, they should seek to justify their rejection of that advice in their reasons. In the absence of any such justification an appeal against their decision will usually be allowed (*Devon County Council* v *Clancy* (1985)).

3. Restrictions on removing children from care

Section 13(1) CCA 1980 places restrictions on the removal of children from the care of local authorities, and provides that persons who do so without the consent of the authority in question are guilty of an offence. Section 13(1) is discussed at page 118.

Chapter 24

Treatment of children in care

Unless otherwise stated this chapter relates to children who are or were in the care of a local authority under s.2 CCA 1980, or by virtue of a care order or a warrant of commitment remanding to the care of a local authority granted under s.23(1) C&YPA 1969 (CCA 1980 s.17).

1. The general duty

In reaching any decision relating to a child in their care a local authority is obliged to give first consideration to the need to safeguard and promote the welfare of the child throughout his childhood. In reaching their decisions the authorities must, as far as practicable, ascertain the wishes and feelings of the child regarding the decision and give due consideration to them, having regard to his age and understanding. Local authorities must make such use of the facilities and services available for children in the care from their own parents as appears reasonable to them in the particular case under consideration. A local authority may act in a manner that may not be consistent with their duty to give first consideration to the needs of the child if it appears necessary to do so for the purpose of protecting members of the public (CCA 1980 s.18).

It is the duty of local authorities to review the case of each child in their care in accordance with Regulations made by the Secretary of State providing for the manner in which cases are to be reviewed, the considerations to which local authorities are to have regard in reviewing cases, and the time when a child's case is first to be reviewed and the frequency of subsequent reviews (CCA 1980 s.20).

2. Accommodation and maintenance

A local authority may discharge its duty to provide accommodation and maintenance for a child in their care in one of the following ways:

(a) by boarding him out on such terms as to payment as the authority may determine, subject to the provisions of the Act and Regulations made under it;

(b) by maintaining him in a community home or in any such home as is referred to in s.80 of the Act — homes for the accommodation of children in need of particular facilities and services;

(c) by maintaining him in a voluntary home other than a community home, the managers of which are willing to receive him; or

(d) *by maintaining him in a children's home registered under the Children's Homes Act 1982 [paragraph (d) will be inserted in this section when CHA 1982 s.15(3) comes into force]*

or by making such other arrangements as seem appropriate to the local authority.

Subject to the provisions of s.18 (requiring the authority to give first consideration to safeguarding and promoting the child's welfare) the authority having care of a child shall secure that any accommodation they provide is, so far as is practicable, near to the child's home (CCA 1980 s.21(1)).

A local authority having the care of a child may also allow him to be under the charge and control of a parent, guardian, relative or friend for a fixed period or until they otherwise determine, subject to any conditions as to charge and control that may have been added to the care order by the court under C&YPA 1969 s.20A (CCA 1980 s.21(2)).

3. Accommodation restricting liberty

(a) Powers to keep child in secure accommodation

As a general rule, a child in the care of a local authority shall not be placed, and if placed shall not be kept, in accommodation provided for the purpose of restricting liberty unless it appears:

(a) that he has a history of absconding and is likely to abscond from other accommodation, and if he absconds, it is likely that his physical, mental or moral welfare will be at risk; or

(b) that if he is kept in any other accommodation he is likely to injure himself or other persons
(CCA 1980 s.21A(1)).

The Secretary of State has used powers granted under this section to regulate:

(a) the maximum period beyond which a child may not be kept in accommodation provided for the purpose of restricting liberty without the authority of a juvenile court; and

(b) the maximum period for which a juvenile court may authorise that a child be kept in such accommodation.

The Regulations made also give juvenile courts the power to authorise a child to be kept in such accommodation for such further periods as the Regulations may specify, and provide for local authorities to make applications to juvenile courts for such orders. The Regulations are made under s.21A(2) and are the Secure Accommodation (No 2) Regulations 1983, SI 1983 No 1808, reproduced at page 270. See page 265 for forms of order.

It is the duty of a juvenile court hearing an application by a local authority to determine whether any relevant criteria for keeping a child in accommodation provided for the purpose of restricting liberty are satisfied in his case. If so, the court must make an order authorising the child to be kept in such accommodation, and specifying the maximum period for which he may be so kept (CCA 1980 s.21A(3)).

A court may adjourn a hearing under subs.3 and on doing so may make an interim order permitting the child to be kept in secure accommodation during the period of the adjournment (CCA 1980 s.21A(4)).

A juvenile court may not exercise any of its powers under s.21A in respect of a child who is not legally represented unless:

(a) he applied for legal aid and his application was refused on the ground that it did not appear that his means were such that required assistance; or

(b) having been advised of his right to apply for legal aid and had the opportunity to do so, he refused or failed to apply.
(CCA 1980 s.21A(6)).

Any appeal against the making of an order under s.21A is to the Crown Court (CCA 1980 s.21A(5)).

(b) Safeguards

No accommodation in a community home may be used as secure accommodation without the specific approval of the Secretary of State, and on giving approval to such use the Secretary of State may impose such terms and conditions as he sees fit (SAR 1983 reg.3). Secure accommodation in a community home may not be used for restricting the liberty of a child under the age of ten unless the local authority has obtained the permission of the Secretary of State prior to such a placement (SAR 1983 reg.4).

If a child is placed in secure accommodation in a community home which is managed by an authority other than that in whose care he is or which is the responsible authority in relation to him, the local authority managing the community home shall inform his care authority or responsible authority as the case may be of the placement within 24 hours thereof (SAR 1983 reg.9).

The maximum periods for which a child may be kept in secure accommodation, with or without the authority of a juvenile court, and the procedure for dealing with applications for authority to keep a child in such accommodation for an extended period are dealt with in Chapter 13 and set out on page 106.

If a child is kept in secure accommodation in a community home and it is intended to make an application to a juvenile court under CCA 1980 s.21A, the child's care authority or responsible authority shall, as soon as possible, inform the child's parent or guardian if practicable, and the child's independent visitor (if one has been appointed — see page 172) of that intention (SAR 1983 reg.15).

Each local authority shall appoint at least two persons to have responsibility to review the case of each child to whom the Regulations apply at intervals not exceeding three months, if the child continues to be kept in secure accommodation in a community home and either:

  (i) he is in the care of that authority, or
  (ii) he falls to be accommodated by that authority, it being the responsible authority
  (SAR 1983 reg.16).

Persons appointed under SAR 1983 reg.16 shall satisfy themselves that the placement in secure accommodation continues to be appropriate, and in doing so they must have regard to the welfare of the child whose case is being reviewed. In undertaking the review referred to in reg.16, the persons appointed shall ascertain and take into account the views of:

  (i)   the child; and
  (ii) the parent or guardian of the child, if practicable; and
  (iii) any other person who has had the care of the child, whose views the persons appointed consider should be taken into account, if practicable; and

    (iv) the child's independent visitor, if one has been appointed; and

    (v) the local authority managing the secure accommodation in which the child is placed, if that authority is a different authority from that specified in reg.16(a) or (b)

(SAR 1983 reg.17)

Whenever a child is placed in secure accommodation in a community home the local authority which manages the accommodation must keep a record. The record must contain the information specified in reg.18 (see page 274).

4. Guarantee of apprenticeships

A local authority may undertake any obligation by way of guarantee under any deed of apprenticeship or articles of clerkship entered into by a child in their care, and they may undertake any such obligation that arises under any deed or articles supplemental thereto, whether or not the person concerned is still in their care (CCA 1980 s.23).

5. Emigration of children in care

With the consent of the Secretary of State, a local authority may procure, or assist in procuring, the emigration of any child in their care. Generally, the Secretary of State shall not give his consent unless satisfied that emigration would benefit the child and that suitable arrangements have been or will be made for the child's reception and welfare in the country to which he is going, that the parents or guardians of the child have been consulted or that it is not practicable to consult them, and that the child consents. However, if the child in question is too young to form or express a proper opinion on the matter, the Secretary of State may consent to his emigration even though the child cannot consent, where the child is to emigrate in company with a parent, guardian, relative or friend of his, or is to emigrate for the purpose of joining such a person.

Section 56 AA 1976, which requires the authority of an order under the Act for the taking or sending abroad for adoption of a child who is a British subject, does not apply in the case of a child who is emigrating with the consent of the Secretary of State given under this section (CCA 1980 s.24)).

For the purposes of s.24 only children in the care of local authorities as a result of an order referred to in s.17 (see page 177) are included in the expression 'any child in their care'.

The reference to 'parents or guardians' in the section includes parents or guardians who have lost their parental rights, but does not include a putative father.

6. Children dying while in care

A local authority may cause the body of any deceased child to be buried or cremated if, immediately before his death, he was in the care of that authority. However, the authority may not cause a body of a child to be cremated if cremation is not in accordance with the practice of the child's religious persuasion.

Where an authority exercises this power in respect of a child who had not attained the age of *sixteen* at the time of his death, they may recover any expenses incurred in exercising that power from any parent of the child, less any amount received by the authority by way of death grant under SSA 1975. Sums recoverable under this section are recoverable as a civil debt (CCA 1980 s.25).

7. Expenses of parents and others

If it appears to a local authority that a parent, guardian or other person visiting a child who is in care, or attending the funeral of a child who had been in care at the time of his death, would not otherwise be able to visit or to attend the funeral without undue hardship and that the circumstances warrant making a payment, they may make a payment to that person in respect of travelling, subsistence or other expenses incurred in visiting the child or attending the funeral (CCA 1980 s.26).

8. Financial assistance for persons over seventeen

The provisions of s.27 apply to any person over compulsory school age but under the age of twenty-one who is, or has at any time after ceasing to be of compulsory school age been in the care of a local authority, being either:

(a) a person who has attained the age of seventeen but has not attained the age of eighteen and who has ceased to be in the care of a local authority; or

(b) a person who has attained the age of eighteen.

In respect of any such person a local authority may make contributions to the cost of accommodation and maintenance in any place near the place where he may be employed, or seeking employment, or receiving education or training (CCA 1980 s.27(1)).

A local authority may make grants to any person who has attained the age of seventeen but not twenty-one and who, at or after attaining the age of seventeen, was in the care of a local authority, to enable him to meet expenses connected with his receiving suitable education or training (CCA 1980 s.27(2)).

Where a person is engaged in a course of education or training at the time he attains the age of twenty-one, or having previously been engaged in a course of education or training which has been interrupted, resumes the course as soon as practicable, a local authority who are, or who were at the time the course was interrupted, making any contribution or grants in respect of him under subs.(1)or(2), shall continue to have the powers under those subsections until the completion of the course (CCA 1980 s.27(3)). This does not prevent a person who has attained the age of eighteen from obtaining further assistance with the cost of further education under EA 1944 s.81, or further help with the cost of training courses in accordance with the Employment and Training Act 1973.

A local authority may provide accommodation for a person who is over compulsory school age but has not attained the age of twenty-one in a community home, if it is provided for children who are over compulsory school age and it is near the place where that person is employed, seeking employment or receiving education or training (CCA 1980 s.72).

9. After-care

If any local authority becomes aware that a child over compulsory school age who, at the time he ceased to be of that age or at any subsequent time was, but no longer is, in the care of a local authority under s.2 CCA 1980, then they shall be under a duty, until he is eighteen, to advise and befriend him, unless satisfied that his welfare does not require it.

Where a child over compulsory school age ceases to be in the care of a local authority under s.2 CCA 1980 and proposes to reside in the area of another local authority, the first authority must inform that other authority of that fact. When it comes to the knowledge of a local authority that has been befriending a child in pursuance under this provision, that he proposes to transfer or has transferred his residence to the area of another local authority, they shall notify that other authority of that fact (CCA 1980 s.28).

'Residence' must be construed in the ordinary way. It means the place where a person lives and has his meals (*Stoke on Trent Corporation* v *Cheshire County Council* (1915)). It is the place where he has his home (*South Shields Corporation* v *Liverpool Corporation* (1943)).

If a person was, at or after the time he attained the age of seventeen, in the care of a local authority under s.2 CCA 1980, but has ceased to be in their care, the authority has a duty to cause him to be visited, advised and befriended, if so requested by him and while he remains under the age of twenty-one. In exceptional circumstances, the authority may be under a duty to give him financial assistance (CCA 1980 s.29).

Chapter 25

Children in the care of voluntary organisations

In Chapter 24 consideration was given to the responsibilities and duties of local authorities to children. In this chapter the role of the voluntary organisations is examined.

1. Boarding out

The power of the Secretary of State under Part III CCA 1980 to make Regulations as to the boarding out of children by local authorities is extended to the boarding out of children by voluntary organisations. In the case of voluntary organisations, any reference to supervision and inspection of children and the premises in which they are boarded out by a local authority, shall be deemed to be a reference to supervision and inspection by either a local authority or, where it is permitted by or under the Regulations, by a voluntary organisation.

Regulations so made may provide that a person who contravenes or fails to comply with them shall be guilty of an offence triable summarily and punishable by a fine not exceeding Level 3 on the standard scale (CCA 1980 s.61). See Boarding-out of Children Regulations 1965 (SI 1965 No 1377) as amended.

2. Arrangements for emigration

The Secretary of State may make Regulations controlling the making and carrying out of arrangements for the emigration of children by voluntary organisations. Regulations made for this purpose may contain any consequential and incidental provisions that the Secretary of State thinks expedient to include. In particular they may include provisons requiring information to be given to the Secretary of State as to the operations or intended operations of the organisation, and for enabling him to be satisfied that suitable arrangements have been or will be made for the children's reception and welfare in the country to which they are going.

Again, such Regulations may provide that any person who contravenes or fails to comply with them shall be guilty of an offence. An offence under these Regulations will be triable summarily and the maximum penalty will be a fine not exceeding Level 3 on the standard scale (CCA 1980 s.62).

3. Restriction on removing children

The provisions of s.13 of the Act (see page 118) apply to children in the care of voluntary organisations as they do to children in the care of local authorities, except that in the case of a child who is not in the care of a local authority references to a local authority shall be construed as references to the voluntary organisation in whose care the child is. Subject to that exception, the provisions of s.13(1) also apply to children who are boarded out by a voluntary organisation. For these purposes, a child is boarded out if he is boarded out by the voluntary organisation in whose care he is with foster parents to live in their home as a member of their family (CCA 1980 s.63).

The effect of this is that any person who removes a child who has been in the care of a voluntary organisation for six months, from a voluntary home or from a family with whom he is boarded out, without the consent of the voluntary organisation, is guilty of an offence, unless he is a parent or guardian of the child and has given the voluntary organisation at least 28 days written notice of his intention to remove the child.

4. General duty of voluntary organisations

When reaching any decision in relation to a child in their care, a voluntary organisation shall give first consideration to the need to safeguard and promote the welfare of the child throughout his childhood. As far as is practicable the organisation shall, in reaching its decisions, ascertain the wishes and feelings of the child in relation to those decisions and give due consideration to those wishes and feelings, having regard to the age and understanding of the child.

Voluntary organisations are also under a duty, in providing for a child in their care, to make such use of facilities and services available for children in the care from their own parents as appears to be reasonable in the case (CCA 1980 s.64A as amended by HASSASSA 1983 Sched.2 para.55).

5. Parental rights and duties

(a) Transfer to voluntary organisation

A local authority may in certain circumstances resolve that parental rights and duties with respect to a child in the care of a voluntary organisation which is an incorporated body shall vest in that organisation. The local authority may so resolve when it appears to them:

(a) that the child is not in the care of any local authority; and

(b) that a condition specified in s.3(1) (see page 169) of the Act is satisfied; and

(c) that it is necessary in the interests of the welfare of the child for the parental rights and duties to be vested in the organisation.

If, immediately before a resolution under this section is passed, the parental rights and duties are vested in the parent in relation to whom the resolution is passed, jointly with any other person, then on the passing of the resolution they shall vest jointly in that other person and the organisation in whose care the child is.

In deciding whether the condition specified in s.3(1)(b)(i) is satisfied, a parent shall be deemed to have abandoned a child if his whereabouts have remained unknown for a period of twelve months.

A local authority may only make a resolution under this section if the child is living in a voluntary home or with foster parents in the area of the local authority and the voluntary organisation has requested the authority to pass the resolution.

Certain parental rights and duties are not vested in the organisation by virtue of a resolution under this section. They are:

(a) the right to consent or to refuse to consent to the making of an application for a freeing for adoption order; and

(b) the right to agree or to refuse to agree to the making of an adoption order.

Regulations made under s.62 (see page 185) shall apply to the emigration of a child notwithstanding that the parental rights and duties relating to the child are vested in the voluntary organisation.

Section 5(2) of the Act (which is concerned with the duration of the resolutions relating to the vesting of parental rights in local authorities) applies in relation to resolutions under this section as if they were resolutions under s.3.

Part 1A of the Act (which is concerned with access to children in care) applies to a child in respect of whom a resolution under this section is in force as it does to a child such as is mentioned in s.12A (see page 173). Consequently, references to a local authority in that part of the Act include references to a voluntary organisation in which the parental rights and duties with respect to a child have vested under such a resolution (CCA 1980 s.64 as amended by HASSASSA 1983 Sched.1, Pt.II para.2).

(b) Assumption of parental rights by local authority

In a case in which parental rights have been vested in a voluntary organisation by resolution under s.64, if it appears to the local authority for the area in which the child is living that, having regard to the interests of the welfare of the child, it is necessary that the parental rights and duties should no longer be vested in that organisation, the local authority shall resolve that they shall be vested in them. Within seven days of passing such a resolution, the local authority must inform the organisation and each parent, guardian or custodian of the child whose whereabouts are known to them that the resolution has been passed. A notice given for the purposes of this section must be in writing (CCA 1980 s.65).

(c) Effect of resolutions

Any resolution made under s.64(1) by which parental rights and duties are vested in a voluntary organisation shall cease to have effect if a resolution is made under s.65(1) that those rights and duties be vested in a local authority (CCA 1980 s.66(1)).

A resolution that has the effect of vesting parental rights and duties in a voluntary organisation is treated in the same way as a resolution vesting those rights and duties in a local authority for the purposes of s.8 CCA 1980. This means that the resolution does not affect any supervision order or probation order previously made in respect of the child in question (CCA 1980 s.66(2)).

Generally, a resolution made under s.65(1) ie a resolution that parental rights and duties previously vested in a voluntary organisation be vested instead in a local authority, is treated as if it were a resolution made under s.3 (see page 187). However, the following provisions do not apply to s.65 resolutions (CCA 1980 s.66(3)):

(i) s.3(2) to (7), relating to notices to be served upon any person whose rights and duties are vested in the authority as a result, if his whereabouts are known;

(ii) s.4(1), which relieves the local authority of the duty imposed by s.2(3) to endeavour to secure that the care of the child is taken over by a parent, guardian, relative or friend; and

(iii) s.5(4), which relates to a juvenile court's powers to determine a resolution upon application.

(d) Parents' rights of appeal

The provisions of s.3(2) to (7) (see page 188), apply to resolutions vesting parental rights and duties in a voluntary organisation under s.64(1) as they do to resolutions made under s.3 (CCA 1980 s.67(1)).

An appeal may be made against a resolution that parental rights and duties be vested in a voluntary organisation, and against a resolution that parental rights previously vested in a voluntary organisation should instead vest in a local authority. In each case the right of appeal is given to the person who would have had those rights and duties if no resolution had been made in relation to the child. Any appeal is to a juvenile court having jurisdiction in the area of the authority which passed the resolution. The appeal may be on the basis that there was no ground for making the resolution, or that the resolution should be determined in the interests of the child (CCA 1980 s.67(2)).

There is a right of further appeal against the decision of the juvenile court. Such appeals are to the High Court (CCA 1980 s.67(3)).

Section 7 of the Act, a section which deals with the appointment of guardians *ad litem* and the submission of written reports, applies to proceedings under this section (CCA 1980 s.67(4)).

6. Visiting

Local authorities have a duty to make sure that children who are in voluntary homes in their area (other than community homes) are visited from time to time in the interests of ensuring their well-being. Persons authorised by the local authority to make such visits may enter voluntary homes in the area of that authority for that purpose (CCA 1980 s.68(1)). Persons authorised to visit may enter voluntary homes outside the area of the authorising local authority if the child being visited is in the care of the authorising authority (CCA 1980 s.68(2)).

The provisions of subs.(1) and (2) do not apply to a voluntary home that is, as a whole, subject to inspection by or under the authority of a government department otherwise than under the general provisions of s.74 (a section that gives the Secretary of State the power to cause inspections of any community home, voluntary home or other premises in which children are living, boarded out or being accommodated or maintained) (CCA 1980 s.68(3)).

Any person who proposes to exercise any power of entry or inspection under this section shall, if so required, produce some properly authenticated document showing his authority to do so (CCA 1980 s.68(4)). A person who obstructs the exercise of any power of entry or inspection commits an offence and is liable on summary conviction to a fine not exceeding Level 2 on the standard scale (CCA 1980 s.68(5)).

The frequency of visits is a matter for the local authority to decide upon. There are no regulations controlling the intervals of time that should pass between visits. Persons authorised to enter premises and inspect them have no authority to use force to effect an entry if entry is denied. Such a person has two remedies. First he may seek a warrant under C&YPA 1933 s.40 if concerned for the welfare of the child. Alternatively or additionally, he may prosecute under s.68(5).

'Obstruction' does not depend upon physical violence (*Hinchliffe* v *Sheldon* (1955)). Standing by passively, in the absence of any duty to act, does not amount to obstruction (*Swallow* v *LCC* (1916)), but doing anything that has the effect of making it more difficult for the authorised person to carry out his duties may amount to obstruction (*Rice* v *Connolly* (1966)).

7. After-care

In Chapter 24 reference was made to the duty of local authorities to give a certain amount of after-care to children formerly in their care. Local authorities also have an after-care responsibility for children formerly in the care of voluntary organisations. If it comes to the knowledge of a local authority that any child over compulsory school age who, at the time he ceased to be of that age or at any subsequent time, was, but is no longer, in the care of a voluntary organisation in their area, they must advise and befriend him until he attains the age of *eighteen*, unless satisfied that his welfare does not require such after-care. If satisfied that the voluntary organisation that formerly had the care of a child has the necessary facilities for advising and befriending him, the authority may make arrangements for him to be advised and befriended by the voluntary organisation rather than by the local authority (CCA 1980 s.69(1)).

To better facilitate the carrying out of the duty imposed by s.69(1), voluntary organisations are required to give notice that a child over compulsory school age has ceased to be in their care to the local authority for the area in which that child proposes to reside. If it comes to the knowledge of a local authority or a voluntary organisation that a child whom they have been advising and befriending under s.69(1) proposes to transfer or has transferred his residence to the area of another local authority, they have a duty to inform that other authority of that fact (CCA 1980 s.69(2) and (3)).

8. Returns by voluntary organisations

The Secretary of State may direct voluntary organisations to transmit to him, at such times and in such form as he may direct, such particulars as he may require with respect to children who are accommodated and maintained in voluntary homes provided by them or who have been boarded out by them. The voluntary organisations are under a duty to comply with such directions (CCA 1980 s.70).

'Boarded out' has the meaning given to it in s.61 (see page 185).

Chapter 26

Community homes

1. Provision and designation of homes

Local authorities are required to make such arrangements as they consider appropriate for securing that homes are available for children in their care, and for purposes connected with the welfare of children, whether in their care or not. Two or more authorities may make the required provisions jointly (CCA 1980 s.31(1) as substituted by HASSASSA 1983 s.4).

In making the necessary arrangements local authorities must have regard to the need to make available accommodation of different descriptions, suitable for different purposes and to the requirements of different descriptions of children (CCA 1980 s.31(2) as substituted by HASSASSA 1983 s.4).

A community home may be provided, managed, equipped and maintained by the local authority; or it may be a home provided by a voluntary organisation but with an instrument of management, providing that the management, equipment and maintenance of it are the responsibility of the local authority or the voluntary organisation. Where the local authority manages a community home provided by a voluntary organisation it is designated a *controlled community home*. Where a voluntary organisation is responsible for the management of a home provided by it, it is designated an *assisted community home* (CCA 1980 s.31(3), (4) and (5) as substituted by HASSASSA 1983 s.4).

2. Instruments of management

The Secretary of State may make instruments of management in respect of controlled or assisted community homes. Where two or more homes are provided by the same voluntary organisation and the same local authority is to be represented on the body of managers, a single instrument of management may be made.

The number of persons constituting the body of managers shall be such multiple of three as may be specified in the instrument. A specified proportion of the managers must be appointed from the local authority. In the case of a controlled home the proportion must be two-thirds; in the case of an assisted home, one-third.

The instrument of management provides for the manner of appointment of foundation managers, ie those who are not appointed by the local authority. Their function is to represent the interests of the voluntary organisation which has provided or is to provide the home, and to secure that, as far as practicable, the character of the home will be preserved and the terms of any trust deed relating to the home will be observed (CCA 1980 s.35 as amended by HASSASSA 1983 Sched.2 para.52).

An instrument of management made by the Secretary of State may not affect the purposes for which the premises comprising the home are held. An instrument of management may contain:

(a) provisions specifying the nature and purpose of the home or each of the homes to which it relates;

(b) provisions requiring a specified number or proportion of the places in the home or homes to be made available to local authorities and other bodies specified in the instrument; and

(c) provisions relating to the management of the home or homes and the charging of fees in respect of children placed there or places made available to any local authority or other body.

If in any case there is any inconsistency between the provisions of any trust deed and the instrument of management relating to a controlled or assisted community home, the instrument of management shall prevail over the provisions of the trust deed in so far as they relate to that home.

The Secretary of State may vary or revoke any provisions of an instrument of management after consultation with the voluntary organisation providing the home and the local authority specified in the instrument of management.

'Trust deed' means any instrument (other than an instrument of management) regulating the maintenance, management or conduct of the home or the constitution of a body of managers or trustees of a home (CCA 1980 s.36 as amended by HASSASSA 1983 Sched. Part I).

3. Management

(a) Controlled homes

The management, equipment and maintenance of a controlled

community home is the responsibility of the local authority specified in the instrument of management for that home. The responsible authority exercise their functions in relation to the home through the body of managers constituted by the instrument of management and anything done, liability incurred or property acquired by the managers shall be done, incurred or acquired by the managers as agents of the responsible authority.

The responsible authority reserves to itself matters relating to the employment of persons at a controlled community home. They may, however, make arrangements with the voluntary organisation which provides the home whereby, upon such terms as may be agreed between them, persons not in the employment of the responsible authority may undertake duties at the home.

The accounting year of the managers of a controlled home is specified by the responsible authority and, before such date in each accounting year as may be specified, the managers submit estimates, in such form as the authority may require, of the expenditure and receipts in respect of the next accounting year. Any expenses incurred by the managers with the approval of the responsible authority are defrayed by that authority.

Managers of a controlled home must keep proper accounts in respect of the home and proper records in relation to the accounts. Where an instrument of management relates to more than one home, one set of accounts may be kept in respect of all the homes to which the instrument relates.
(CCA 1980 s.37)

(b) Assisted homes

The management, equipment and maintenance of an assisted community home is the responsibility of the voluntary organisation by which the home is provided. The organisation exercises its functions in relation to the home through the body of managers constituted by the instrument of management. Anything done, liability incurred or property acquired by the managers shall be done, incurred or acquired by the managers as agents for the responsible organisation.

The employment of persons at an assisted community home is a matter for the responsible organisation but, subject to certain exceptions in s.38(5), the responsible organisation must consult the local authority specified in the instrument of management before engaging any person to work at the home or terminating a person's employment at the home without notice. If the local authority so directs, the responsible organisation shall not carry out its proposal without the consent of the authority. The local authority may, after consultation with the responsible organisation, require the organisation to terminate the employment of a person at the home. However, these provisions do not apply in such cases or circumstances as may be specified by notice in writing given by the local authority to the responsible organisation, or in relation to the employment of any person or class of persons specified in the instrument of management.

The powers of a local authority in relation to the staff of an assisted community home give a measure of control over persons who will, if employed, be in regular contact with the children in the home. Local authorities may wish to waive their rights where the employment in question is of maintenance or other staff unlikely to have regular contact with the children. In such cases local authorities may give notice in writing authorising the responsible organisation to proceed with such appointments without consultation.

The responsible organisation must specify the accounting year of the managers and before such date in each year as may be so specified, the managers submit to the organisation estimates, in such form as the organisation may require, of expenditure and receipts in respect of the next accounting year. All expenses incurred by the managers with the approval of the responsible organisation shall be defrayed by the organisation.

The managers of an assisted community home must keep proper accounts in respect of that home and proper records in relation to those accounts. Where an instrument of management relates to more than one assisted community home, one set of accounts may be kept in respect of all of the homes to which the instrument relates. (CCA 1980 s.38).

4. Conduct

The Secretary of State may make Regulations with respect to the conduct of community homes and for securing the welfare of children in those homes. Such Regulations may:

(a) impose requirements as to accommodation, equipment and medical arrangements to be made for protecting the health of children in the home;

(b) impose requirements as to facilities to be provided for religious instruction;

(c) require the approval of the Secretary of State for the provision of accommodation to be used for restricting the liberty of children in community homes, and impose other requirements as to the placing of children in accommodation of that nature, including a requirement to obtain the permission of the local authority in whose care the child is;

(d) authorise the Secretary of State to give and revoke directions requiring:

    (i) the local authority providing the home or specified in the instrument of management for the home, or

    (ii) the voluntary organisation by which an assisted community home is provided,

to accommodate in the home a child in the care of a local authority for whom no places are made available in that home or to take such action in relation to a child accommodated in the home as may be specified in the directions;

(e) prescribe standards to which premises used for community homes are to conform;

(f) require the approval of the Secretary of State to the use of buildings for the purpose of community homes and to the doing of anything (whether by way of addition, diminution or alteration) which materially affects the buildings or grounds or other facilities or amenities for children in community homes; and

(g) provide that, to such extent as may be provided for in the Regulations, the Secretary of State may direct that any provision of Regulations under this section which is specified in the direction and makes any such provision as is referred to in paragraph (a) (e) or (f) above shall not apply in relation to a particular community home or the premises used for it, and may provide for the variation or revocation of any such direction by the Secretary of State

(CCA 1980 s.39 as amended by CJA 1982 Sched.14 para.46 and HASSASSA 1983 Sched.2 Part I). See Community Homes Regulations 1972.

The Secretary of State's powers to give directions under this section enable him to require the accommodation of a child in a community home in order to protect the public. In such a case, the home need not be in the area of the authority having the care of the child.

5. Closure

Premises that have been used as a community home may cease to be used for that purpose, and the closure may come about in one of three ways. First, the Secretary of State is empowered by s.40 CCA

1980 to direct that the premises shall no longer be used for the purpose. Secondly, the voluntary organisation providing the community home may, after giving notice to the Secretary of State and the local authority, cease to provide the home. Finally, the local authority specified in the instrument of management may, after giving notice to the Secretary of State and the voluntary organisation providing the premises, withdraw their designation of the home as a controlled or assisted community home.

(a) Direction by Secretary of State

If it appears to the Secretary of State that premises used for the purposes of a community home are unsuitable for those purposes, or that the conduct of the home is not in accordance with Regulations made by him under s.39 of the Act or is otherwise unsatisfactory, he may by written notice to the responsible body give a direction that from a date specified in the notice, the premises shall not be used for those purposes. Where a direction under this section has not been revoked, the Secretary of State may at any time, by order, revoke the instrument of management for that home.

For these purposes the responsible body shall be:

  (i) in the case of a home provided by a local authority, that local authority;

  (ii) in the case of a controlled community home, the local authority specified in the instrument of management; and

  (iii) in the case of an assisted home, the voluntary organisation by which the home is provided.

  (CCA 1980 s.40).

(b) Discontinuance by a voluntary organisation

If a voluntary organisation that has provided a controlled or assisted community home wishes to cease to provide the home it must give not less than two years' notice in writing to the Secretary of State and to the local authority specified in the instrument of management of its intention. The notice must specify the date from which the organisation intends to cease to provide the home. Where such notice has been given and has not been withdrawn before the date specified in it, the instrument of management shall cease to have effect on that date and the home shall cease to be a controlled or assisted community home.

If the body of managers of a home to which such a notice relates give notice that they are unable or unwilling to carry on as managers of the home until the date specified in the notice given by the voluntary organisation, the Secretary of State may by order:

(i) revoke the instrument of management; and

(ii) require the local authority specified in the instrument to conduct the home until the date specified in the notice given by the voluntary organisation, or until such earlier date as may be specified in the order, as if it were a community home provided by that local authority.

If the Secretary of State makes an order of this type:

(i) nothing in the trust deed for the home shall affect the conduct of the home by the local authority; and

(ii) the Secretary of State may by order direct that for the purposes of any provision specified in the direction and made by or under any enactment relating to community homes other than this section, the home shall, until the date given in the notice served by the voluntary organisation of the earlier date specified in the order made by the Secretary of State, be treated as an assisted community home or as a controlled community home, but except in so far as the Secretary of State directs, the home shall until that date be treated for the purposes of any such enactment as a community home provided by the local authority; and

(iii) on the date or the earlier date specified in the order made by the Secretary of State, the home shall cease to be a community home

(CCA 1980 s.43 as amended by HASSASSA 1983 Sched.10 Part I).

(c) Closure by local authority

A local authority specified in the instrument of management for a controlled or assisted community home may give the Secretary of State and the voluntary organisation that has provided the home notice of their intention to withdraw their designation of the home as a controlled or assisted community home. Not less than two years notice may be given, and it must be given in writing. It must also specify the date on which the designation is to be withdrawn.

If a notice of intention to withdraw a designation is given and the body of managers for the home in question give notice in writing to the Secretary of State that they are unable or unwilling to continue as managers until the date on which designation is to be withdrawn, then, unless their notice is withdrawn, the Secretary of State may by order revoke the instrument of management from such earlier date as may be specified in his order. Before making an order revoking an instrument of management the Secretary of State must consult the local authority and the voluntary organisation.

When a notice has been given of an intention to withdraw designation and that notice is not withdrawn, the instrument of management for the home in question shall cease to have effect on the relevant date and accordingly the home shall cease to be a controlled or assisted community home on that date (CCA 1980 s.43A as amended by HASSASSA 1983 s.5).

6. Exemption of controlled and assisted homes from statutory controls

While any voluntary home is designated a controlled or an assisted community home the provisions of ss.57 to 60 CCA 1980 do not apply to it. These sections relate to registration procedures for voluntary homes, and regulations as to the conduct of voluntary homes (CCA 1980 s.41).

A 'voluntary home' is defined in s.56 of the Act. It means any home or other institution for the boarding, care and maintenance of poor children, being either:

(a) a home or other institution supported wholly or partly by voluntary contributions, or

(b) a home or other institution supported wholly or partly by endowments, not being a school within the meaning of EA 1944.

'Voluntary home' does not, for the purposes of CCA 1980, include a nursing home or mental nursing home within the meaning of NHA 1975, or a residential care home within the meaning of HASSASSA 1983 Sched.4 Part I.

Chapter 27

Fostering

The fostering of children is regulated by the Foster Children Act 1980. It consolidates earlier legislation relating to the fostering of children by private individuals in England and Wales. Provisions which enable the Secretary of State to make Regulations with regard to fostering, formerly contained in the Children Act 1975 which is repealed in as much as it relates to England and Wales, are included in FCA 1980.

1. Definition of foster children

A child below the upper limit of the compulsory school age is a foster child if his care and maintenance are undertaken by a person who is not a relative, guardian or custodian of his (FCA 1980 s.1). However, a child is not a foster child:

    (a) while he is in the care of any person:

        (i) in premises in which any parent, adult relative or guardian of his is for the time being residing;

        (ii) in any voluntary home within the meaning of CCA 1980;

        (iii) in any school within the meaning of EA 1944 in which he is receiving full-time education;

        (iv) in any hospital, or in any nursing home registered or exempted from registration under NHA 1975; or

        (v) in any home or institution not specified in s.2(2) or (5) but maintained by a public or local authority (FCA 1980 s.2(2));

    (b) at any time while his care and maintenance are undertaken by a person:

        (i) who is not a regular foster parent and at that time does not intend to, and does not in fact, undertake his care and maintenance for a continuous period of more than 27 days; or

(ii) who is a regular foster parent but at that time does not intend to, and does not in fact, undertake his care and maintenance for a continous period of more than 6 days (FCA 1980 s.2(3));

(c) while he is in the care of any person in compliance with a supervision order within the meaning of C&YPA 1969 (FCA 1980 s.2(4));

(d) while he is liable to be detained or subject to guardianship under MHA 1983, or is resident in a residential care home within the meaning of Sched.4 Part 1 HASSASSA 1983 (FCA 1980 s.2(5));

(e) while he is in the care and possession of a person who proposes to adopt him under arrangements made by an adoption agency within the meaning of s.1 of the Adoption Act 1976; and

(f) while he is a protected child within the meaning of Part III of the Adoption Act 1976 (FCA 1980 s.2(6)).

In addition to the specific situations set out above in which a child is not a foster child, the Act provides that a child is not a foster child while he is in the care of a local authority or a voluntary organisation or is boarded out by a local authority or a local education authority (FCA 1980 s.2(1)).

2. Duties of local authorities

Local authorities have a general duty to satisfy themselves as to the well-being of foster children within their area. For that purpose they must make sure that the children are visited by officers of the authority in accordance with the regulations made under s.3(2) (see below), and that such advice as appears to be needed in relation to the care and maintenance of the children is given (FCA 1980 s.3(1)).

Regulations made by the Secretary of State may require that foster children in a local authority's area are to be visited by an officer of the authority on specified occasions or within specified periods of time (FCA 1980 s.3(2)). No Regulations have been made as at April 1987. Until such time as Regulations are made, the duty to visit is in the terms, 'that, so far as appears to the authority to be appropriate, the children are visited from time to time by officers of the authority' (FCA 1980 s.3(3)).

3. Notices

Section 4 FCA 1980 gives the Secretary of State power to make Regulations requiring parents of children who are to be fostered to give information about the proposed fostering to the local authority for the area in which it is proposed they should be fostered. At the time of going to press (April 1987) no Regulations have been made under the section.

Any person proposing to foster a child not already in his care must notify the local authority in whose area the premises in which the child is to live are situated of his intention to do so. The notification must be in writing and, unless the child is received by the foster parent in an emergency, it must be given not less than two and not more than four weeks before the child is to be received (FCA 1980 s.5(1)).

Foster parents maintaining a foster child who was received in an emergency, or who became a foster child while in the care of those persons, have a duty to give notice in writing to the local authority not later than 48 hours after the child becomes a foster child. Again, the local authority to be notified is the one in whose area the premises in which the child is to live are situated (FCA 1980 s.5(2)).

Notices given under s.5(1) or (2) must specify the date on which it is intended that the child should be received, or the date on which the child was in fact received or became a foster child, and the premises in which the child is to be or is being kept. If a person who is maintaining one or more foster children changes his permanent address or the premises in which those children are being kept, he must give the local authority written notice of the change not less than two weeks nor more than four weeks before it is to take place, unless the change is to take place in an emergency, when notice must be given no later than 48 hours after it has taken place. The notice must specify the new address or premises and if the new premises are in the area of a different local authority, the authority to whom the notice is given must inform that other authority, and give them such of the following particulars as are known:

(a) the name, sex and date and place of birth of the child; and

(b) the name and address of every person who is a parent or guardian or acts as a guardian of the child or from whom the child was or is to be received

(FCA 1980 s.5(3)-(5)).

Service of notices under s.5 may be by post (s.20).

There seem to be several situations in which a child may become a foster child while already in the care of the person who proposes to become his foster parent. One example would be where a child remained with a foster parent for a period that took him outside the exception mentioned in s.2(3). Another example might be where a parent of a child leaves a household and the child continues to reside there and is maintained by another person at those premises.

A person who ceases to be the foster parent of a child is also under a duty to give written notice to the local authority of the circumstances in which he has ceased to be a foster parent. Notice must be given within 48 hours of the event. This duty to notify arises:

(a) if a foster child dies (in which case written notice must also be given to the person from whom the child was received); and

(b) where a person who has been maintaining a foster child ceases to maintain the child in circumstances which do not require notification under the provisions of s.5(4) or s.6(1) (FCA 1980 s.6(1) and (2)).

A person need not give the notice required by s.6(2) if, at the time he ceases to maintain the child at his premises he intends to resume maintenance of the child at those premises with 27 days. However, if having had such an intention, he subsequently abandons it or the period of 27 days expires without him giving effect to it, he must then give the required notice within 48 hours of that event (FCA 1980 s.6(3)).

Should any foster child be removed or remove himself from the care of the foster parent maintaining him, the foster parent must give the local authority, at their request, the name and address, if known, of the person into whose care the child has been removed (FCA 1980 s.6(4)).

Again, notices referred to in s.6 may be served by post (s.20).

4. Disqualification

Certain persons are disqualified from keeping foster children. A person shall not maintain a child as a foster child if:

(a) an order removing a child from his care has been made against him under this Act or under Part I of the Children Act 1958; or

(b) an order has been made under C&YPA 1933 or 1969 and by virtue of that order a child was removed from his care; or

(c) he has been convicted of an offence specified in Schedule 1 to the C&YPA 1933 or he has been placed on probation or discharged conditionally or absolutely for such an offence; or

(d) his rights and powers with respect to a child have been vested in a local authority under s.2 of the Children Act 1948 or s.3 CCA 1980; or

(e) an order under s.1(3) or (4) of the Nurseries and Child-Minders Regulation Act 1948 has been made against him refusing the registration of any premises occupied by him or his registration, or an order has been made under s.5 of that Act cancelling such registration; or

(f) an order has been made under s.43 of the Adoption Act 1958 or s.34 of the Adoption Act 1976 for the removal of a protected child who was being kept or was about to be received by him,

unless he has disclosed that fact to the local authority and has obtained their written consent (FCA 1980 s.7(1)).

References in s.7 to related Scottish law have been omitted from the text above, but readers should be aware that orders made under those related Statutes will also disqualify a person from becoming a foster parent.

Where any person is disqualified by virtue of s.7(1), any other person who lives in the same premises as he does, or who lives in premises at which he is employed, will be similarly disqualified (FCA 1980 s.7(2)).

5. Local authority powers

(a) Inspection of premises

Any officer of a local authority so authorised may inspect the whole or any part of any premises in the area of the authority that are being used for the fostering of children. An officer making such an inspection must produce some authenticated document showing that he is an authorised inspector (FCA 1980 s.8).

The inspectors' powers are not limited to an inspection of the room in which the child sleeps. He is specifically authorised to inspect the whole of any premises in which a foster child is kept.

(b) Power to impose requirements

Local authorities may impose requirements upon premises that are used wholly or partly for the purpose of keeping foster children. The requirements may be as to:

(i) the number, age and sex of the foster children who may be kept at any one time in the premises or any part of them;

(ii) the accommodation and equipment to be provided for the children;

(iii) the medical arrangements to be made for protecting the health of the children;

(iv) the giving of particulars to the person for the time being in charge of the children;

(v) the number, qualifications or experience of persons employed in looking after the children;

(vi) the keeping of records;

(vii) the fire precautions to be taken in the premises; and

(viii) the giving of particulars of any foster child received in the premises and of any change in the number or identity of the foster children kept in them.

A requirement imposed may be limited to a particular class of foster child, and requirements of the types envisaged by paras (ii) to (viii) above may be limited so as to apply only when the number of foster children kept in the premises exceeds a specified number.

After such time as may be specified by the local authority, a person must comply with any requirement imposed on him under this provision whenever a foster child is kept in the premises in question.

Requirements are imposed by notice in writing addressed to the person on whom it is imposed. The notice must also inform him of his right to appeal against the requirement and of the time within which he must make his appeal (FCA 1980 s.9). Appeals are to a juvenile court (see page 206). Requirements imposed are of no effect while the appeal is pending (FCA 1980 s.11).

(c) Prohibition on keeping of foster children

If a local authority is of the opinion that premises in which it is proposed to keep foster children are unsuitable, or that the person who proposes to keep foster children is not a suitable person to have the care and maintenance of foster children, or that it would be detrimental to any child to be kept by a particular person or in particular premises, it may impose a prohibition on the person who is proposing to keep foster children in those premises. A prohibition imposed may:

   (i)   prohibit a person from keeping any foster child in the specified premises; or

  (ii)   prohibit him from keeping any foster child in *any* premises in the area of the local authority; or

 (iii)   prohibit him from keeping a particular child specified in the prohibition in premises so specified

(FCA 1980 s.10(1) and (2)).

If the circumstances change a local authority that has imposed a prohibition may cancel it, either of their own motion or on the application of the person on whom it was imposed (FCA 1980 s.10(3)).

Where a local authority has imposed a requirement on any person under s.9, they may prohibit him from keeping foster children in his premises until that requirement has been complied with (FCA 1980 s.10(4)).

A prohibition is imposed by notice in writing addressed to the person on whom it is imposed. It must inform him of his right to appeal against the prohibition and of the time within which he may appeal against it (FCA 1980 s.10(5)). Appeals are to a juvenile court (see below). If notice of appeal is given the prohibition is, nevertheless, effective pending the determination of the appeal.

(d) Appeals against impositions of requirements or prohibitions

Any person aggrieved by a requirement imposed under s.9, or by a prohibition under s.10, may appeal to a juvenile court. The appeal must be lodged within 14 days from the date on which he is notified of the requirement or prohibition or, in the case of a prohibition imposed under s.10(2), within 14 days of the refusal by the local authority to accede to an application by him for the cancellation of the prohibition. Where the appeal is against the imposition of a requirement under s.9, the requirement is of no effect while the appeal is pending (FCA 1980 s.11(1)).

The juvenile court's powers, on hearing an appeal, are not limited to cancelling the requirement or prohibition imposed, or dismissing the appeal. The court may vary a requirement, or allow more time for compliance. It may also substitute for an absolute prohibition a prohibition on using the premises after such time as the court may specify unless such specified requirements as the local authority had power to impose under s.9 are complied with. Any requirement or prohibition so specified or substituted shall be deemed for the purposes of the Act to have been imposed by the local authority under s.9 or s.10 (FCA 1980 s.11(2) and (3)).

There is a further right of appeal against decisions of the juvenile court to the Crown Court (FCA 1980 s.14(2)).

The right of appeal is given to any person who is aggrieved by a requirement or prohibition made by a local authority. It seems that it is not restricted to the person upon whom the requirement or prohibition is imposed, and that a person who has placed or who wishes to place a child with another person as a foster parent might have a right of appeal if he is aggrieved by the terms of a requirement or a prohibition which has the effect of preventing that placement. However, 'person aggrieved' has been said to be a person who has suffered a legal grievance, or against whom a decision has been pronounced which has wrongfully deprived him of something, or wrongfully affected his title to something (*Re Baron, ex p The Debtor* v *Official Receiver* (1943)). On this definition, it is difficult to see how the right of appeal given by s.11 can extend to anybody other than the person on whom the requirement of prohibition has been imposed.

(e) Removal of foster children from unsuitable surroundings

A local authority can make a complaint to a juvenile court for an order for the removal of a foster child to a place of safety, until he can be restored to a parent, relative or guardian of his, or until other arrangements can be made with respect to him. The court may make such an order if satisfied that a foster child is being kept or is about to be received:

  (i) by any person who is unfit to have his care, or
 (ii) in contravention of s.7 or of any prohibition imposed under s.10, or
(iii) in any premises or any environment detrimental or likely to be detrimental to him

(FCA 1980 s.12(1)). See page 266 for a form of order.

If there is proof that there is imminent danger to the health or well being of the child, the powers vested in the juvenile court may be exercised by a justice of the peace on the application of a person authorised to visit foster children (FCA 1980 s.12(2)).

An order made under s.12 on the ground that a prohibition under s.10 has been contravened, may also require that all the children kept at the premises in question be removed from them (FCA 1980 s.12(3)).

The order may be executed by a person who is authorised to visit foster children, or by any constable (FCA 1980 s.12(4)).

Any child who has been removed from premises under such an order may be received into care by a local authority under s.2 CCA 1980, whether or not the circumstances are such that they fall within s.2(1) (a) to (c), and notwithstanding that he appears to the local authority to be over the age of seventeen (FCA 1980 s.12(5)).

Where a child is removed under these provisions the local authority is under a duty, if practicable, to inform a parent or guardian of the child, or any person who acts as his guardian, that he has been removed (FCA 1980 s.12(6)).

(f) Search warrants

Officers of local authorities who are refused permission to premises or to any part of premises in which foster children are kept, or who apprehend that such refusal is likely, may obtain a warrant for the purpose of inspecting the premises. Warrants for this purpose may be issued on one of two bases. First, a justice of the peace may grant a warrant if satisfied that there is reasonable cause to believe that a foster child is being kept in any premises or any part of premises and admission has been refused, or a refusal of admission is apprehended, or that the occupier is temporarily absent from the premises. The warrant granted will authorise the officer to enter the premises, by force if need be, at any reasonable time within 48 hours of the issue of the warrant, for the purpose of inspecting the premises. Secondly, a refusal to allow the visiting of a foster child or the inspection of premises by a person authorised to do so shall be treated as giving reasonable cause for suspicion of unnecessary suffering caused to, or certain offences committed against, a child, for the purposes of C&YPA 1933 s.40. This likewise gives grounds for a warrant (FCA 1980 s.13). See page 267 for a form of information and warrant.

6. Prohibition on advertising

No advertisement indicating that a person will undertake, or will arrange for, the care and maintenance of a child shall be published unless it truly states that person's name and address (FCA 1980 s.15(1)).

The Secretary of State may make Regulations prohibiting parents and guardians from publishing or causing to be published any advertisement indicating that foster parents are sought for a child (FCA 1980 s.15(2)).

The Secretary of State may also make Regulations that prohibit:

   (a) a member of a class of persons specified in the Regulations, or

(b) a person other than a person specified in the Regulations, or other than a member of a class of persons so specified,

from publishing or causing to be published any advertisement indicating that he is willing to undertake, or arrange for, the care and maintenance of a child. Regulations made under this section may make different provisions for different cases or classes of cases and may exclude specified cases or classes of case (FCA 1980 s.15(3) and (4)).

At April 1987, no Regulations have been made.

7. Offences under the Act

A person is guilty of an offence under FCA 1980 if:

(a) being required to give any notice or information, he:

    (i) fails to give the notice within the specified time limit, or

    (ii) fails to give the information within a reasonable time, or

    (iii) knowingly makes, or causes or procures another person to make, any false or misleading statement in the notice or information; or

(b) he refuses to allow:

    (i) the visiting of any foster child by a duly authorised officer of the local authority, or

    (ii) the inspection of any premises under s.8; or

(c) he maintains a foster child in contravention of s.7; or

(d) he fails to comply with a requirement imposed by a local authority under this Act or keeps any foster child in any premises in contravention of a prohibition so imposed; or

(e) he refuses to comply with an order under this Act for the removal of any child or obstructs any person in the execution of such an order; or

(f) he wilfully obstructs a person entitled to enter any premises by virtue of a warrant under s.13(1); or

(g) he causes to be published or knowingly publishes any advertisement in contravention of s.15 or of any Regulations made under that section.

A person guilty of an offence is liable on summary conviction to a fine not exceeding Level 5 on the standard scale and/or to a term of imprisonment not exceeding 6 months.

A person who lives in or on premises in which a person who is disqualified from keeping foster children lives or works and who is, therefore, himself disqualified from keeping them, is not guilty of an offence of maintaining a child in contravention of s.7 if he proves that he did not know and has no reasonable ground for believing, that a person living or employed in the premises in which he lives was a person who was disqualified for keeping foster children under s.7.

Proceedings may be instituted by a local authority, and where the offence is concerned with a failure to give a notice within a specified time, the proceedings may be brought at any time within six months from the date when evidence of the offence came to the knowledge of the authority, notwithstanding the provisions of s.127(1) MCA 1980 (which lays down time limits for proceedings and generally restricts the laying of informations to six months from the date of the offence) (FCA 1980 s.16).

For cases on the interpretation of the expression 'obstructs' see page 190.

8. Extension of the Act to other children

If a child below the upper limit of compulsory school age resides in a school within the meaning of EA 1944 which is not maintained by a local education authority, during school holidays for a period in excess of two weeks, the provisions of FCA 1980 apply in relation to him despite s.2(2) (see page 200), but subject to the following modifications:

(a) s.5(1)-(4) (notifications to be given to local authority by person maintaining or proposing to maintain a foster child); s.6 (notifications to authority by a person ceasing to maintain a foster child); s.9 (local authority power to impose requirements); s.10 (power of a local authority to impose prohibitions); and s.18 (extension of Act to children over compulsory school age) shall not apply, but

(b) the person undertaking the care and the maintenance of children in the school during school holidays shall give written notice to the local authority that children to whom this Act applies will reside in the school during those holidays.

Any notice given under paragraph (b) above shall be given not less than two weeks before the Act shall apply to the children, and it must state the estimated number of children to whom the Act will apply (FCA 1980 s.17(1) and (2)).

A local authority may exempt any person from the duty of giving such notices. Any exemption given may be for a specified period or indefinitely and it may be revoked at any time by notice in writing (FCA 1980 s.17(3)).

The provisions of the Act apply in relation to a foster child who attains the upper limit of compulsory school age until:

(a) he would, apart from that limit, have ceased to be a foster child; or

(b) he reaches the age of eighteen; or

(c) he lives elsewhere than with the person with whom he was living when he attained the said limit,

whichever event comes first (FCA 1980 s.18).

9. Life assurance

For the purposes of the Life Assurances Act 1774 a person who maintains a foster child for reward is to be regarded as a person who has no interest in the life of the child (FCA 1980 s.19).

Chapter 28

Children's homes

Local authorities have a responsibility in relation to children's homes to which the Children's Homes Act 1982 apply. The statute provides for the registration, inspection and conduct of those homes.

The Act applies to any home or other institution providing accommodation and maintenance wholly or mainly for children other than:

(a) community homes provided under CCA 1980 s.32;

(b) voluntary homes as defined by CCA 1980 s.56;

(c) homes registered under NHA 1975 or Part I of Schedule 4 to HASSASSA 1983;

(d) any health service hospital within the meaning of NHSA 1977 and any accommodation provided by a local authority and used as a hospital by or on behalf of the Secretary of State;

(e) homes and other premises managed by a government department or provided by a local authority; and

(f) any school (other than an independent school providing accommodation for fifty children or less and not for the time being approved by the Secretary of State under EA 1981 s.11(3)(a)) within the meaning of EA 1944

(CHA 1982 s.1 as amended by HASSASSA 1983 Sched.4 Pt II para 4. NB: no date has yet been appointed for the commencement of s.1).

1. Prohibition on unregistered homes

Local authorities may not place children in their care in any children's home or allow any child to remain in any children's home unless it is registered under the Act (a 'registered children's home'). Any person who carries on a children's home which is not registered but in which are accommodated one or more children in the care of a local authority, commits an offence and is liable on summary conviction to a fine not exceeding Level 5 on the standard scale (CHA 1982 s.2. NB: no date has yet been appointed for the commencement of this section).

2. Registration of homes

(a) Application

An application for registration of a children's home must be made by the person carrying on, or intending to carry on, the home, and shall be made to the local authority for the area in which the home is, or is to be, situated. Applications must be made in the prescribed manner and must be accompanied by such particulars as may be prescribed and such reasonable fee as the local authority may determine.

If a local authority are satisfied that a children's home in respect of which an application for registration has been made will comply with such requirements as may be prescribed and with such other requirements as appear to the authority to be appropriate, they shall grant the application either unconditionally or subject to conditions imposed under s.4 of the Act. The local authority shall also give to the applicant notice that the home has been registered by the authority under the Act from such date as may be specified in the notice. If the authority is not so satisfied it must refuse the application.

If an application has not been granted or refused by a local authority within the period of twelve months beginning with the date when it was served on them it shall be deemed to have been refused, and the applicant shall be deemed to have been notified of the refusal at the end of that period.

A school registered under s.1(3) shall not cease to be a children's home by reason only of a subsequent change in the number of children for whom it provides accommodation.

(CHA 1982 s.3 as amended by HASSASSA 1983 Sched.10 Pt.1. NB: no date has yet been appointed for the commencement of this section).

(b) The imposition of conditions

A local authority may impose such conditions relating to the conduct of the home as they think fit when granting an application for registration under the Act. From time to time the authority may vary any condition in force or impose any additional condition, either on the application of the person carrying on the home or without such application.

The person carrying on the home is guilty of an offence if any condition imposed or varied under this section is not complied with. On summary conviction such a person will be liable to a fine not exceeding Level 4 on the standard scale. (CHA 1982 s.4 as amended by HASSASSA 1983 Sched.4 Pt.II para.45. NB: No date has yet been appointed for the commencement of this section).

(c) Review of registrations

Local authorities who have registered a children's home under the Act must review the registration at the end of the period of twelve months beginning with the date of registration and annually thereafter. The purpose of the review is to determine whether the registration should continue in force or be cancelled under s.6(2). If the local authority is satisfied that the home is being carried on in accordance with the relevant requirements they shall determine that the registration of the home should continue in force. The authority gives notice of their determination to the person carrying on the home, and the notice must require him to pay such reasonable fee as the authority may determine in respect of carrying out the annual review. It is a condition of the home's continued registration that the fee is so paid before the expiry of the period of twenty-eight days beginning with the date on which the notice is received by the person carrying on the home.

'The relevant requirements' means any requirements of the Act and of any Regulations made under s.8 and any conditions imposed under the provisions of s.4.

(CHA 1982 s.5. NB: No date has yet been appointed for this section to come into force.)

(d) Cancellation of registrations

The person carrying on a registered home may at any time make an application for the cancellation by the responsible authority of the registration of the home. The application must be made in such manner and include such particulars as may be prescribed. If the responsible authority are satisfied either that no child in the care of a local authority is for the time being accommodated in the home, or, in the case of a school registered under s.1(3) that it is no longer a school to which the provision applies, the authority shall give to the person carrying on the home notice that the registration of the home has been cancelled by the authority as from the date of the notice.

If on any annual review conducted under s.5, or at any other time, it appears to the responsible authority that a registered home is being carried on otherwise than in accordance with the relevant requirements, they may determine that the registration of the home should be cancelled. Similarly, the responsible authority may at any time determine that the registration of a home should be cancelled on the ground that the person carrying on the home has been convicted of an offence under this Act or any Regulations made under s.8, or on the ground that any other person has been convicted of such an offence in relation to the home.

'Relevant requirements' has the same meaning as in s.5, see above.

(CHA 1982 s.6 as amended by HASSASSA 1983 Sched.10 Pt.I. NB: no date has yet been appointed for the commencement of this section.)

(e) Registration procedures

Where a person applies for registration of a children's home and the local authority propose to grant the application, they shall give him written notice of their proposal and of the conditions subject to which they propose to grant the application. However, the authority need not give notice of such a proposal if they propose to grant it subject only to conditions which the applicant specified in his application, or subject only to conditions which the authority and the applicant have subsequently agreed.

An authority must give notice to an applicant of any proposal to refuse his application, and of any proposal to cancel the registration, or to vary any condition in force in respect of the home, or to impose any additional condition.

Any notice under these provisions must include a statement of the authority's reasons for their proposal.

(CHA 1982 s.6A as amended by HASSASSA 1983 Sched.4 Pt.II para.46. This section is in force)

A notice under s.6A shall state that within 14 days of the service of the notice, any person on whom it is served may require the local authority to give him the opportunity to make representations to them concerning the matter. The requirement must be made in writing. The local authority must not then determine the matter until:

    (i)   any person on whom the notice was served has made representations to them concerning the matter; or

   (ii) the period during which any person could have required the authority to give him an opportunity to make representations has elapsed without their being required to give such an opportunity; or

  (iii) the conditions specified in subs.(3) are satisfied, ie:

- that a person on whom the notice was served has required the local authority to give him an opportunity to make representations to them concerning the matter;

- that the local authority have allowed him a reasonable period to make his representations; and

- that he has failed to make them within that period.

A person who wishes to make representations under this section may choose whether to make them orally or in writing. If he informs the local authority that he wishes to make his representations orally, the local authority shall give him the opportunity of appearing before and of being heard by a committee or sub-committee of the local authority (CHA 1982 s.6B as amended by HASSASSA 1983 Sched.4 Pt.II para. 46. This section is in force)

If the local authority decides to adopt the proposal, they shall serve notice of their decision, in writing, on any person on whom they were required to serve notice of the proposal. A notice served under this section must be accompanied by a note explaining the right of appeal under s.6D.

A decision of a local authority, other than a decision to grant an application for registration subject only to such conditions as are mentioned in s.6A(2) or to refuse an application for registration, shall not take effect until the expiration of the period of 28 days from the date of the service of the notice if no appeal is brought. In any case in which an appeal is brought the decision shall not take effect until the appeal is determined or abandoned (CHA 1982 s.6C as amended by HASSASSA 1983 Sched.4 Pt.II para.46. This section is in force).

(f) Appeals

An appeal against a decision of a local authority under this Act shall lie to a Registered Homes Tribunal. An appeal shall be brought by notice in writing given to the local authority within 28 days of the date on which the notice of decision was served.

On hearing an appeal the Tribunal has power to confirm the local authority's decision or to direct that it shall have no effect. In addition, the Tribunal has the power to:

(i) vary any condition for the time being in force in respect of the home to which the appeal relates;

(ii) direct that any such condition shall cease to have effect; or

(iii) direct that any such condition as it thinks fit shall have effect in respect of the home.

A local authority is under a duty to comply with any directions given by a Tribunal under this section. (CHA 1982 s.6D as amended by HASSASSA 1983 Sched.4 Pt.II para.46. This section is in force.)

(g) Prohibition on further applications

Generally, where an application for the registration of a home is refused, no further application for the registration of the home may be made within a period of six months beginning with the date when the applicant is notified of the refusal. However, where an appeal against the refusal has been determined or abandoned the reference to the date on which the applicant is notified of the refusal shall be treated as if it were a reference to the date on which the appeal was abandoned or determined.

Where the registration of a home is cancelled, no application for the registration of the home shall be made within the period of six months beginning with the date of cancellation except where an appeal is brought against such cancellation, in which case the six month period begins on the date on which the appeal is determined or abandoned (CHA 1982 s.6E as amended by HASSASSA 1983 Sched.4 Pt.II para 46. This section is in force.)

3. Regulations relating to registered homes

The Secretary of State may make Regulations as to the registration of children's homes, the conduct of registered homes and for securing the welfare of the children in registered homes. In particular, Regulations made under this section may:

(a) make provision as to the carrying out of annual reviews under s.5;

(b) impose requirements as to the accommodation, staff and equipment to be provided in registered homes and as to the arrangements for medical (including psychiatric) and dental care which are to be made for protecting the health of children in such homes;

(c) make provisions for children accommodated in registered homes to receive a religious upbringing appropriate to the religious persuasion to which they belong;

(d) authorise the responsible authority to limit the number of children who may be accommodated in any particular registered home;

(e) impose requirements as to the keeping of records and giving of notices in respect of such children; and

(f) require notice to be given to the responsible authority of any change of the person carrying on a registered home or of the premises used by such a home.

The Regulations may make different provisions for different cases.

Any Regulations made may provide that a contravention or failure to comply with any specified provision of the Regulations shall be an offence. Any person guilty of such an offence shall be liable on summary conviction to a fine not exceeding Level 4 on the standard scale. (CHA 1982 s.8 as amended by CJA 1982 ss.37 and 46. NB: no date has yet been appointed for the commencement of this section).

4. Inspection of homes

Any person who has been authorised by a local authority to inspect registered homes may enter and inspect them at all reasonable times. The powers granted by this section include the power to enter and inspect not only registered homes but also any premises which the officer has reasonable cause to believe are being used as part of such a home. The officer may inspect any child accommodated in the home and require the production of, and inspect, any records required to be kept in accordance with any regulations made under s.8. A person who proposes to exercise powers granted under this section must produce some authenticated documentation of his authority if he is required to do so.

If any person obstructs an officer of the local authority in the execution of his powers, without reasonable cause, he is guilty of an offence and liable on summary conviction to a fine not exceeding Level 4 on the standard scale.

Any refusal to allow an officer duly authorised to enter premises shall be deemed to be a reasonable cause to suspect that a child in the home or premises is being neglected in a manner likely to cause him unnecessary suffering or injury to health, for the purposes of C&YPA 1933 s.40 (issue of search warrants, see page 208).

(CHA 1982 s.9 as amended by CJA 1982 ss.37 and 46. NB: no date has yet been appointed for the commencement of this section).

5. Disqualified persons

Any person who has been convicted of any offence specified in C&YPA 1933 Sched.1 or who has been placed on probation or discharged conditionally or absolutely for any such offence is disqualified from carrying on or being employed in a registered home (CHA 1982 s.10(1)).

The reference to probation and conditional and absolute discharges in the last paragraph is made because, even though such orders are not usually to be regarded as 'convictions', they do nevertheless give rise to a disqualification under this section. No reference has been made to related Scottish law but readers are reminded that convictions recorded under such Statutes also give rise to disqualification for the purposes of the section.

A person who is disqualified by virtue of s.10 may not carry on or be otherwise concerned in the management of, or have any financial interest in, a registered home unless he has:

(a) disclosed to the responsible authority the fact that he has been convicted or otherwise dealt with as mentioned in s.10(1), and

(b) obtained the written consent of that authority.

No disqualified person may be employed in a registered home unless the employer has:

(a) disclosed to the responsible authority that that person has been convicted or otherwise dealt with as mentioned in subs.(1), and

(b) obtained the written consent of that authority.
(CHA s.10(2) and (3)).

Any person who contravenes subs.(2) or (3) commits an offence and is liable on summary conviction to a fine not exceeding Level 5 on the standard scale and/or a term of imprisonment not exceeding six months (CHA 1982 s.10(4) as amended by CJA 1982 ss.37 and 46. NB: no date has yet been fixed for the commencement of s.10).

6. Proceedings under the Act

Proceedings for offences under the Act or any Regulations made under it may be brought by a local authority. If an offence is committed by a body corporate and it is proved that the offence has been committed with the consent or connivance of or to be attributable to any neglect on the part of any director, manager, secretary or other similar officer of the body, or any person who was purporting to act in any such capacity, he as well as the body corporate shall be guilty of the offence and shall be liable to be proceeded against and punished accordingly.

Where a person is charged with an offence under s.2(2) — carrying on an unregistered children's home, or s.4(3) — failing to comply with a condition attached to registration, or Regulations made under s.8, it shall be a defence to prove that he took all reasonable precautions and exercised all due diligence to avoid the commission of the offence by himself or any person under his control (CHA 1982 s.11. NB: no date has yet been fixed for the commencement of this section).

Chapter 29

Nurseries and child-minders

Local authorities have certain duties in relation to nurseries and persons who act as child-minders. They are imposed by the Nurseries and Child-Minders Regulation Act 1948 the purpose of which is to ensure the well-being of children in the care of day nurseries or child-minders.

1. Registration

Every local social services authority is under a duty to keep registers:

(a) of premises in their area (other than premises wholly or mainly used as private dwellings) where children are received to be looked after for the day or part or parts thereof, for a duration, or an aggregate duration, of two hours or for any longer period not exceeding six days; and

(b) of persons in their area who for reward receive into their homes children under the age of five to be looked after as aforesaid.

The registers must be open to inspection at all reasonable times (N&CMRA 1948 s.1(1)).

Persons receiving or proposing to receive children as described above may apply to the local social services authority for registration. On receipt of any application the local social services authority must register the premises to which or person to whom the application relates unless:

(a) they are satisfied that any person employed or proposed to be employed in looking after children at the premises is not fit to look after children; or

(b) where the premises were not at the commencement of the Act in use for the reception of children as mentioned in subs.(1)(a), they are satisfied that the premises are not fit to be used for that purpose (whether because of the condition of the premises or of the equipment in the premises or for any reason connected with the situation, construction or size of the premises or with other persons in the premises),

in which cases the authority may, by order, refuse to register the premises; or

(c) they are satisfied that the person applying for registration or any person employed or proposed to be employed by him in looking after children, is not a fit person to look after children; or

(d) they are satisfied that the premises in which the children are received or proposed to be received are not fit to be used for that purpose (whether because of their condition or the condition of any equipment in the premises or for any reason connected with the situation, construction or size of the premises or with other persons in the premises),

in which cases the authority may, by order, refuse to register the applicant (N&CMRA 1948 s.1(2) and (3) as amended by LGA 1972 Sched.23 para.4(1) and HS&PHA 1968, s.60(1), (2), (5) and (6)).

Where premises that are wholly or mainly used as private dwellings are also used for the purpose of receiving and looking after children, they are not to be registered as nurseries, but whichever of the occupants carries on the business of looking after children on those premises must be registered as a child-minder, if the children received are under five. Whether premises are 'mainly used as a private dwelling house' is a matter of fact for a court to determine. The word 'mainly' is to be given its ordinary meaning, ie 'for the most part; chiefly; principally' (*Miller* v *Ottilie (Owners)* (1944)). Sleeping and eating upon premises are facts that are residential in nature but they cannot be said to prove conclusively that a house is a dwelling house (*Macmillan and Co Ltd* v *Rees* (1946)).

An application for registration of premises must contain a statement of each person employed or to be employed in the premises in looking after children, and of each person who has attained the age of sixteen and is normally resident on the premises (HS&PHA 1968 s.60(7)).

A local social services authority that intends to make an order refusing registration must give notice of their intention to the applicant or to the occupier of the premises not less than fourteen days before making the order of refusal. Every notice served must contain a statement of the grounds on which the authority intends to make the order, and must advise the person to whom it is sent that he may within fourteen days after receipt of the notice inform the authority in writing of his desire to show cause why the order should not be made. If the person on whom the notice is served gives such an indication, the authority must give him the opportunity, in person or by a representative, to show cause why an order should not be made before they make the proposed order (N&CMRA 1948 s.6(1) and (2)).

There is a provision for persons who are aggrieved by decisions or the local social services authorities to appeal to the magistrates' court (see page 225).

2. Power to impose requirements on registration

The local social services authority may make orders as to the maximum number of children who may be received into nurseries and as to the maximum number of children that a child-minder may receive into his home having regard to the number of any other children who may from time to time be in the home (N&CMRA 1948 s.2(1) and (2)).

Orders may also be made by the local social services authority in relation to any premises or person registered under the Act requiring precautions to be taken against the exposure of the children on the premises to infectious diseases (N&CMRA 1948 s.2(3)).

Requirements may also be imposed by order of the local social services authority in relation to any premises registered as a nursery with the object of securing:

(a) that a person with such qualifications as may be specified by the authority shall be in charge of the premises and of the persons employed there;

(b) that the premises shall be adequately staffed, both as respects the number and as respects the qualifications and experience of the persons employed, and adequately equipped;

(c) in the case of premises that were used as a nursery at the date of the commencement of the Act, that such repairs, alterations or additions as may be specified in the order be carried out or made;

(d) that the premises be kept safe and adequately maintained and the equipment be adequately maintained;

(e) that there shall be adequate arrangements for feeding the children received and for providing them with suitable diets;

(f) that the children received are under medical supervision; and

    (g) that records, containing such particulars as the authority
        may specify, be kept in relation to the children received at
        the premises
(N&CMRA 1948 s.2(4)).

An order requiring repairs, alterations or additions to premises that
were in use as a nursery at the time the Act came into force may be
made on registration, or at any time within one month thereafter.
Other orders may be made on registration or at any subsequent time
(N&CMRA 1948 s.2(5)). Authorities have the power to vary or
revoke requirements contained in orders made under s.2 by means
of a subsequent order (N&CMRA 1948 s.2(6)).

No requirements of a type mentioned in paragraphs (a) to (c) above
may require anything to be done in the case of premises that were in
use as a nursery at the time the Act came into force before the
expiration of a reasonable time from the commencement of the Act
(N&CMRA 1948 s.2(7)).

Requirements imposed under s.2 must be specified in the certificate
of registration issued in accordance with s.3. The time within which
the requirement is to be fulfilled should be stated. In any case in
which an applicant or occupier considers that the time allowed for
compliance with any requirement is too short he may inform the
authority of that fact in writing in accordance with the appeal
procedures contained in s.6 (see page 225).

3. Registration certificates

The certificates of a registration granted under s.1 must be issued by
the authority granting them. Such certificates should specify the
situation of the premises to which, or the name and address of the
person to whom, the registration relates, and any requirements
imposed under s.2. If any changes occur which affect the particulars
stated in the certificate, the local social services authority should
issue an amended certificate. An authority may issue a copy of a
registration certificate, on payment of such reasonable fee as they
may determine, if satisfied that any certificate has been lost or
destroyed (N&CMRA 1948 s.3).

The address of any registered child-minder will ordinarily be the
address at which children are received by him.

The only change in circumstances that any person is required to
notify to the local social services authority under the Act is the
acquisition of a new home by a registered child-minder (s.4(3)). The
Act does not contain any provision requiring a certificate holder to
deliver it up on cancellation or registration under s.5. It is likely,

therefore, that most changes in circumstances that might give rise to the issue of amended certificates of registration will be those discovered by authorised officers on the exercise of their powers of entry and inspection (see page 226).

4. Cancellation of registration

Social services authorities may, by order, cancel any registration certificate that they have issued in respect of any premises or any person who is a registered child-minder in any case in which:

(a) there has been a contravention of, or non-compliance with, any requirement imposed under s.2; or

(b) it appears to the authority that circumstances exist which would justify a refusal to register the premises or the person in question under the provisions of s.1(3) or (4).

However, the registration of premises shall not be cancelled, in a case in which there has been a requirement to carry out repairs or to make alterations or additions in accordance with s.2(4)(c), on the ground that the premises are not fit to be used for the reception of children, if the time limit referred to in s.2(7) for complying with the requirement has not expired, and it is shown that the condition of the premises is due to repairs not having been carried out or the alteration or additions not having been made. (N&CMRA 1948 s.5).

5. Appeals

Not later than fourteen days before any order is made refusing an application for registration, cancelling any registration or imposing any requirement under s.2, the local social services authority must send to the applicant, to the registered person or to the occupier of the registered premises, notice of their intention to make the order. Any such notice must set out the grounds on which the authority intends to make the order. It must also state that if, within fourteen days of the receipt of the notice, the applicant, registered person or occupier informs the authority in writing of his desire to show cause, in person or by representative, why the order should not be made, the authority must give him the opportunity to do so before making the order (N&CMRA 1948 s.6(1) and (2)).

If a local social services authority, after giving the applicant, registered person or the occupier of registered premises the opportunity to show cause why the order should not be made, decides to proceed to make the order, they shall make the order and send a copy of it to that person (N&CMRA 1948 s.6(3)).

Any person who is aggrieved by an order made under the provisions of the Act may appeal to a magistrates' court having jurisdiction in the place where the premises are situated or where the applicant resides: Any order of cancellation shall not take effect until the time allowed for appeal has expired or if an appeal has been lodged, until such appeal has been determined (N&CMRA 1948 s.6(4)).

Notices and orders that are required to be sent under the provisions of the Act may be sent by registered post (or by personal service) (N&CMRA 1948 s.6(6)).

See page 207 for authorities on the interpretation of the expression 'person aggrieved'.

6. Inspection of premises

Persons who have been authorised for that purpose by a local social services authority may enter any premises in the area of the authority which are used for the reception of children as mentioned in s.1(1)(a), at all reasonable times, and inspect them and the children received therein, the arrangements for their welfare and any records relating to them kept in accordance with the Act. Similarly, authorised persons may enter the homes of registered child-minders at all reasonable times and may inspect them and any children received in them as mentioned in s.1(1)(b), the arrangements for their welfare and any records relating to them and kept in accordance with the Act (N&CMRA 1948 s.7(1)).

If any authorised person has reasonable cause to believe that children are being received in a person's home or in any other premises in contravention of s.4 of the Act, he may apply to a justice of the peace and if the justice is satisfied on a written information confirmed on oath or affirmation, that there is reasonable cause to believe that children are being so received, he may grant a warrant authorising the applicant to enter the home or other premises and carry out an inspection. If required to do so, a person proposing to exercise any power of entry or inspection shall produce some duly authenticated document confirming his authority to exercise the power (N&CMRA 1948 s.7(2) and (3)).

It is an offence for any person to obstruct the exercise of any power of entry and inspection granted under this Act. The offence is triable summarily and punishable by a fine not exceeding Level 2 on the standard scale (N&CMRA 1948 s.7(4)).

7. Exempt institutions

Certain institutions are exempt from the provisions of the Act. In particular, hospitals and other homes and institutions mentioned in FCA 1980 s.2 are exempt. Nothing in the Act applies to the reception of children in any school even though they may have been received to be looked after and not for educational purposes N&CMRA 1948 s.8(1) and (2) as amended by FCA 1980 Sched.2 para 1.

The provisions of the Act do not apply to the reception of children in a nursery school which is maintained or assisted by a local education authority or one in respect of which payments are made by the Minister of Education under EA 1944 s.100. Nor do they apply to the reception of children in any play centre maintained or assisted by a local education authority under EA 1944 s.53 (N&CMRA 1948 s.8(3) as amended by LGA 1958 Sched.8 para.30).

Note: References to the corresponding provisions in the Education (Scotland) Act 1946 have been omitted from the text.

'Hospital' has the same meaning as in NHSA 1977 s.128(1). 'School', except in the expression 'nursery school', means an institution which has the sole or main purpose of providing education for children of compulsory school age (N&CMRA 1948 s.13(2)).

Appendix A

Forms

Contents

Legal Aid

Appeal

Local Authorities

Care proceedings

1. Notice of care proceedings

IN . . . .

Petty Sessional Division of . . . .

To the Clerk of the Juvenile Court sitting at . . . .

TAKE NOTICE that . . . . of . . . .
(hereinafter called the relevant infant) who is believed to be a [child] [young person], is to be brought before the Court under section 1 of the Children and Young Persons Act 1969 on the grounds hereinafter mentioned;

It is alleged that the following condition is satisfied with respect to the relevant infant, that is to say (*State grounds briefly, referring to s. 1*(2)(*a*) *to* (*f*)).

It is further alleged that the relevant infant is in need of care or control which he is unlikely to receive unless an order is made under the said section 1;

In pursuance of Rule 14 of the Magistrates' Courts (Children and Young Persons) Rules 1970 a copy of this notice is being sent to each of the following persons, that is to say, to: ....

Dated the .... day of ...., 19.....

.... (on behalf of the Council of the County

of ....)

(a constable)

(an authorised person)

2. Authority to remove to a place of safety

IN...........................

Petty Sessional Division of...............

.... of ....

(hereinafter called the applicant) has this day applied under section 28(1) of the Children and Young Persons Act 1969 for authority to detain and take to a place of safety .... of ....

a child (young person) hereinafter called the relevant infant;

And I, the undersigned justice of the peace, am satisfied that the applicant has reasonable cause to believe (*Specify belief in terms of s.28(1)(a), (b) or (c)*)

and hereby grant the said application;

And the relevant infant may be detained in a place of safety by virtue of this authorisation for a period of ...... days beginning with the date hereof.

Dated the .... day of ...., 19.....

.... Justice of the Peace for ....

3. Interim care order

IN...........................

Before the Juvenile Court sitting at ....

To each and all of the constables of .... and to the council of the county of ....

.... (hereinafter called the relevant infant) who is believed to have been born on the .... day of ...., 19.....,

[was this day] [was on the .... day of ...., 19.....],

brought before the court under section 1 of the Children and Young Persons Act 1969;

or

The Court having made a direction under section 2(9) of the Children and Young Persons Act 1969.................... of....................

.... (hereinafter called the relevant infant) who is believed to have been born on the .... day of ...., 19.....,

[was this day] [was on the .... day of ...., 19.....],

deemed to have been brought before the court under section 1 of the said Act of 1969;

[And the court is not in a position to decide what order, if any, ought to be made under the said section 1];

[And the court has directed that the relevant infant be brought before a Juvenile Court acting for the . . . . petty sessional area];

IT IS HEREBY DIRECTED that the relevant infant be committed for a period of . . . . days to the care of the said council in whose area it appears that [the relevant infant resides] [the circumstances in consequence of which this order is made arose];

IT IS FURTHER ORDERED [subject to the direction hereinafter given] that the said council shall bring the relevant infant before [the Court] [a Juvenile Court acting for the . . . . petty sessional area (hereinafter called the specified court)] on the expiration of this order or at such earlier time as the [specified] court may require;

[By reason [of the relevant infant being under the age of five years] [of the illness of the relevant infant] [of an accident to the relevant infant], it is hereby directed that the relevant infant shall only be brought before the [specified] court as aforesaid if the [specified] court so requires];

And you the said constables are hereby required, unless the relevant infant is forthwith received into the care of a person authorised by, and acting on behalf of, the said council, to deliver the relevant infant, together with this order, into the care of a person authorised and acting as aforesaid.

Dated this . . . . day of . . . . , 19 . . . . .

By order of the Court

Justice of the Peace for . . . .
Clerk of the Court

4. Interim care order: Proceedings in respect of supervision order

IN . . . .
Petty Sessional Division of . . . .

Before the Juvenile Court sitting at . . . .

To each and all of the constables of . . . . and to the council of the county of . . . .

. . . . of . . . . (hereinafter called the relevant infant) who is believed to have been born on the . . . . day of . . . . , 19 . . . . . , [was this day] [was on the . . . . day of . . . . , 19 . . . . . ,] on an application under section 15(1) of the Children and Young Persons Act 1969 brought before the court under [a warrant issued under section 16(2)] [an interim care order made under section 16(3)] of that Act;

[The Court considers that it is likely to exercise its powers under the said section 15(1) to make an order in respect of the relevant infant but seeks information which it considers is unlikely to be obtained unless an interim care order is made];

And the relevant infant [being present] [not being present the Court is satisfied that the relevant infant is under the age of five years/cannot be present by reason of illness/accident];

IT IS HEREBY ORDERED that the relevant infant be committed for a period of .... days to the care of the said council in whose area it appears that [the relevant infant resides] [the circumstances in consequence of which this order is made arose];

IT IS FURTHER ORDERED [subject to the direction hereinafter given] that the said council shall bring the relevant infant before [the Court] [a Juvenile Court acting for the .... petty sessional area (hereinafter called the specified Court)] on the expiration of this order or at such earlier time as the [specified] court may require;

[By reason [of the relevant infant being under the age of five years] [of the illness of the relevant infant] [of an accident to the relevant infant], it is hereby directed that the relevant infant shall only be brought before the [specified] court as aforesaid if the [specified] court so directs];

And you the said constables are hereby required, unless the relevant infant is forthwith received into the care of a person authorised by and acting on behalf of, the said council, to deliver the relevant infant, together with this order, into the care of a person authorised and acting as aforesaid.

Dated this .... day of ...., 19.....

By order of the Court

Justice of the Peace for ....
Clerk of the Court

5. Interim care order following arrest on warrant

IN ....
Petty Sessional Division of ....

To each and all of the constables of .... and to the council of the county of ....

.... of .... (hereinafter called the relevant infant) who is believed to have been born on the .... day of ...., 19....., is detained in pursuance of a warrant issued in pursuance of section [2(4)] [16(2)] of the Children and Young Persons Act 1969;

In pursuance of the said warrant the relevant infant was this day brought before me, the undersigned justice of the peace;

IT IS HEREBY ORDERED that the relevant infant be committed for a period of .... days to the care of the said council in whose area it appears that [the relevant infant resides] [the circumstances in consequence of which this order is made arose];

IT IS FURTHER ORDERED [subject to the direction hereinafter given] that the said council shall bring the relevant infant before [the Court] [a Juvenile Court acting for the .... petty sessional area (hereinafter called the specified court)] on the expiration of this order or at such earlier time as the [specified] court may require;

[By reason [of the relevant infant being under the age of five years] [of the illness of the relevant infant] [of an accident to the relevant infant], it is hereby directed that the relevant infant shall only be brought before the [specified] court as aforesaid if the [specified] court so requires];

And you the said constables are hereby required, unless the relevant infant is forthwith received into the care of a person authorised by and acting on behalf of, the said council, to deliver the relevant infant, together with this order, into the care of a person authorised and acting as aforesaid.

Dated this .... day of ...., 19.....

By order of the Court

Justice of the Peace for ....

Clerk of the Court

6. Interim care order following detention in place of safety

IN ....

Petty Sessional Division of ....

[Before the Court sitting at ....]

To each and all of the constables of .... and to the council of the county of ....

.... of .... (hereinafter called the relevant infant) who is believed to have been born on the .... day of ...., 19...., is detained in pursuance of [section 40 of the Children and Young Persons Act 1933] [section 7 of the Children Act 1958] [section 43 of the Adoption Act 1958] [section 28 of the Children and Young Persons Act 1969];

Application has been duly made to [the Court] [me, the undersigned justice of the peace] for an interim care order in respect of the relevant infant;

And the relevant infant [being present] [not being present, [the Court is] [I am] satisfied that the relevant infant [is under the age of five years] [cannot be present by reason of illness/accident]];

IT IS HEREBY ORDERED that the relevant infant be committed for a period of .... days to the care of the said council in whose area it appears that [the relevant infant resides] [the circumstances in consequence of which this order is made arose];

IT IS FURTHER ORDERED [subject to the direction hereinafter given] that the said council shall bring the relevant infant before [the Court] [a Juvenile Court acting for the .... petty sessional area (hereinafter called the specified court)] on the expiration of this order or at such earlier time as the [specified] court may require;

[By reason [of the relevant infant being under the age of five years] [of the illness of the relevant infant] [of an accident to the relevant infant], it is hereby directed that the relevant infant shall only be brought before the [specified] court as aforesaid if the [specified] court so requires];

And you the said constables are hereby required, unless the relevant infant is forthwith received into the care of a person authorised by, and acting on behalf of, the said council, to deliver the relevant infant, together with this order, into the care of a person authorised and acting as aforesaid.

Dated this . . . . day of . . . ., 19. . . . .

By order of the Court

Justice of the Peace for . . . .
Clerk of the Court

7. Further interim order

IN . . . .
Petty Sessional Division of . . . .

Before the Juvenile Court sitting at . . . .

To each and all the constables of . . . . and to the council of the county of . . . .

. . . . of . . . . (hereinafter called the relevant infant) who is believed to have been born on the . . . . day of . . . ., 19. . . . ., was committed to the care of a local authority by an interim care order made on the . . . . day of . . . ., 19. . . . ., and the said order has not yet expired;

And the relevant infant [being present] [not present, the Court is satisfied that the relevant infant [is under the age of five years] [cannot be present by reason of illness/accident]];

IT IS HEREBY ORDERED that the relevant infant be committed for a period of . . . . days to the care of the said council in whose area it appears that [the relevant infant resides] [the circumstances in consequence of which this order is made arose];

IT IS FURTHER ORDERED [subject to the direction hereinafter given] that the said council shall bring the relevant infant before [the Court] [a Juvenile Court acting for the . . . . petty sessional area (hereinafter called the specified court)] on the expiration of this order or at such earlier time as the [specified] court may require;

[By reason [of the relevant infant being under the age of five years] [of the illness of the relevant infant] [of an accident to the relevant infant], it is hereby directed that the relevant infant shall only be brought before the [specified] court as aforesaid if the [specified] court so requires];

And you the said constables are hereby required, unless the relevant infant is forthwith received into the care of a person authorised by, and acting on behalf of, the said council, to deliver the relevant infant, together with this order, into the care of a person authorised and acting as aforesaid.

Dated this .... day of .... , 19.....

By order of the Court

Justice of the Peace for ....
Clerk of the Court

8. Offence condition finding

IN............................
Petty Sessional Division of ....

Before the Juvenile Court sitting at ....

.... of .... (hereinafter called the relevant infant) who is believed to have been born on the .... day of .... , 19....., [was this day] [was on the .... day of .... , 19.....] brought before the Court under section 1 of the Children and Young Persons Act 1969;

And it was alleged that the following condition was satisfied with respect to the relevant infant, that is to say, that the relevant infant was guilty of [an] offence[s], namely (*State briefly particulars of offence(s)*), ...
....
....
IT IS HEREBY ADJUDGED that the relevant infant is [not] guilty of the said offence[s].

Dated this .... day of .... , 19.....

By order of the Court

Justice of the Peace for ....
Clerk of the Court

9. Care order

IN............................
Petty Sessional Division of ....

Before the Juvenile Court sitting at ....

To each and all the constables of.................. and to the council of the county of ....

.... of .... (hereinafter called the relevant infant) who is believed to have been born on the .... day of .... , 19....., [was this day] [was on the .... day of.......... , 19.....,] brought before the Court under section 1 of the Children and Young Persons Act 1969;

And the Court is satisfied that the following condition is satisfied with respect to the relevant infant, that is to say, (*Specify in the terms of s.1(2) (a) to (f) identifying in the case of para (f) the offence*) ....
....
....
and also that the relevant infant is in need of care or control which the relevant infant is unlikely to receive unless an order under the said section is made in respect of the relevant infant;

IT IS HEREBY ORDERED that the relevant infant be committed to the care of the said council in whose area it appears that the [relevant infant resides] [circumstances in consequence of which this order is made arose, it not appearing that the relevant infant resides in the area of any local authority in England or Wales];

And you, the said constables, are hereby required, unless the relevant infant is forthwith received into the care of a person authorised by, and acting on behalf of, the said council, to deliver the relevant infant, together with this order, into the care of a person authorised and acting as aforesaid.

Dated this .... day of ...., 19.....

By order of the Court

Justice of the Peace for ....
Clerk of the Court

10. Care order made on discharge of a supervision order

IN..............................
Petty Sessional Division of ....

Before the Juvenile Court sitting at ....

To each and all the constables of.................. and to the council of the county of ....

The Juvenile Court sitting at..
on the .... day of ...., 19....., made a supervision order within the meaning of the Children and Young Persons Act 1969 in respect of .... of .... (hereinafter called the supervised person) who is believed to have been born on the .... day of..........., 19.....;

[The said supervision order was varied by an order made by the Juvenile Court sitting at ....
on the .... day of ...., 19.....;]

The said supervision order [as so varied] names the [county] [borough] of .... and the .... petty sessional area as the areas in which it appears the supervised person resides or will reside and places the supervised person under the supervision of [the council of the said county/borough] [a probation officer appointed for or assigned to the said petty sessional area] (hereinafter called the supervisor) and unless previously discharged, ceases to have effect on........................ (*Specify date*)

[The supervised person] [...................... a [parent] [guardian] of the supervised person on the supervised person's behalf] [the supervisor] has applied for the discharge of the said supervision order;

And the Court is satisfied that the supervised person is unlikely to receive the care and control that he needs unless this order is made;

IT IS HEREBY ORDERED that the said supervision order be discharged but that the supervised person be committed to the care of the council first above mentioned in whose area it appears that [the supervised person resides] [circumstances in consequence of which this order is made arose, it not appearing that the supervised person resides in the area of any local authority in England or Wales];

And you, the said constables, are hereby required, unless the supervised person is forthwith received into the care of a person authorised by, and acting on behalf of, the council first above mentioned, to deliver the supervised person, together with this order, into the care of a person authorised and acting as aforesaid.

Dated this .... day of ...., 19.....

By order of the Court

Justice of the Peace for ....
Clerk of the Court

11. Order extending or discharging care order

IN..............................
Petty Sessional Division of ....

Before the Juvenile Court sitting at ....

The Juvenile Court sitting at...
on the .... day of ...., 19....., made a care order in respect of .... of ....
(hereinafter called the relevant infant) who is believed to have been born on the .... day of ...., 19.....;

The said order commits the relevant infant to the care of the council of the county of.................;

[The said order, unless extended or discharged, would, in pursuance of section 20(3)(b) of the Children and Young Persons Act 1969, cease to have effect when the relevant infant attains the age of 18 years;

The relevant infant is accommodated in [a community home] [a home provided by the Secretary of State] and it appears to the Court that by reason of the relevant infant's mental condition or behaviour it is in the [relevant infant's] [public] interest for the relevant infant to be so accommodated after attaining the age of 18 years;]

[The said council] [the relevant infant] [................... a parent or guardian of the relevant infant on the relevant infant's behalf] has applied for the [extension] [discharge] of the said order;

IT IS HEREBY ORDERED that the said order shall [continue in force until the relevant infant attains the age of 19 years] [be discharged].

Dated this . . . . day of . . . ., 19 . . . . .

By order of the Court

> Justice of the Peace for . . . .
> Clerk of the Court

12. Supervision order

IN . . . .

Petty Sessional Division of . . . .

Before the Juvenile Court sitting at . . . .

. . . . of . . . . (hereinafter called the relevant infant) who is believed to have been born on the . . . . day of . . . ., 19 . . . ., [was this day] [was on the . . . . day of . . . ., 19 . . . . .,] brought before the Court under section 1 of the Children and Young Persons Act 1969;

And the Court is satisfied that the following condition is satisfied with respect to the relevant infant, that is to say, (*Specify in the terms of s. 1(2)(a) to (f) identifying, in the case of para. (f), the offence*) . . . .
. . . .
and also that the relevant infant is in need of care or control which the relevant infant is unlikely to receive unless an order under the said section is made in respect of the relevant infant;

It appears to the Court that the relevant infant [resides] [will reside] in the [county] [county borough] of . . . . and in the petty sessional area of . . . . ;

IT IS ORDERED that the infant is placed under the supervision of [the council of [the said county/district] [the non-metropolitan county/county district of . . . .] who have agreed to be designated as the supervisor] [a probation officer appointed for or assigned to the said petty sessions area] [for the period of . . . . beginning with the date of this order] [until the infant attains the age of eighteen years].

The infant shall comply, so long as the order is in force, with the requirements specified in the Schedule hereto.

Dated this . . . . day of . . . ., 19 . . . . .

By order of the Court

> Justice of the Peace for . . . .
> Clerk of the Court

Schedule

Requirements imposed by the court should be listed in the terms of C&YPA 1969 s.12 (as amended) or Rule 28 of the MCCR 1970.

13. Supervision order made on discharge of care order

IN . . . .
Petty Sessional Division of . . . .

Before the Juvenile Court sitting at . . . . (Code) . . . . .

Date: . . . .

Infant: . . . .   Age . . . . years

Address: . . . .

The . . . . Juvenile Court on . . . . made a care order committing the infant to the care of the council of the [non-metropolitan county] [metropolitan district] of . . . .

[The infant] [. . . . a parent/guardian of the infant on his behalf] [the said council] has applied for the discharge of the said order.

It appears to the court that the infant [resides] [will reside] in the non-metropolitan county/metropolitan district of . . . . and in the . . . . petty sessions area.

[It appears to the court that the infant is in need of care and control and the court is satisfied he will receive that care and control through the making of a supervision order.]

The care order is discharged and the infant is placed under the supervision of [the council of [the said county/district] [the non-metropolitan county/metropolitan district of . . . .] who have agreed to be designated as the supervisor] [a probation officer appointed for or assigned to the petty sessions area] [for the period of . . . . beginning with the date of this order] [until the infant attains the age of eighteen years]. [And the infant shall comply, so long as this order is in force, with the requirement(s) specified in the Schedule hereto.]

By order of the Court

Justice of the Peace for . . . .
Clerk of the Court

Schedule

Requirements imposed by the court should be listed in the terms of C&YPA 1969 s.12 (as amended) or Rule 28 of the MCCR 1970.

14. Order varying or discharging supervision order

IN . . . .
Before the [Juvenile] [Magistrates'] Court sitting at . . . .

The Juvenile Court sitting at . . . . on the
. . . . day of . . . . , 19 . . . . . , made a supervision order within
the meaning of the Children and Young Persons Act 1969 in respect of
. . . . of . . . . (hereinafter
called the supervised person) who is believed to have been born on the
. . . . day of . . . . , 19 . . . . . ;

[The said supervision order was varied by an order made by the Juvenile
Court sitting at . . . . on the . . . . day of
. . . . , 19 . . . . . ,];

The said supervision order [as so varied] names the [county] [county
borough] of . . . . and the . . . .
petty sessional area as the areas in which it appears the supervised person
resides or will reside and places the supervised person under the supervision
of [the council of the said [county] [county borough]] [the council of the
[county] [county borough] of . . . .] [a probation officer
appointed for, or assigned to, the said petty sessional area] and, unless
previously discharged, ceases to have effect on the . . . .
day of . . . . , 19 . . . . .]

The said supervision order [as so varied] in pursuance of sections 12 and
18(2)(b) of the said Act of 1969 contains certain requirements including the
following requirements (*Specify requirements to be varied*) . . . .
. . . .

[The supervised person] [. . . . a [parent] [guardian]
of the supervised person on behalf of the supervised person] [the supervisor]
has applied for the [variation] [discharge] of the said supervision order;

[The supervisor has referred to the Court a report from a medical
practitioner in pursuance of section 15(5) of the said Act of 1969 proposing
that a mental health treatment requirement should be [cancelled] [varied]
for the following reasons (*Specify in the terms of s.15(5)*) . . . .
. . . .

IT IS HEREBY ORDERED that the said supervision order [varied as aforesaid]
shall be [discharged] [varied] [further varied] as follows:

. . . .
. . . .

Dated . . . . day of . . . . , 19 . . . . .

By order of the Court

Justice of the Peace for . . . .

Clerk of the Court

15. Order of recognizance to keep the peace etc.

IN THE COUNTY OF ....
Petty Sessional Division of ....

Before the Juvenile Court sitting at ....

.... of ...., a young person who is believed to have been born on ...., [was this day] [was on the .... day of ...., 19.....,] brought before the Court under section 1 of the Children and Young Persons Act 1969;

And the Court is satisfied that the following condition is satisfied with respect to the said young person, that is to say, he is guilty of an offence, namely .... and also that he is in need of care or control which he is unlikely to receive unless an order under the said section is made in respect of him.

IT IS ORDERED that the said young person, who has consented to the making of this order, do forthwith enter into a recognizance in the sum of .... to [keep the peace] [and] [be of good behaviour] for a period of .... from the date of this order.

Dated .... day of ...., 19.....

By order of the Court

Justice of the Peace for ....
Clerk of the Court

16. Remittal order

IN ....
Petty Sessional Division of ....

Before the Juvenile Court sitting at ....

.... of .... (hereinafter called the relevant infant) who is believed to have been born on the .... day of ...., 19....., [was this day] [was on the .... day of ...., 19.....,] brought before the Court under section 1 of the Children and Young Persons Act 1969;

And it was alleged that the following condition was satisfied with respect to the relevant infant, that is to say, (*Specify in the terms of s.1(2)(a) to (f) identifying in the case of para. (f), the offence*) ....
....

[IT IS HEREBY ADJUDGED that the relevant infant is guilty of the said offence]; It appearing to the Court that the relevant infant resides in the [county] [county borough] of .... and in the ....
.... petty sessional area, IT IS HEREBY DIRECTED that the relevant infant be brought before a Juvenile Court acting for that petty sessional area;

[Accordingly, it shall be the duty of the council of the said [county] [county borough] to give effect within twenty-one days to the aforesaid direction] (*Omit this paragraph in cases where an interim order is made*)

Dated . . . . day of . . . . , 19 . . . . .

By order of the Court

Justice of the Peace for . . . .
Clerk of the Court

17. Notice of appointment of guardian ad litem

. . . . Magistrates' Court

Date: . . . .

Name of child or young person: . . . .

(hereinafter called the infant)

Address: . . . .

. . . .

TAKE NOTICE that . . . .

of . . . .

has been appointed guardian *ad litem* of the above-named infant in proceedings which are in the list for hearing at this Juvenile Court on (*date*) . . . . at (*time*) . . . .

In pursuance of rule 14A(5) of the Magistrates' Courts (Children and Young Persons) Rules 1970 a copy of this notice is being sent to each of the following persons:

Clerk of the Court

Address of Court: . . . .

Telephone number: . . . .

18. Notice of order depriving parent or guardian of right to represent child or young person

. . . . Magistrates' Court

Date: . . . .

Name: . . . .

Address: . . . .

. . . .

TAKE NOTICE that it appears to the Court that in the proceedings concerning the child/young person named . . . .

(hereinafter called the infant) of whom you are a parent/guardian, which are in the list for hearing at this Juvenile Court on (*date*) . . . .

at (*time*) . . . . there is or may be a conflict on relevant matters between your interests and those of the said infant. Accordingly the Court has ordered that in relation to the proceedings you are not to be treated as representing the infant or as otherwise authorised to act on the infant's behalf.

Clerk of the Court

Address of the Court: ....

Telephone number:...

19. Hospital order – care proceedings

IN..............................

Petty Sessional Division of ....

Before the Juvenile Court sitting at ....

.... of .... (hereinafter called the relevant infant) who is believed to have been born on the .... day of ...., 19....., was this day [was on the .... day of ...., 19.....,] brought before the Court under section 1 of the Children and Young Persons Act 1969.

And the Court is satisfied that the following condition is satisfied with respect to the relevant infant, that is to say, (*Specify in the terms of s.1(2)(a) to (f) identifying the offence in the case of (f)*) and also that the relevant infant is in need of care or control which the relevant infant is unlikely to receive unless an order under the said section is made in respect of the relevant infant.

And the Court has heard [considered] the [written] evidence of two medical practitioners (*Insert names and addresses*) ....
....

[each] [the first-mentioned] of whom is approved, for the purposes of section 28 of the Mental Health Act 1959, by a local health authority as having special experience in the diagnosis or treatment of mental disorders, and each of the said practitioners has described the relevant infant as suffering from [mental illness] [psychopathic disorder] [subnormality] [severe subnormality].

And the Court is satisfied that the relevant infant is suffering from the following forms of mental disorder within the meaning of the said Act of 1959, namely, [mental illness] [psychopathic disorder] [subnormality] [severe subnormality] and that the disorder is of a nature or degree which warrants the relevant infant's detention in a hospital for mental treatment and is satisfied that arrangements have been made for the relevant infant's admission to the hospital hereinafter specified within twenty-eight days of this date and that the most suitable method of disposing of the case is by means of a hospital order.

IT IS HEREBY ORDERED that the relevant infant be admitted to and detained in ....

(And that the relevant infant be conveyed to the said hospital by ....
....).

(AND IT IS DIRECTED that pending admission to the said hospital the relevant infant shall be detained in a place of safety, namely, ...
. . . .)
(and shall be conveyed there by . . . .).

Dated this . . . . day of . . . . , 19. . . . .

By order of the Court

Justice of the Peace for . . . .
Clerk of the Court

Criminal cases

20. Summons: Offence

IN THE COUNTY OF . . . .
Petty Sessional Division of . . . .

To . . . . of . . . . (hereinafter called the defendant) [and . . . . his [parent] [guardian]]

Information has this day been laid before me the undersigned [Justice of the Peace] [Clerk to the Justices] by . . . . that you the defendant, who are believed to be a [child] [young person], on the . . . . day of . . . . , 19. . . . . , at . . . . in the [county] aforesaid [or of . . . .] (*State briefly particulars of offence*) . . . .
. . . .

[And information has further been laid by . . . . that you . . . . are the [parent] [guardian] of the defendant]

YOU ARE THEREFORE HEREBY SUMMONED [each of you] to appear on . . . . day the . . . . day of . . . . , 19. . . . . , at the hour of . . . . in the . . . . noon before the [Juvenile] [Magistrates'] Court sitting at . . . . to answer the said information.

Dated this . . . . day of . . . . , 19. . . . . ,

[Justice of the Peace for the [county] aforesaid]
[Clerk to the Justices for the Petty Sessional Division aforesaid]

21. Summons: Parent or guardian

IN THE COUNTY OF ....
Petty Sessional Division of ....

To .... of ....
.... who is believed to be a [child] [young person], of whom
you are stated to be the [parent] [guardian], is charged for that [he] [she]
on the .... day of ...., 19....., at .... in
the [county] aforesaid [or of ....] (*State briefly
particulars of offence*)

YOU ARE THEREFORE HEREBY SUMMONED to appear before the [Juvenile]
[Magistrates'] Court sitting at .... on .... day, the
.... day of ...., 19....., at the hour of .... in the
.... noon and during all stages of the proceedings.

Dated the .... day of ...., 19.....

[Justice of the Peace for the [county] aforesaid]
[Clerk to the Justices for the Petty Sessional Division aforesaid]

22. Attendance centre order

.... Juvenile Court
Date: ....
Accused: .... Age .... years
Address: ....
Offence: ....

The accused was on (*date*) .... found guilty of the above
offence which is punishable on summary conviction in the case of an adult
with imprisonment.

The court has been notified by the Secretary of State that the attendance
centre specified herein is available for the reception from the court of
persons of the accused's class or description.

The court is satisfied that the attendance centre is reasonably accessible to
the accused, having regard to the age of, and the means of access available
to, the accused and any other circumstances.

[The court is of the opinion that twelve hours' attendance would be
[excessive, having regard to [the accused's age] [the following
circumstances: ....
....
the accused being under fourteen years of age] [inadequate, having regard
to all the circumstances]]

Order: That the accused attend at the ....
attendance centre on the first occasion (*date*)................. at (*time*)
.... and subsequently at such times as shall be fixed by the officer
in charge of that centre, until the accused shall have completed a period of
attendance of .... hours.

Dated this .... day of ...., 19.....

By order of the Court

Justice of the Peace for ....
Clerk of the Court

Note: The present address of the attendance centre specified above is:

....

23. Care order

IN............................
.... Juvenile Court   Code No ....
Date: ....
Defendant: .... d.o.b. ....
Address...
Offence(s): ....

To each and all the constables of .... and to the
council of the county of...

The defendant, who is believed to have been born on the date mentioned
above was [today] [on ....] found guilty of the above
offence(s) which is/are punishable in the case of an adult with
imprisonment.

And the court is of opinion that a care order is appropriate because of the
seriousness of the offence(s) and that the defendant is in need of care or
control which he is unlikely to receive unless the court makes a care order.

It is hereby ordered that the defendant be committed to the care of the said
council in whose area it appears that (the defendant resides) (the offence(s)
was/were committed, it not appearing that the defendant resides in the area
of any local authority in England and Wales).

Direction: And you the constables are hereby required, unless the defendant
is forthwith received into the care of a person authorised by, and acting on
behalf of, the said council, to deliver the defendant, together with this
order, into the care of a person authorised and acting as aforesaid.

Dated .... day of ...., 19.....

By order of the Court

Justice of the Peace for ....
Clerk of the Court

24. Supervision order

IN . . . .
Petty Sessional Division of . . . .
Before the Juvenile Court sitting at . . . .

. . . . of . . . . (hereinafter
called the defendant) who is believed to have been born on the . . . .
day of . . . ., 19 . . . . ., [is this day] [was on the . . . .
day of . . . ., 19 . . . . .,] found guilty of an offence, namely
(*State briefly particulars of offence*) . . . .
. . . .
It appears to the Court that the defendant [resides] [will reside] in the
[county] [county borough] of . . . . and in the
. . . . petty sessional area.

IT IS HEREBY ORDERED that the defendant be placed under the supervision
of [the council of the said [county] [county borough]] [the council of the
[county] [county borough] of . . . . who have agreed
to be designated as the supervisor] [a probation officer appointed for or
assigned to the said petty sessional area] (hereinafter called the supervisor)
[for the period of . . . .] beginning with the date of this order.
[And the defendant shall comply, so long as this order is in force, with the
requirement[s] specified in the Schedule hereto.]

Dated . . . . day of . . . ., 19 . . . . .

By order of the Court

Justice of the Peace for . . . .
Clerk of the Court

Schedule

*Any requirement(s) imposed by the court should be listed here. These
should be in the terms of s.12 C&YPA 1969 as amended, or r.28 MCCR
1970, as appropriate.*

25. Order of recognizance to keep proper care etc.

IN THE COUNTY OF . . . .
Petty Sessional Division of . . . .

Before the [Juvenile] [Magistrates'] Court sitting at . . . .
. . . . of . . . . (hereinafter called
the defendant), who is believed to have been born on . . . .
[is this day] [was on the . . . . day of . . . ., 19 . . . . .]
found guilty of an offence, namely, ...
. . . .
It is hereby ordered that . . . . of . . . .
. . . . a [parent] [guardian] of the defendant who has consented
to the making of this order, do forthwith enter into a recognizance in the

sum of .... to take proper care of, and exercise proper control over, the defendant [for the period of ....] [until the defendant attains the age of eighteen].

Dated this .... day of ...., 19.....

By order of the Court

Justice of the Peace for ....

Clerk of the Court

26. Remittal order

IN...............................

Petty Sessional Division of ....

Before the Magistrates' Court sitting at ....

.... of................ (hereinafter called the defendant) has this day been found guilty by the said Court of (*State the offence*) ....

The defendant is a [child] [young person] who is believed to have been born on the.............. day of................, 19.....;

IT IS HEREBY ORDERED that the case be remitted to the Juvenile Court sitting at .... acting [for the same place as the Court] [for the place where the defendant resides];

AND IT IS DIRECTED that the defendant [be committed to ....

.... until brought before that Juvenile Court] [be released upon unconditional/ conditional bail] to appear at that Juvenile Court on............. day, the................. day of................., 19....., at the hour of .... in the .... noon].

Dated this .... day of ...., 19.....

By order of the Court

Justice of the Peace for ....

Clerk of the Court

27. Warrant of commitment — detention centre

IN.............................

.... Court   Code No ....

Date:.........................

Accused: .... Age: .... years

Address: ....

Offence(s): The accused was on .... [convicted] [found guilty] of the offence(s) particulars of which are set out in the Schedule hereof, which are punishable with imprisonment in the case of a person aged 21 years or over, and the court is of opinion, for the following reason, that no method of dealing with the accused other than a detention centre order is appropriate because [(a) it appears to the court that the accused is unable or unwilling to respond to non-custodial penalties]

[(b) a custodial sentence is necessary for the protection of the public]

[(c) the offence(s) was/were so serious that a non-custodial sentence cannot be justified because (*state reasons*)...................................
....]

[The court considered that it was unnecessary to obtain a social inquiry Report because (*state reasons*) ....
....]

Decision: That the accused be subject to a detention centre order for the period(s) set out in the Schedule hereto.

Direction: You, the constables of the .... Police Force are hereby required to convey the accused to the detention centre at..................... and there deliver the accused to the Governor thereof, together with this warrant; and you the Governor, to receive into your custody and keep the accused for the said period(s).

By order of the Court

Justice of the Peace for ....
Clerk of the Court

Schedule

Offence No 1
Term of detention...
Offence No 2
Term of detention.................................... concurrent*
Offence No 3
etc

* If consecutive terms ordered, strike out 'concurrent' and add 'to begin on the expiration of the term of detention imposed in respect of Offence No...'

28. Warrant of commitment − youth custody

IN.............................
.... Court   Code No ....

Date: ....
Accused: .... Age: .... years
Address: ....

Offence(s): The accused was on .... [found guilty] [convicted] of the offence(s) particulars of which are set out in the Schedule hereto, which are punishable with imprisonment in the case of a person aged 21 years or over, and the court is, for the following reason, of the opinion that no method of dealing with the accused other than a term of youth custody is appropriate because

(a) the accused is unable or unwilling to respond to non-custodial penalties;

[(b) a custodial sentence is necessary for the protection of the public; or]

(c) the offence(s) was/were so serious that a non-custodial sentence cannot be justified

because (*state reasons*) ....

....

[The court considered that it was unnecessary to obtain a social inquiry report because (*state reasons*) ....

....]

The court passed a sentence of youth custody on the accused because it considered that his detention in a detention centre would be unsuitable because of his mental condition.

Decision: That the accused serve a term of youth custody for the period(s) set out in the Schedule hereto.

Direction: You, the constables of the................ Police Force are hereby required to convey the accused to .... YOUTH CUSTODY CENTRE/PRISON and there deliver the accused to the Governor thereof, together with this warrant; and you, the Governor, to receive into your custody and keep the accused for the said period(s).

By order of the Court

Justice of the Peace for ....
Clerk of the Court

Schedule

Offence No 1
Term of youth custody...
Offence No 2
Term of youth custody............................... concurrent*
Offence No 3
etc.

* If term is to be consecutive delete 'concurrent' and add 'to begin at the expiration of the term of youth custody imposed for Offence No .... above'.

29. Attendance centre order on failure to comply with requirements of supervision order

Court: .... Code No: ....

Date: ....
Supervised person: .... Age .... years
Address: ....
Supervision order made on: ....
by the: .... Juvenile Court.
(Varied on: .... by the: .... Juvenile Court.)

Local Authority area:...
Petty Sessions area: .... for the time being named in the supervision order.

Supervisor: [.......................... Council] [a probation officer appointed for, or assigned to, that petty sessions area]

On the application of the supervisor the court is satisfied that the supervised person has failed to comply with the following requirement(s) of the supervision order

Requirements of supervision order contravened: The court has been notified by the Secretary of State that the attendance centre specified herein is available for the reception from the court of persons of the supervised person's class or description.

The court is satisfied that the attendance centre is reasonably accessible to the supervised person, having regard to the age of, and the means of access available to, the supervised person and any other circumstances.

[The court is of the opinion that twelve hours attendance would be inadequate having regard to all the circumstances]

Order: That the supervision order be [discharged] [varied] as follows:—

AND that the supervised person attend at the .... attendance centre on the first occasion on (*date*)............ at (*time*)...........
and subsequently at such times as shall be fixed by the officer in charge of that centre, until the supervised person shall have completed a period of attendance of .... hours.

By order of the Court

Clerk to the Justices

Note: The present address of the attendance centre specified above is:
....

Legal aid

30. Application for Legal Aid (Legal Aid Act 1974, s.28; Legal Aid in Criminal Proceedings (General) Regulations)

Application for Legal Aid
PLEASE USE BLOCK CAPITALS

  1. Name ....
     Address ....
     .... Date of Birth ....
  2. I apply for legal aid at the Crown/Magistrates'/Juvenile Court sitting
     at...
     My case is due to be heard on ....
     at .... a.m./p.m.
  3. Is any other person charged with you in these proceedings? YES/NO

4. The solicitor I wish to act for me is (*state name and address*) ....
....

5. Describe shortly what it is you are accused of doing, eg. "stealing £50
   from my employer", "kicking a door causing £50 damage".
....

I understand that I (or my parents if I am under 16) may be required by the
Supplementary Benefits Commission to supply further information about
my means. I also understand that the court may order me to make a
contribution to the costs of legal aid or to pay the whole costs if it considers
that my means enable me to do so and, if I am under 16, may make a similar
order with respect to my parents.

Signed .... Dated ....

Reasons for wanting Legal Aid
When deciding whether to grant you legal aid, the court will need to know
the reasons why it is in the interests of justice for you to be represented. You
are therefore *requested* to complete the remainder of this form to avoid the
possibility of legal aid being refused because the court does not have
sufficient information about the case. *If you need help in completing the
form and especially if you have previous convictions, you should see a
solicitor*. He may be able to advise you free of charge or at a reduced fee.
If you plead *not guilty*, the information in this form will not be made known
to the magistrates who try your case, unless they convict you. If you are
acquitted the financial information will be given to them.

6. I am in real danger of a custodial sentence because (*give brief reasons*):
....

7. If you were convicted of the present charge, would you be in breach of
   any court order, ie suspended sentence of imprisonment, conditional
   discharge, probation, community service; or are you subject to a
   deferred sentence? (*give brief details so far as you are able including the
   date(s) on which the sentence(s) was/were imposed*):
....
....

8. I am in real danger of losing my livelihood or suffering serious damage
   to my reputation because (*give brief reasons*):
....
....

9. A substantial question of law is involved (*give brief details*):
....

10. I shall be unable to follow the proceedings because:
    (a) My knowledge of English is inadequate   YES/NO
    (b) I suffer from a disability, namely ....
....

11. Witnesses have to be traced and interviewed on my behalf (*state
    circumstances*):
....
....

253

12. The case involves expert cross-examination of a prosecution witness (*give brief details*):

   ....

13. The case is a very complex one, for example, mistaken identity (*explain briefly*):

   ....

14. Any other reason (*give full particulars*):

   ....
   ....

Statement of Means by Applicant or Appropriate Contributor for Legal Aid Purposes
(General Reg. 4(1))

To apply for criminal legal aid you must complete this form. If you are not yet sixteen, then your mother or father may also be asked to complete one. If you have applied for legal aid for your child, and your child is sixteen years old or over, then **you** do not need to fill in this form. **Your child** should complete it, giving details of his or her **own income**.

This information is needed before legal aid can be granted, so to avoid any delay in your application being considered, please complete this form as fully and as carefully as possible.

SECTION 1 – PERSONAL DETAILS

1. Full name (*block letters please*) ....

2. Date of birth ....

3. Home address ....
   ....

4. Marital status (*please tick one box*)
   ☐ single   ☐ divorced
   ☐ married   ☐ widow(er)
   ☐ married but separated

5. Occupation (*state 'unemployed' if appropriate*)
   List here **all** your jobs, including any part-time work and your employer's name and address. (If you have more than one job, give the name and address of each employer; if self-employed state 'self').

   ....
   ....

SECTION 2 – PERSONAL DETAILS (DEPENDENT CHILD)

If legal aid is being sought for a dependent child, and he or she is not yet sixteen, please answer the following questions about him or her.

1. Full name (*block letters please*) ....

2. Date of birth ....

3. Home address (*if different from yours*) ....
   ....

4. Your relationship to him or her (*e.g. father*) ....

SECTION 3 – FINANCIAL DETAILS

Part A – Income
Please give below details of your net income (*i.e. after the deduction of tax and national insurance*) from all sources for the three months immediately before this form is completed. If you are married and living with your wife or husband, then you have to provide details of his or her income as well. The court may ask you to provide proof of the information you give in this form.

Your contribution, if any, will be assessed and collected on a **weekly** basis, so if you are paid monthly, please give **weekly** figures.

1. Do you receive Supplementary Benefit?

   ☐ Yes— *You do not need to complete the rest of this form, simply turn to the declaration section and sign it.*

   ☐ No— *Please go on to question two.*

2. Do you receive Family Income Supplement?

   ☐ Yes— *There is no need to complete any more of Part A, so please turn to Part B – Capital and Savings.*

   ☐ No— *Please go on to question three.*

3. Please give details of your INCOME in the table below.

Description of INCOME	Amount		Remarks
	Your income	Income of husband/wife	
(a) Weekly earnings or salary, including overtime, commission or bonuses. (Please give net figures). Please attach with this form your last six wage slips. If you do not have that many, please attach as many as you can.			
(b) If your earnings change from week to week, give the amounts for the last 13 weeks. (If you do not have this information, please give the amounts for as many weeks as you can, and at least the last 6 weeks. You should if possible attach wage slips).			
(c) Income from any part-time job not included at (a) above. (Please give gross and net figures).			
(d) Income from state benefits — e.g. family allowance (*please specify below here*).			
(e) Gross income from subletting house, rooms, etc.			
(f) Any other income (*please give details below here*).			
(g) If in a business of your own, please attach the most recent accounts available.			

IMPORTANT: If the information you have given in the table above is going to change soon, please give details of the change in section 5 of this form.

Part B — Capital and Savings
Please give details of **all** your capital and savings. If you are married and living with your husband or wife, also give details of his or her capital and savings. You should give particulars of savings with the National Savings Bank or with other banks. National Savings Certificates, cash stocks and shares or any other investments. Please also give details of any property you own, such as houses or flats apart from the house or flat in which you live.

1. Please give details of your *CAPITAL and SAVINGS* in the table below.

Description of CAPITAL and SAVINGS	Amount		Remarks
	You	Husband/Wife	
(a) Do you own house property (apart from your main or only dwelling)? (*Answer YES or NO*)	YES/NO	YES/NO	
(b) if YES state: (i) The value (*i.e. the approximate selling price*) (ii) The amount of any outstanding mortgage.			
(c) Give details of your savings. (*State saving Institution below here*)			
Give details of any articles of value that you own (*e.g. jewellery, furs, paintings*) with their approximate value.			

SECTION 4 — ALLOWANCES AND DEDUCTIONS

In assessing your means for legal aid purposes, the court will make allowances for the cost of supporting your husband or wife, children and any other dependent relatives, and also for your accommodation costs and travelling expenses. If there are any other expenses which you think the court should make allowance for, please give details at question 4 below.

1. Please give the NUMBER of dependants who are *LIVING WITH YOU*.

Husband or wife	Children 18 and over	Children 16 and 17	Children 11 to 15	Children under 11	Other *(specify below)*

2. If you pay maintenance to a dependant who does not live with you, please give details of the amounts you pay to support them.

Age of dependant	Your relationship to him or her	Amount you pay per week

3. You may claim for the HOUSING EXPENSES of you and your wife or husband. Please give the amounts you pay each week. If you own more than one house, only give details connected with the house in which you live. If you are paying the housing expenses of (a) dependant(s) who do(es) not live with you, please give both amounts.

Description of payment	Amount per week	Amount per week for dependant(s)
Rent		
Mortgage repayment		
Ground rent		
Service charge		
Rates		
Board and lodging		
Bed and breakfast		

4. The TRAVELLING EXPENSES of you and your husband or wife may be taken into account. You may claim for the actual amounts that you and your husband or wife spend per week travelling to and from your place(s) of employment.

	You	Your husband or wife
Amount spent		

5. Please give details of any OTHER EXPENSES which you think the court should know about.

Description of expenditure	Amount spent per week

6. Allowance for contributions in respect of LEGAL ADVICE AND ASSISTANCE under the "green form" scheme.
   You may already have been given some advice and assistance by a solicitor under the "green form" scheme, and you may have paid, or been asked to pay, a contribution towards that advice. If this is the case, then the amount of your legal aid contribution will be reduced by the amount of "green form" contribution you have paid.

Name and address of the solicitor who gave the advice and assistance	Amount of contribution paid (or to be paid)

SECTION 5 — FURTHER INFORMATION

This part of the form is set aside for you to give any financial information that you think the court should have when deciding upon your application for legal aid. You may also use this part of the form to tell the court of any future changes in circumstance that might alter your financial position.

SECTION 6 — DECLARATION

Anyone who has knowingly or recklessly made a statement which is false in any way, or has knowingly withheld information is liable to be prosecuted and, if convicted, to either imprisonment for a term not exceeding four months, or to a fine or both. After your application has been considered by the court, you may be asked to give further information or to clarify information that you have already given. In particular you may be required to provide documentary proof of the information you have given (e.g. wage slips, rent books, etc.)

I declare that to the best of my knowledge and belief, I have given a complete and correct statement of my income, savings and capital (and that of my husband or wife)* (and that of my child)**.

Date .... Signed ....

   * Delete if you are not living with your husband or wife, or if you are single.
** Delete if legal aid is not sought for your child.

Appeal

31. Notice of appeal

IN THE COUNTY OF ....
Petty Sessional Division of ....

To The Clerk to the Justices, ...
And to .... (*other party to the proceedings*)
I,........................... of...........................
do hereby give you and each of you notice that it is my intention at the Crown Court, ... to appeal against a certain conviction of me [and/or the sentence imposed upon me] [order made against me] by the .... Juvenile Court sitting at .... in the said county on the .... day of............., 19....., for having on the .... day of ...., 19..... at ....
(*State shortly offence(s)*) ....
....
And that the general grounds of such appeal are....................
....
and that I am not guilty of the said offence and/or that my sentence was too severe.

Dated this .... day of............., 19.....
.... (*Appellant's signature*)
Note: The appellant is required to serve a copy of this notice upon (1) the Clerk to the Justices, and (2) the person who prosecuted the case in the Juvenile Court, and such notice must be served either personally or by registered post or recorded delivery within *twenty-one days* of the date of the Justices' decision. Leave to appeal out of time (that is to say more than 21 days after the adjudication) must be sought from the Chief Clerk, Crown Court, ...).

Local authorities

32. Information/warrant to search for child or young person absent from remand home, place of safety etc. (s.32 C&YPA 1969)

.... Magistrates' Court

Date: ....

The information of: ....

Address: ....

Telephone Number: ....

who upon oath or affirmation states that he has reasonable grounds for believing that (*specify name*) .... a child or young person to whom section 32 of the Children and Young Persons Act 1969 applies, is absent from the place where he is required to be, and that the said child/young person is in the premises at (*specify address*) ....
....
(Informant's signature) ....

Taken and sworn before me,

Justice of the Peace

To each and all of the Constables of ....

Date: ....

The information of the above-named informant who states upon oath that he has reasonable grounds for believing that [*specify name*] ....
a child/young person to whom section 32 of the Children and Young Persons Act 1969 applies, is absent from the place where he is required to be, and that the said child/young person is in the premises at (*specify address*) ....

YOU ARE HEREBY AUTHORISED to enter and search the said premises and if the said child/young person is found, to arrest him without warrant under the authority of the said section 32 and conduct him to the premises where he should be or to such other premises as may be directed.

Justice of the Peace

33. Information for warrant for search for or of removal of child or young person (s.40 C&YPA 1933)

IN ....

Petty Sessional Division of ....

Date: ....

The information of: ....

Address: ....

Telephone no: ....

who upon oath or affirmation states that there is reasonable cause to suspect that .... (*specify name and address of child/young person*) is a child/young person who (*specify grounds in terms of s.40(1)(a) or (b)*)

wherefore application is made for a warrant to search for and remove the child/young person to a place of safety.

Informant's signature: ....
Taken and sworn before me,

Justice of the Peace

34. Warrant for search for or removal of child or young person (s.40 C&YPA 1933)

IN ....
Petty Sessional Division of ....

To each and all of the constables of ....
Information on oath [affirmation] has this day been laid before me, the undersigned justice of the peace, by ....
of .... a person acting in the interests of a child or young person, namely, ... (hereinafter called the relevant infant) that there is reasonable cause to suspect (*specify ground in terms of s.40(1)(a) or (b)*).

YOU ARE HEREBY AUTHORISED to search for the relevant infant and, if it is found that (*specify in terms of s.40 (1)*) to take him/her to a place of safety;

YOU ARE HEREBY AUTHORISED to remove the relevant infant with or without search to a place of safety;

And for the purposes hereof YOU ARE HEREBY AUTHORISED to enter (*specify address of premises*)

IT IS HEREBY DIRECTED that when executing this warrant you shall not be accompanied by the said informant [shall be accompanied by a duly qualified medical practitioner];

And the relevant infant may be detained in a place of safety by virtue of this warrant until he/she can be brought before a juvenile court, except that the relevant infant shall not be so detained for a period exceeding .... days.

Dated this .... day of ...., 19.....

By order of the Court

Justice of the Peace for ....
Clerk of the Court

35. Information for search warrant and warrant to search under s.67 Children Act 1975

IN. . . . .
. . . . Magistrates' Court

Date: . . . .
The information of: . . . .
Address: . . . .
Telephone Number: . . . .

an officer of the . . . . County Council who upon oath
states that he has reasonable grounds for believing that. . . . .
a child within the meaning of the Children Act 1975 and to whom section 67
of that Act applies who is in the care of the said local authority is absent
from the place where he is required to be, and that the said child is in the
premises at

(Informant's signature) . . . .

Taken and sworn before me

Justice of the Peace

To . . . .
an officer of the local authority namely the. . . . . County Council

The information of: . . . . an officer of the . . . .
County Council, who upon oath states that he has reasonable grounds for
believing that . . . . a child within the meaning of the
Children Act 1975 and to whom section 67 of that Act applies who is in the
care of the said local authority is absent from the place where he is required
to be, and that the said child is in the premises at . . . .

YOU ARE THEREFORE HEREBY AUTHORISED to enter and search the said
premises and if the said child is found, to place him in such accommodation
as the said local authority may provide.

Dated . . . . day of. . . . . , 19. . . . .

By order of the Court

Justice of the Peace for . . . .
Clerk of the Court

36. Access Order

. . . . Juvenile Court   Code. . . . .
Date: . . . .
Name of child: . . . .
On the complaint of . . . . of . . . .
made under section 12C of the Child Care Act 1980 that the Council, to
whose care the child is committed, has terminated arrangements for access
to the child by the complainant or refused to make such arrangements and
that an access order should be made, it is adjudged that the complaint is true
and it is ordered that the said Council is hereby required to allow the

263

complainant, being the child's [parent] [guardian] [custodian], access to the child [subject to the following condition[s]]

Dated . . . . day of . . . . , 19 . . . . .

By order of the Court

Justice of the Peace for . . . .
Clerk of the Court

37. Emergency order suspending access order

. . . . Juvenile Court   Code . . . .

Date: . . . .

Name of child: . . . .

On . . . . the . . . . Juvenile Court made an access order requiring the . . . . Council to allow access to the child by (*specify name of parent, guardian or custodian*)

Application having been made by . . . . I am satisfied that continued access to the child by . . . . in accordance with the terms of the said access order will put the child's welfare seriously at risk:

The operation of the said access order is hereby suspended for a period of (*specify number of days*) beginning with the date of this order.

Dated . . . . day of . . . . , 19 . . . . .

By order of the Court

Justice of the Peace for . . . .
Clerk of the Court

NOTE: *If during the above-mentioned period for which the access order is suspended the above-named Council make an application to a juvenile court for variation or discharge of that access order, the operation of the said access order will be further suspended until the date on which such application is determined or abandoned.*

38. Order varying or discharging access order

. . . . Juvenile Court   Code . . . .

Date: . . . .

Name of child . . . .

On . . . . [this] [the . . . .] Juvenile Court made an access order requiring the . . . . Council to allow access to the child by . . . .

On the complaint of . . . . of . . . . made under section 12D of the Child Care Act 1980 for the variation or discharge of the said order it is adjudged that the complaint is true and it is ordered that the said order is hereby [discharged] [varied as follows]

Justice of the Peace
[By order of the Court
Clerk of the Court]

39. Interim order authorising use of secure accommodation

.... Juvenile Court   Code.....................
Date: ....
Relevant infant: .... Age .... years
Address: ....

The relevant infant is [in the care of] [accommodated by] the ....
.... Council in pursuance of (*specify statutory provision*).
On the application of .... for an order authorising the
keeping of the relevant infant in secure accommodation, the court is not in
a position to determine whether in the case of the said infant the criteria set
out in section 21A of the Child Care Act 1980 or in regulations made under
that section or section 39 of that Act are satisfied.

The said application is hereby adjourned. The applicant shall bring the
relevant infant before the above court on (*date*) ....
at (*time*) .... or at such earlier time as the court may require.
During the period of the adjournment the relevant infant may be kept in
secure accommodation.

Justice of the Peace
[By order of the Court
Clerk of the Court]

40. Order authorising the use or further use of secure accommodation

.... Juvenile Court   Code.....................

Date: ....
Relevant infant: .... Age .... years.
Address: ....

The relevant infant is [in the care of] [accommodated by] the ....
.... Council in pursuance of (*specify statutory provision*)
*[On.................. on an application of.................. [this]
[the .... Juvenile Court] determined that in the case of the
relevant infant the criteria set out in section 21A of the Child Care Act 1980
or in Regulations made under that section or section 39 of that Act were
satisfied and made an order authorising the retention of the relevant infant
in secure accommodation for a period not exceeding .... days]

On the *[further] application of .... the court has determined that *[it remains the case that] the relevant infant:

[has a history of absconding and is likely to abscond from accommodation
other than that provided for the purpose of restricting liberty, and that if he
absconds it is likely that his physical, mental or moral welfare will be at risk]

[is likely to injure himself or other persons if he is kept in accommodation
other than that provided for the purpose of restricting liberty]

[has been committed to the care of the said council under section 23 of the
Children and Young Persons Act 1969]

[has been charged with or convicted of an offence imprisonable in the case of a person aged 21 or over for 14 years or more]

[that he has been charged with or convicted of an offence of violence, or has previously been convicted of such an offence]

[that either he is likely to abscond from accommodation other than that provided for the purpose of restricting liberty or he is likely to injure himself or other people if he is kept in any other description of accommodation and that in either case all other descriptions of accommodation are inappropriate]

The relevant infant may be retained in secure accommodation during a *[further] period of .... days beginning with the date of this order.

Justice of the Peace
[By order of the Court
Clerk of the Court]

* Delete if application is the first application for an order.

41. Order for removal of foster child or protected child to place of safety

IN ....

Petty Sessional Division of ....

.... Juvenile Court

Date: ....

To each and all the constables of .... and to ...., a person authorised to visit foster/protected children

[Complaint having been made today by the Council of the County/County Borough of ....] [Application having today been made to me, the undersigned Justice of the Peace] by ...., a person authorised to visit foster/protected children on the ground that .... of ...., a foster/protected child (referred to hereafter as the child) is (*State grounds of complaint or application briefly*)

[Proof having been given that there is imminent danger to the health or well-being of the child]

IT IS HEREBY ORDERED that the child [and all other foster children kept at ....] be removed to a place of safety

AND THE CHILD [and any other foster children so removed] may be detained in a place of safety by virtue of this order until restored to a parent, relative or guardian or until other arrangements can be made, except that the child [and any other foster child so removed] shall not be detained for a period exceeding .... days.

[Justice of the Peace]
[By order of the Court
Clerk of the Court]

42. Information/warrant to enter and inspect premises in which foster child is kept (s.13 FCA 1980)

.... Magistrates' Court

Date:....................................

The information of .... of ....

Telephone number:.......................

who upon oath or affirmation states that there is reasonable cause to believe that ...., a foster child, is being kept in premises at .... and

[admission to those premises or the part of those premises in which the foster child is being kept has been refused to a duly authorised officer of the local authority]

[a refusal of admission to those premises to a duly authorised officer of the local authority is apprehended]

[the occupier of those premises is temporarily absent]

Informant's signature: ....

Justice of the Peace

To:.............., an authorised officer of the.............. Council

Date:....................................

The information of the above-named informant who states upon oath [affirmation] that there is reasonable cause to believe that that ....

.............., a foster child, is being kept in premises at ....

and (*specify ground set out in information*)

YOU ARE HEREBY AUTHORISED to enter the said premises (by force if need be) within 48 hours of the issue of this warrant for the purpose of inspecting those premises.

Justice of the Peace

Appendix B

Statutory Instruments and other source material

Contents

Children and Young Persons (Definition of Independent Persons) Regulations 1971
(SI 1971 No 486)

1. These regulations may be cited as the Children and Young Persons (Definition of Independent Persons) Regulations 1971 and shall come into operation on 1st April 1971.

2. —(1) In these regulations "the Act" means the Children and Young Persons Act 1969.

(2) The Interpretation Act 1889 shall apply to the interpretation of these regulations as it applies to the interpretation of an Act of Parliament.

3. For the purposes of section 24(5) of the Act a local authority to whose care a person is committed by a care order may appoint as an independent person to be a visitor to that person any person other than the following:

(1)   any person having any connection with that authority by reason of
    (a) being a member, or a member of a committee or sub-committee, whether elected or co-opted; or
    (b) being an officer or person appointed; or
    (c) holding a paid office or appointment for profit; or
    (d) being employed under a contract to supply goods or services to that authority; or
    (e) being a spouse of any such person.

(2)   any person having a connection with a community home managed by a local authority under the provisions of the Act by reason of
    (a) being a member, or a member of a social services committee or sub-committee, whether elected or co-opted; or
    (b) being an officer or person appointed to perform services for the benefit of the authority in respect of the functions of its social services committee; or
    (c) holding a paid office or appointment for profit, the object of which is the performance of services for the benefit of the authority in respect of the functions of its social services committee; or
    (d) providing services, whether paid or unpaid, in or in connection with any community home; or
    (e) being employed under a contract to supply goods or services to a community home managed by the authority; or
    (f) being the spouse of any such person.

(3)   any person having any connection with a community home provided by a voluntary organisation under the provisions of the Act by reason of
    (a) being a member of any body of management of such a voluntary organisation; or
    (b) holding any paid office or appointment for profit which is in the gift of any such organisation, the object of which is the performance of services for the benefit of that organisation in respect of a community home; or
    (c) providing services, whether paid or unpaid, in or in connection with any community home provided by such an organisation; or
    (d) being a member of a body of management of any community home constituted under section 39 of the Act; or
    (e) being employed under a contract to supply goods or services to a community home managed by such an organisation; or
    (f) being a spouse of any such person.

The Secure Accommodation (No 2) Regulations 1983
(SI 1983 No 1808) as amended by the Secure Accommodation (No 2) (Amendment) Regulations 1986, SI 1986 No 1591

Operative 1 January 1984

The Secretary of State for Social Services in relation to England and the Secretary of State for Wales in relation to Wales in exercise of the powers conferred upon them by sections 21A and 39 of the Child Care Act 1980(**a**) and of all other powers enabling them in that behalf hereby make the following regulations:—

Citation and commencement
1. These regulations may be cited as the Secure Accommodation (No. 2) Regulations 1983 and shall come into operation on 1st January 1984.

Interpretation
2.— (1) In these regulations, unless the context otherwise requires—
"the 1980 Act" means the Child Care Act 1980;
"responsible authority" means a local authority which arranges for a child to be accommodated by virtue of an enactment specified in the Schedule to these regulations;
"care authority" means a local authority which has in its care a child to whom Part III of the 1980 Act applies by virtue of section 17 of that Act;
"independent visitor" means a person appointed under section 11 of the 1980 Act;
"secure accommodation" means accommodation provided for the purpose of restricting the liberty of children.

(2) Any reference in these regulations to any provisions made by or contained in any enactment or instrument shall, except insofar as the context otherwise requires, be construed as including a reference to any provision which may re-enact or replace it with or without modification.

(3) Any reference in these regulations to a numbered regulation shall be construed as a reference to the regulation bearing that number in these regulations, and any reference in a regulation to a numbered paragraph is a reference to the paragraph bearing that number in that regulation.

Approval by Secretary of State of secure accommodation in a community home
3. Accommodation in a community home shall not be used as secure accommodation unless it has been approved by the Secretary of State for such use and in approving such accommodation for use as secure accommodation the Secretary of State may impose such terms and conditions as he sees fit.

Placement of a child aged under 10 in secure accommodation in a community home
4. Subject to regulation 10(3) a child under the age of 10 years shall not be placed by a local authority in secure accommodation in a community home unless that authority has obtained the permission of the Secretary of State prior to such placement.

Children to whom section 21A of the 1980 Act shall apply
5. Section 21A of the 1980 Act (use of accommodation for restricting liberty of children in the care of a local authority), shall apply also to children committed to the care of a local authority by a judge exercising the inherent wardship jurisdiction, whether in the High Court or in wardship proceedings transferred to a county court under s.38 of the Matrimonial and Family Proceedings Act 1984 and to children of a description specified in the Schedule to these regulations.

Children to whom section 21A of the 1980 Act shall not apply
6. Section 21A of the 1980 Act shall not apply to a child to whom the said section would otherwise apply if that child is detained under any provision of the Mental Health Act 1983(**a**) or if any of the following provisions apply to that child—

(*a*) section 53 of the Children and Young Persons Act 1933(**b**) (punishment of certain grave crimes),

(*b*) section 28(4) or section 29(3) of the Children and Young Persons Act 1969(**c**) (detention of child or young person in place of safety and further detention of arrested child or young person respectively),   ·

(*c*) section 72 of the Child Care Act 1980 (accommodation of persons over school age in convenient community home).

Description of children to whom section 21A of the 1980 Act shall have effect subject to modifications
7.—(1) Section 21A(1) of the 1980 Act shall have effect subject to the modifications specified in paragraph (2) in relation to a child committed to the care of a local authority under section 23 of the Children and Young Persons Act 1969 (remand to care of local authority) in the following cases—

(*a*) where the child is charged with or convicted of an offence imprisonable in the case of a person aged 21 or over for 14 years or more, or

(*b*) where the child is charged with or convicted of an offence of violence, or has been previously convicted of an offence of violence.

(2) In a case to which paragraph (1) applies, for the words "unless it appears" to the end of sub-section (1) of section 21A of the 1980 Act there shall be substituted the following words—

"unless it appears that any accommodation other than that provided for the purpose of restricting liberty is inappropriate because —

(*a*) the child is likely to abscond from such accommodation, or
(*b*) the child is likely to injure himself or other people if he is kept in any such accommodation."

Applications to juvenile court to be made by local authorities
8. Applications to a juvenile court under section 21A of the 1980 Act shall be made—

(a) by the care authority, or

(b) in the case of a child to whom the Schedule to these regulations applies, by the responsible authority.

Duty to give information of placement
9. Where a child is placed in secure accommodation in a community home which is not managed by his care authority or, in the case of a child to whom the Schedule to these regulations applies, by his responsible authority, the local authority which manages that accommodation shall inform his care authority or as the case may be his responsible authority of the placement within 24 hours thereof.

Maximum period in accommodation for restricting liberty without juvenile court authority
10.—(1) Subject paragraph (3) and to regulation 11, the maximum period beyond which a child to whom these regulations apply may not be kept in secure accommodation without the authority of a juvenile court is 72 hours, whether consecutively or 72 hours in aggregate in any period of 28 consecutive days.

(2) Where authority of a juvenile court to keep a child in secure accommodation has been given, any period during which the child has been kept in such accommodation before the giving of that authority shall be disregarded for the purposes of any further placement in such accommodation after the period authorised by the juvenile court has expired.

"(3) A child who is a ward of court may be placed or kept in secure accommodation only pursuant to the direction of a judge exercising wardship jurisdiction, whether in the High Court or in wardship proceedings transferred to a county court under section 38 of the Matrimonial and Family Proceedings Act 1984; and paragraph (1) shall not apply in respect of a ward of court so kept pursuant to such a direction.".

Different provision as to maximum period in accommodation for restricting liberty without juvenile court authority.
11. Where a child was placed in secure accommodation at any time between 12 midday on the day before and 12 midday on the day after a public holiday or a Sunday, and

(a) during that period the maximum period specified in regulation 10(1) expires, and

(b) the child had, in the 27 days before the day on which that placement was made, been placed and kept in such accommodation for an aggregate of more than 48 hours,

the maximum period shall be treated as if it did not expire until 12 midday on the first day, which is not itself a public holiday or a Sunday, after the public holiday or Sunday.

Maximum period of authorisation by a juvenile court
12. Subject to regulations 13 and 14, the maximum period for which a juvenile court may authorise a child to whom these regulations apply to be kept in secure accommodation is three months.

Further periods of authorisation by a juvenile court
13.—(1) Subject to regulation 14, a juvenile court may from time to time authorise a child to whom these regulations apply to be kept in secure accommodation for a further period.

(2) Any period authorised by a juvenile court under this regulation shall not exceed six months.

Maximum periods of authorisation by a juvenile court for remanded children
14. The maximum period for which a juvenile court may from time to time authorise a child who has been remanded and committed to the care of a local authority under section 23 of the Children and Young Persons Act 1969 to be kept in secure accommodation is the period of the remand, so however that any such period of authorisation shall not extend beyond the period of his remand.

Duty to inform parents and others in relation to children in secure accommodation in a community home.
15. Where a child to whom these regulations apply is kept in secure accommodation in a community home and it is intended that an application will be made to a juvenile court to keep the child in that accommodation, the child's care authority or, in the case of a child to whom the Schedule to these regulations applies the responsible authority, shall as soon as possible inform the child's parent or guardian, if practicable, and the child's independent visitor, if one has been appointed, of such intention.

Appointment of persons to review placement in secure accommodation in a community home.
16. Each local authority shall appoint at least two persons who shall review at intervals not exceeding three months the case of each child to whom these regulations apply where the child continues to be kept in secure accommodation in a community home and either—

    (*a*) is in the care of that authority, or

    (*b*) falls to be accommodated by that authority, being the responsible authority.

Review of placement in secure accommodation in a community home
17.—(1) The persons appointed under regulation 16 in addition to satisfying themselves in relation to each case that the criteria for keeping the child in secure accommodation continue to apply, shall satisfy themselves that the placement in such accommodation in a community home continues to be appropriate and in doing so shall have regard to the welfare of the child whose case is being reviewed.

(2) In undertaking the review referred to in regulation 16 the persons appointed shall ascertain and take into account the views of—

    (*a*) the child, and

    (*b*) the parent or guardian of the child, if practicable, and

    (*c*) any other person who has had the care of the child, whose views the persons appointed consider should be taken into account, if practicable, and (*d*) the child's independent visitor, if one has been appointed, and

(*e*) the local authority managing the secure accommodation in which the child is placed if that authority is a different authority from that specified in regulation 16(a) or (b).

(3) The local authority shall, if practicable, inform all those whose views are required to be taken into account under paragraph (2) of the outcome of the review.

"(4) Where the persons appointed under regulation 16 satisfy themselves that the criteria for keeping a child who is a ward of court in secure accommodation no longer apply, or that the placement of such a child in secure accommodation is no longer appropriate, the local authority shall as soon as practicable notify the court exercising wardship jurisdiction in relation to that child of the outcome of the review and seek the further directions of the court.".

Records to be kept in respect of a child in secure accommodation in a community home
18. Whenever a child is placed in secure accommodation in a community home the local authority which manages that accommodation shall ensure that a record is kept as to:—

(*a*) the name, date of birth and sex of that child, and

(*b*) the care order or other statutory provision by virtue of which the child is in the community home and in either case particulars of any other local authority involved with the placement of the child in that home, and

(*c*) the date and time of his placement in secure accommodation, the reason for his placement, the name of the officer authorising the placement, and where the child was living before such placement, and

(*d*) all those informed by virtue of regulations 9, 15 and 17, court orders made by virtue of section 21A of the 1980 Act any direction referred to in regulation 10(3) and reviews undertaken in respect of the child by virtue of regulation 17, and

"(*dd*) the date and time of any occasion on which a child is locked on his own in any room in the secure accommodation other than his bedroom during usual bedtime hours, the name of the person authorising this action, the reason for it and the date and time the child ceases to be locked in that room, and".

(*e*) the date and time of his discharge and his residence following discharge from secure accommodation

and these records shall be available for inspection by the Secretary of State who may require that copies of them be sent to him at any time.

Revocation of Secure Accommodation Regulations 1983
19. The Secure Accommodation Regulations 1983(**a**) are hereby revoked.

SCHEDULE *Regulation 5*

CHILDREN TO WHOM SECTION 21A OF THE 1980 ACT SHALL APPLY

Section 21A of the 1980 Act (use of accommodation for restricting liberty of children in the care of a local authority) shall apply also to a child who falls to be accommodated by a local authority by virtue of any of the following enactments—

(*a*) section 40 of the Children and Young Persons Act 1933 (warrant to search for or remove a child or young person),

(*b*) paragraph 6 or 7 of Schedule 5A to the Army Act 1955 (reception orders and committal into care),

(*c*) paragraph 6 or 7 of Schedule 5A to the Air Force Act 1955 (reception orders and committal into care),

(*d*) paragraph 6 or 7 of Schedule 4A to the Naval Discipline Act 1957 (reception orders and committal into care),

(*e*) section 43 of the Adoption Act 1958 (removal of protected children from unsuitable surroundings),

(*f*) section 10(1) and (4) of the Matrimonial Proceedings (Children) Act 1958 (power of court in Scotland in actions of divorce to commit care of child to local authority),

(*g*) section 7(4) of the Children Act 1958 (removal in Scotland of foster children kept in unsuitable surroundings),

(*h*) section 2(1) of the Matrimonial Proceedings (Magistrates' Courts) Act 1960 (order by a magistrates' court in matrimonial proceedings),

(*i*) section 15 or 74 of the Social Work (Scotland) Act 1968 (provisions as to care of children, parent of child in residential establishment under supervision requirement moving from Scotland),

(*j*) section 7(2) of the Family Law Reform Act 1969 (committal of wards of court to care of local authority),

(*k*) section 2(5) or (10), 16(3), 25(1), 26(2) or 28(1) of the Children and Young Persons Act 1969 (place of safety order, interim order, place of safety for supervised person, transfers between England or Wales and Northern Ireland, transfers between England or Wales and the Channel Islands or Isle of Man, detention of child or young person in place of safety),

(*l*) section 43(1) of the Matrimonial Causes Act 1973 (power to commit to care of local authority),

(*m*) section 2(2)(*b*), 11(1) or (5) of the Guardianship Act 1973 (committal of minor to care of local authority in guardianship proceedings, jurisdiction and orders in Scotland relating to care and custody of children),

(*n*) sections 17, 34(5) in its application to section 2(2)(b) of the Guardianship Act 1973, 36(2) or (3)(*a*) of the Children Act 1975 (care of child on refusal of adoption order, interim order in custodianship care of child on revocation of custodianship order),

275

(*o*) section 10(1) of the Domestic Proceedings and Magistrates' Courts Act 1978 (powers of court to commit children to care of local authority),

(*p*) section 12 of the Foster Children Act 1980 (removal of foster children kept in unsuitable surroundings).

Access (Notice of Termination and Refusal) Order 1983 *(SI 1983 No 1860)*

Operative 30 January 1984

The Secretary of State for Social Services in exercise of the powers conferred on him by Section 12B(1) of the Child Care Act 1980 and in exercise of all other powers enabling him in that behalf, hereby makes the following Order:—

Citation and interpretation

1.—(1) This Order may be cited as the Access (Notice of Termination and of Refusal) Order 1983 and shall come into operation on 30 January 1984. (2) In this Order the expression 'the 1980 Act' means the Child Care Act 1980.

Form of notice

2.—(1) The form of notice to be given to a parent, guardian or custodian by a local authority or voluntary organisation of termination of arrangements for access to a child, to whom Part IA of the 1980 Act applies, shall be form 1 in the schedule to this Order. (2) The form of notice to be given to a parent, guardian or custodian by a local authority or voluntary organisation of refusal to make arrangements for access to a child, to whom Part IA of the 1980 Act applies, shall be form 2 in the schedule to this Order.

Signed by authority of the Secretary of State for Social Services.

SCHEDULE

Article 2

FORM 1

NOTICE OF TERMINATION OF ARRANGEMENTS FOR ACCESS

CHILD CARE ACT 1980: SECTION 12B

FROM: [LOCAL AUTHORITY/VOLUNTARY ORGANISATION]

TO: [NAME OF PARENT/GUARDIAN/CUSTODIAN]

NAME OF CHILD:

... [Name of child] of whom you are the ... [parent/guardian/custodian] is in the care of this ... [authority/organisation]. The purpose of this notice is to advise you that the ... [authority/organisation] have decided that the arrangements for you to have access to ... [name of child] should be terminated. Your access will be terminated from the date this notice is served on you. You have a right under section 12C of the Child Care Act 1980 to apply to the juvenile court at ... [name of court] for an order granting you access to ... [name of child].

The application must be made within six months of the date this notice is served on you. If you wish to apply to the court for an order granting you access or if you need any help in connection with this notice, you are advised to seek legal advice as soon as possible. Depending on your financial circumstances, you may be entitled to free or low-cost help under the Legal Aid or Legal Advice and Assistance schemes. Your local Citizens Advice Bureau will be able to give you the names of solicitors in the area who operate these schemes.

Dated ....

[signed]

An officer authorised to sign on
behalf of the local authority/
voluntary organisation.

FORM 2

NOTICE OF REFUSAL OF ARRANGEMENTS FOR ACCESS

CHILD CARE ACT 1980: SECTION 12B

FROM: [LOCAL AUTHORITY/VOLUNTARY ORGANISATION]

TO: [NAME OF PARENT/GUARDIAN/CUSTODIAN]

NAME OF CHILD:

... [Name of child] of whom you are the ... [parent/guardian/custodian] is in the care of this ... [authority/organisation]. The purpose of this notice is to advise you that the ... [authority/organisation] have decided that your request for arrangements for access to ... [name of child] should be refused. You have a right under section 12C of the Child Care Act 1980 to apply to the juvenile court at ... [name of court] for an order granting you access to ... [name of child].

The application must be made within six months of the date this notice is served on you. If you wish to apply to the court for an order granting you access or if you need any help in connection with this notice, you are advised to seek legal advice as soon as possible. Depending on your financial circumstances, you may be entitled to free or low-cost help under the Legal Aid or Legal Advice and Assistance schemes. Your local Citizens Advice Bureau will be able to give you the names of solicitors in the area who operate these schemes.

Dated ....

[signed]

An officer authorised to sign on
behalf of the local authority/
voluntary organisation.

Guardians Ad Litem and Reporting Officers (Panels) Regulations 1983
(SI 1983 No 1908 as amended by SI 1986 No 3)

Citation, commencement and interpretation
1.—(1) These regulations may be cited as the Guardians Ad Litem and Reporting Officers (Panels) Regulations 1983 and shall come into operation on 27th May 1984.

(2) Any reference in these regulations to any provision made by or contained in any enactment shall, except insofar as the context otherwise requires, be construed as including a reference to any provision which may re-enact or replace it, with or without modification.

(a) Made by the Secretary of State for Social Services in exercise of the powers conferred by section 103(1)(*a*) of the Children Act 1975.

Panels of guardians ad litem and reporting officers
2.—(1) There shall be established in the area of each local authority a panel of persons appointed in accordance with the provisions of regulation 3 of these regulations from whom guardians ad litem and reporting officers may be appointed for the purposes specified in section 103(1)(*a*) of the Children Act 1975.

(2) A local authority shall ensure that the number of persons appointed to the panel established in its area is sufficient for the purposes specified in the said section 103(1)(*a*) in the area in which the panel is established.

Appointments to panels
3.—(1) Members of a panel shall be appointed by the local authority in whose area the panel is established.

(2) Before appointing a person to be a member of a panel the local authority shall invite nominations from—

    (*a*) any probation committee established in its area by virtue of Schedule 2 to the Powers of the Criminal Courts Act 1973,

    (*b*) the clerk of each magistrates' court in its area,

    (*c*) any local authority whose area adjoins its area and

    (*d*) any other person as it considers appropriate.

(3) The local authority shall decide whether the qualifications and experience of any person nominated by any of the bodies referred to in paragraph (2) or by itself are suitable for the purposes of that person's appointment as a guardian ad litem or reporting officer.

(4) Before making an appointment to the panel, the local authority shall consult such organisations and persons from whom nominations were invited under paragraph (2) above as it thinks fit, in respect of those persons whom it proposes to appoint to the panel.

(5) The appointment of a person to a panel shall be for a period not exceeding three years, so however that the local authority may terminate that person's membership of the panel at any time where the local authority considers that he is unable or unfit to carry out the functions of a guardian ad litem or reporting officer.

(6) A local authority shall maintain a record of those persons whom it has appointed to be members of the panel established in its area.

Expenses, fees and allowances of members of panels
4.—(1) Local authorities shall in respect of the purposes specified in section 103(10)(*a*) of the Children Act 1975 defray expenses incurred by members of the panels established in their areas and pay fees and allowances for members of such panels.

(2) No expenses, fees and allowances as referred to in paragraph (1) shall be defrayed or paid by local authorities by virtue of paragraph (1) in respect of a member of a panel who is employed by a local authority or probation committee for 30 hours or more a week.

The Magistrates' Courts (Child Abduction and Custody) Rules 1986
(SI 1986 No 1141)

Operative 1 August 1986

The Lord Chancellor, in exercise of the power conferred upon him by section 144 of the Magistrates' Courts Act 1980, as extended by sections 10 and 24 of the Child Abduction and Custody Act 1985, after consultation with the Rule Committee appointed under the said section 144, hereby makes the following Rules:—

Citation and commencement
1.   These Rules may be cited as the Magistrates' Courts (Child Abduction and Custody) Rules 1986 and shall come into operation on 1st August 1986.

Interpretation
2.   In these Rules:—

"complaint" includes an application under Rule 14 of the Magistrates' Courts (Children and Young Persons) Rules 1970(**c**);

"Contracting State" means a Contracting State defined in section 2 of the 1985 Act;

"the 1985 Act" means the Child Abduction and Custody Act 1985;

"the Hague Convention" means the Convention defined in section 1(1) of the 1985 Act;

"the High Court" means the High Court in England and Wales or the High Court in Northern Ireland.

Stay of proceedings pending in a magistrates' court
3.   Where any proceedings in which a decision falls to be made on the merits of rights of custody (as construed under section 9 of the 1985 Act) are pending in a magistrates' court and that court receives notice from the High Court or the Court of Session that an application in respect of the child concerned has been made under the Hague Convention, the magistrates' court shall order that all further proceedings in the proceedings pending before it shall be stayed, and shall cause notice to be given to the parties to the proceedings accordingly.

Dismissal of complaint
4.   Where a magistrates' court which has stayed any proceedings under Rule 3 above receives notice from the High Court or the Court of Session that an order has been made under Article 12 of the Hague Convention for the return of the child concerned, the court shall dismiss the complaint and cause notice to be given to the parties to the proceedings accordingly.

Resumption of proceedings after stay

5. Where a magistrates' court which has stayed any proceedings under Rule 3 above receives notice from the High Court or Court of Session that an order for the return of the child concerned has been refused (other than in the circumstances set out in the third paragraph of Article 12 of the Hague Convention), the court shall order that the stay be lifted, shall so notify the parties to the proceedings, and shall proceed to deal with the complaint accordingly.

Further stay of proceedings or dismissal of complaint

6. Where a magistrates' court which has stayed any proceedings under Rule 3 above receives notice from the High Court or Court of Session that an order has been made under the third paragraph of Article 12 of the Hague Convention staying or dismissing the application thereunder, the court shall continue the stay on the proceedings pending before it or, in a case where the High Court or Court of Session has dismissed the application, dismiss the complaint, and shall cause notice to be given to the parties accordingly.

Notice of registration of order in respect of a child

7. Where any proceedings such as are mentioned in section 20(2)(*a*), (*b*) or (*c*) of the 1985 Act are pending in a magistrates' court and that court receives notice from the High Court or the Court of Session that an application has been made under section 16 of that Act for the registration of a decision made in respect of the child in proceedings commenced before the proceedings which are pending (other than a decision mentioned in section 20(3) of the 1985 Act) or that such a decision has been registered under the said section 16, the court shall cause notice to be given to the parties to those proceedings that it has received notice of the application or of the registration, as the case may be.

Authenticated copy of magistrates' court order

8.—(1) A person who wishes to make an application under the Hague Convention in a Contracting State other than the United Kingdom and who wishes to obtain from a magistrates' court an authenticated copy of a decision of that court relating to the child in respect of whom the application is to be made shall apply in writing to the justices' clerk for that court.

(2) An application under paragraph (1) above shall specify:—

(*a*) the name and date or approximate date of birth of the child concerned;

(*b*) the date or approximate date of the proceedings in which the decision of the court was given, and the nature of those proceedings;

(*c*) the Contracting State in which the application in respect of the child is to be made;

(*d*) the relationship of the applicant to the child concerned;

(*e*) the postal address of the applicant.

(3)   A justices' clerk who receives an application for an authenticated copy of a decision under this rule shall send by post to the applicant at the address indicated in the application for the purposes an authenticated copy of the decision concerned.

(4)   For the purposes of paragraph (3) of this rule a copy of a decision shall be deemed to be authenticated if it is accompanied by a statement signed by the justices' clerk that it is a true copy of the decision concerned.

Application for declaration of unlawful removal of a child
9.   An application to a magistrates' court under section 23(2) of the 1985 Act (declaration that the removal of a child from the United Kingdom has been unlawful) may be made orally or in writing in the course of the custody proceedings (as defined in section 27 of that Act).

Extract from DHSS Guide for Guardians Ad Litem in the Juvenile Court

Enquiries concerning this guide may be addressed to Children's Division B; telephone (01) 407 5522, Exts. 6212/7531.

34.   The guardian ad litem has a duty to 'so far as it is reasonably practicable, investigate all circumstances relevant to the proceedings' and, in order to do this, to 'interview such persons and inspect such records and obtain such professional assistance' as he thinks appropriate.

35.   The guardian ad litem will need to establish the child's history to determine the agencies and individuals he will need to approach. Often, a number of agencies may have been involved in the child's care. There may be other agencies who have assisted the family: the consent of family members may be needed before such agencies are able to help. The guardian ad litem will normally, of course, want to interview the child's parents and the foster parents or residential care staff who have cared for him. He should not overlook other adults with whom the child has established a relationship or who may be able to comment on his needs. Legal aid will usually be available to pay for expert advice or reports from specialists such as educational psychologists, doctors or child psychiatrists (see paragraphs 28 and 101).

36.   It is hoped that the guardian ad litem will enjoy the confidence and co-operation of local authorities and other agencies. Sometimes the local authority may be considering or reviewing plans for the child in the period before the hearing. The guardian ad litem needs to be aware of any changes in circumstances which may influence his view of the case. He must be able to keep in touch with, although he cannot participate in, the development of plans and decision making.

37.   It would not be appropriate for the guardian ad litem to look for compromise with other parties or to seek to influence their actions in respect of the child, although he will want to identify any common ground. However, he may properly decide to share his findings and conclusions with other parties and it may often be constructive to do so, always bearing in mind that his written report may be given to parties only by or with the permission of the court (see paragraph 44).

38.   The guardian ad litem's first and paramount consideration must be the need to safeguard the child's best interests until he achieves adulthood. He is also under a duty to take into account the child's wishes and feelings, having regard to his age and understanding and to ensure that his wishes and feelings are made known to the court. It is, of course, essential to the investigation − and to the discharge of the guardian ad litem's function as a whole − that he should find out and understand the child's wishes and feelings and make them known to the court.

Access to records

39.   The guardian ad litem has a duty, as part of his investigation, to inspect such records as he thinks appropriate. The effect of Regulation 15 of the Adoption Agencies Regulations is to give guardians ad litem and reporting officers in adoption proceedings unrestricted access to adoption records in a particular case. There is no corresponding provision in respect of other confidential records which guardians ad litem will need to examine. It is hoped that local authorities and other agencies will allow guardians ad litem access to records, in view of the guardian's status as an officer appointed by the court. However, except in the case of adoption records, the Rules give guardians ad litem no right of access. Where access is refused to information or documents which the guardian ad litem believes are relevant to the case, he can instruct the solicitor to apply for a witness summons to secure the attendance of any witness or to ask any person to attend court with a particular document (section 97 of the Magistrates' Courts Act 1980). However, there is no legal machinery in the magistrates' court to force anyone simply to disclose a document. The law provides for the attendance of a person with the document at the court: the question of whether the document should be disclosed depends on whether it has been referred to in evidence or is shown to be relevant to the proceedings.

40.   The juvenile court has no power to order a local authority to disclose the entire contents of its case file; nor can the local authority claim blanket privilege for non-disclosure. It is the practice, in these circumstances, for the court to be shown the documents in issue and to decide after representations from the parties whether or not privilege does apply to the documents.

Preparing the report

41.   The investigation, assessment and recommendations of the guardian must be reported in writing to the court. The report should be in part descriptive, setting out of the process of the guardian ad litem's enquiry; and the child's circumstances and history. It should also be analytical, teasing out and weighing the key considerations. And should aim to assist the court by making clear recommendations, wherever possible, as to how the child's interests can best be protected and promoted. The merits and disadvantages of alternative courses of action may need to be balanced. It will be helpful if any areas of agreement between the parties can be identified.

42.   The guardian ad litem should include in the report a separate section which deals with the wishes and feelings of the child. It may be appropriate for the guardian ad litem to interpret and comment on these in terms of the child's developmental and emotional state. Nevertheless, the guardian ad litem should always seek faithfully to reflect the child's stated views. The manner and circumstances in which these have been expressed should be described and whether these views have been consistent.

Appendix C

Standard scale of penalties

Level 1 .... £50

Level 2 .... £100

Level 3 .... £400

Level 4 .... £1,000

Level 5 .... £2,000

(Criminal Justice Act 1982 s.37(2)).

Maximum fines that may be imposed on:

Children (under 14)	£100
Young persons (14–16)	£400

(MCA 1980 ss.24(3) and (4), 36(1) and (2))

Index